MY GRAPE VILLAGE

A Memoir by

LAURA BRADBURY

Published by Grape Books

www.laurabradbury.com

ISBN 13: 978-0-9921583-4-7

À mon pirate et mes trois princesses, cette aventure n'existerait pas sans vous.

.

"Tous pour un, un pour tous."

-Alexandre Dumas

CHAPTER 1

"Are they going to survive?" I asked Franck.

I clutched the metal gate as I watched our two daughters make their way through the preschool playground. I had never seen such a place of utter lawlessness.

Despite the larger than life statue of the Virgin Mary that loomed over the courtyard, French children punched and taunted each other. Here was the *laissez-faire* philosophy in action. A cluster of teachers stood well off to the side of the mayhem. They chatted and sipped, espressos out of china cups. It would have been entertaining to watch if not for the fact that Franck and I had just jettisoned our daughters into the deep end of it all.

Two and a half year old Camille in her yellow sundress and white sandals glanced back at us and furrowed her eyebrows. She lowered her head and marched straight to her classroom door, making eye contact with no-one. She disappeared inside. I couldn't take it, I had to make sure-

I opened the gate, and winced as the rusty metal screeched.

"*Non Madame Germain!*" One of the teachers in the cluster shook her finger at me. "No parents allowed in the courtyard during school hours!"

"How did she see me?" I turned to Franck. "She didn't even turn around when that red -haired kid beat that other little boy to a pulp."

"They see what they want to see," Franck said, putting his hand over mine as he closed the gate. There was more metallic squealing and the teachers heads all snapped in our direction.

"I bet they don't oil the gate on purpose," I muttered. I glanced down at Franck's hand over mine. His knuckles were white.

"*Allez*," he said. "We must leave them."

I caught sight of four and a half year old Charlotte walking to her classroom, located at the far end of the schoolyard. Her blond hair was pulled up with two ladybug barrettes and she rolled a *cartable* – her French school bag - behind her. She smiled at a little boy wearing a chic little mint green Lacoste polo shirt who ran toward her. He shoved her as he ran past, knocking over both her and her *cartable*. Charlotte picked herself up. She looked stricken for a moment and then continued to walk to her class again with a brave smile plastered on her face. A girl with angelic blond braids had the temerity to stick her tongue out at my precious eldest daughter. Charlotte blinked back tears and when she reached the classroom door gave us a small wave that was so courageous it splintered my heart in two.

Franck dragged me back up the path and out the heavy wooden doors of the school. The doors were promptly locked behind us.

Once we were in the parking lot I threw myself against his chest. "We've made a terrible mistake," I mumbled into his T-shirt.

The girls weren't even supposed to be going to Saint Coeur, or Sainted Heart, in Beaune. They had been signed up to attend the village schools in Magny-les-Villers and Villers-la-Faye. Three days ago, a teacher friend of Franck's phoned to tell him they couldn't take Charlotte. There were simply too many children in her year. We scrambled to find a school for the girls so we could have time to work. Franck thought of Saint Coeur because it was where I went to school during my year as a Rotary exchange student in Burgundy when I was seventeen. They luckily – or so I thought at the time – had spots for both of our daughters. Now I knew the truth. Saint Coeur wasn't full like other schools because this place was where Burgundian society put all the hardened future criminals.

Franck kissed the top of my head. "We just need to give it time Laura. We all have to adapt. I went to preschool in France and, *régardez!* I'm still here."

I stared at the locked doors. "I can't stand the thought of my girls trapped in there with all of those horrible French children and the teachers who don't care if they get kill…"

"We had good reasons for moving back to France," Franck interrupted. "Not just for us, but for them."

Maybe we did, but my daydreams of familial bonding at Beaune's Saturday market, introducing the girls to *pain au chocolat* and *escargots*, and becoming fluent in French had shriveled up in the last ten minutes.

"I can't remember why those reasons were so compelling, can you?" I asked Franck.

"Not at the moment, to be honest." Franck glanced at the closed doors and frowned. "I do know one thing though."

"What?"

"Stéphanie told me about a Judo class that Tom takes. I'm going to sign our girls up right away."

"I never thought self-defense was something the girls would have to learn over here."

Franck pulled me towards the car. "It may be the most important thing," he said.

CHAPTER 2

After we dropped off the girls, Franck and I made a beeline for the cottage we purchased several months previously in Franck's village of Villers-la-Faye. It was nestled right across a quiet lane along the back wall of chez Germain – the house where Franck's grandfather and great-grandfather had been born, the house where Franck had grown up, and the house where Franck's parents still lived.

The cottage had a massive old grapevine growing up one corner and along the side of the roofline. The cottage, as a consequence, had always been known in the village as *La Maison de la Vieille Vigne* or "The House of the Old Vine." The wall behind it was stained green where the local winemakers sprayed copper on it to empty their tanks on the way back from the vineyards.

Luc, a local guy who had done a fabulous and dirt-cheap renovation of the upstairs of Franck's sister Stéphanie's house in the neighbouring village of Magny-les-Villers, was waiting for us in a white *camionette* when we pulled up. He was almost as white as his vehicle, being covered from head to toe in a fine white powder that I recognized, even from a distance, as drywall dust. He smoked a cigarette and looked dubiously at the poorly shingled roof of the cottage.

Franck and I had had our eye on *La Maison de la Vieille Vigne* ever since we realized a year or two into renting out our first house in the nearby village of Magny-les-Villers as a vacation rental to visitors to France that this lark of ours had the potential to turn into a full-time gig.

"That would be the perfect vacation rental," I often commented to Franck as we walked past the closed-up cottage on our way from his family home to the vineyards.

Six years before, Franck and I bought our first house opposite the Roman church in Magny-les-Villers. I was tormented by panic attacks brought on by two stressful years of studying law at Oxford and began to admit to myself that if I continued with a legal career, it might make us financially comfortable but it would also kill my soul. Neither of us had a source of income but the house was cheap and we both welcomed a project – any project – while we attempted to figure out how we were going to embark on our new life as a married couple.

After four months of frenzied renovations we welcomed our first paying guests in the home we baptized *La Maison des Deux Clochers*. Managing a vacation rental in France turned out to be not only successful, but perfectly suited to our combined talents. On every vacation back to Burgundy we searched for a second property but none intrigued us as much as the little cottage behind Franck's family home.

Through the village gossip network i.e. the *boulangerie* across from chez Germain, Franck quickly found out about the owner, a man from Dijon who was friendly with local winemakers, and who decamped to Villers-la-Faye with his wife every summer. Franck contacted him but he had no interest in selling. We kept calling, however, on every visit to France – the time we came for Charlotte's baptism, when I had just found out I was pregnant with Camille, when Camille was five months old and we had to cancel her baptism because she caught the measles. Over time, Franck and the cottage owner became friendly. During their phone calls they would reminisce about the village characters, and those lazy, indolent, wine soaked summers of the past. Finally, just when we were used to making the phone call more out of habit than anything else, he surprised us by saying he was ready to sell. His wife had passed away that winter and he wanted to move South to be with his daughter. He suggested a price and Franck accepted. So here we were, late for meeting with the handyman whom we hoped would help us create a charming vacation rental out of a ramshackle sixteenth century ruin.

"Luc?" Franck enquired.

Luc stuck out his hand. "That's me. Nice to meet you." He shook my hand and smiled. I wasn't expecting to like him, mainly because I couldn't imagine anyone helping us except our friend Gégé who had been our partner in crime throughout the four-month renovation of *La Maison des Deux Clochers*.

Franck fished a large metal key out of his pocket. "Do you want to come in?" he asked Luc.

Gégé didn't have any spare time to help friends do renovations anymore. He had found the love of his life, a chain-smoking travel agent named Audrey with a voice like Edith Piaf. They moved in together, and last I heard were traveling in Morocco. Gégé sent us a postcard of teetering piles of djalabas at the Souk in Marrakesh and scribbled "Looks like a bigger mess than your new project! Glad I'm in Morocco!" I was overjoyed that Gégé had found his soulmate but that didn't stop me from missing him terribly.

Luc picked a thread of tobacco off his lip. "Oh yes. Even from the outside it looks like quite a project." He had a trustworthy face and kind brown eyes that crinkled at the corners. At least he had a sense of humour. *Merci Dieu*. That was essential.

Franck opened the long shutters that were locked over the front door.

Franck and Luc went inside first and I followed after, treading cautiously. Strange things could spring out of closed up houses in France. I'd heard stories of bats and feral cats and I had seen for myself a nest of albino spiders.

Thankfully, there was no overpowering stench of mothballs like there had been in *La Maison des Deux Clochers*. Still, the dust and mustiness was enough to make me sneeze. I went to every window and opened them as well as the shutters.

"*Dis-donc...*" Luc murmured, taking in the hideous and poorly laid tile on the floor and the strange mezzanine above us that looked like it was mainly constructed out of particleboard. "Looks like there was a handyman that lived here."

"Or a not so handy man," Franck said.

We toured the house and Luc pointed out everything that needed to be changed. The roof needed replacing, the floor ripped up, the mezzanine and several interior walls removed, and the kitchen and bathroom, which sported a bright yellow toilet and matching bidet, needed to be gutted. For no discernable reason, the oil furnace was located in the middle of the house in a hallway between the main room and the bedroom. That had to go, if only for esthetic reasons.

"New windows, roof, floor, fixtures, doors and shutters." Luc took copious notes on the piece of paper clipped on his clipboard.

"Do you mean to tell me we basically need to rebuild this cottage from the ground up?" Franck asked, when we finally worked our way back to the front door.

Luc read over his notes. "Pretty much, except for the oak beams and the stone walls."

Franck and I exchanged a worried look. Somehow, even though we went over the list of work, neither of us had realized until this second that the renovations of *La Maison de la Vieille Vigne* amounted more or less to building an entirely new house.

"Do you think it's possible to complete all that by July?" Franck ventured.

It was September now. That gave us just over ten months. It seemed like a luxury compared to the four months we had to renovate *La Maison des Deux Clochers*. Franck and I embarked on that adventure with no renovation experience, very little money, and no-one to help us but the disaster-loving Gégé. Despite being newly married, Franck and I grew apart during my two stressful years at Oxford law school. Being thrown together in such an epic project would either make or break us. Luckily, it not only drew us closer, but it made our lives take a completely new and unexpected turn. French vacation rentals became our future, and even though neither of us had ever contemplated such a career before, it was perfect for both of us. Things were different this time. Not only was the magnitude of work at *La Maison de la Vieille Vigne* four or five times that of our vacation rental in Magny, but we were parents now – even though neither Franck nor I had completely adjusted to that reality yet.

Luc stared at Franck, incredulous. "July? *Non, ce n'est pas possible…*I mean, maybe if the trades worked day and night and you already had your building permits…"

"We don't." Franck couldn't lie to save his life.

"Then *non*, I don't think it's at all possible," Luc said, clearly possessor of the same trait.

"It has to be," I said. "I've already rented out this cottage starting on July 12th. The first guests have already paid us their deposit."

Luc stared at me, trying to divine if I was joking. His eyes widened when he realized I was serious. "How can you possibly rent it out when the renovations haven't even begun? That is crazy. A million things could go wrong."

I shrugged. I had always had the tendency, for better or for worse, of going through life in what my father called a 'Ready.Fire.Aim' fashion.

"My wife is very forward thinking," Franck said, apologetic. "Can you help us?"

Luc drew his eyebrows together and scanned the main room once more. "I can try, but I refuse to make any promises."

"We don't need promises," Franck said. "Try is enough for us."

"All right then." Luc began scribbling more notes. "First we'll need to line up a roofer."

That evening Franck and I waited at the doors of Saint Coeur by four -thirty. School wasn't over until almost five. Even preschoolers went for a full day, although every school child enjoyed a full two hour lunch break. When we picked Charlotte and Camille up for lunch they didn't want to go back. I entertained the wildy optimistic hope that their afternoon had been better.

After our fruitful morning with Luc at the cottage, we did not wile away the afternoon making love or tasting the newest vintage of Volnay or anything one might expect newcomers to do Instead, we spent the hours between lunch and picking up the girls trolling the used car lots of Beaune in the wilting heat of early September.

We finally decided to buy not a French car, but a roughed up Ford Mondeo the same colour as an avocado left in the open air for too long. Franck took it for a test drive and assured me the gears were *comme du beurre*. More than anything else, we bought it because it was cheap, we were overheated, and eager to check "get a car" off our ever-growing "to-do" list.

As for the gears changing "like butter" I had to take Franck's word. Even though I had been driving since I was sixteen, I never learned to drive standard. That was another item on our "to-do" list for the following week, once the girls settled in at school.

Franck checked his watch. "When are they going to open the door?"

I eyed the thick stone walls that encircled the school. Why did schools in France resemble maximum security prisons? Had they ever considered that maybe that was why most of the children inside mostly behaved as though they belonged in one? Charlotte's preschool in Canada had been wide open and parents could wander in and out on a whim. The walls of Saint Coeur were at least twelve feet tall – too high for a desperate parent to scale, at least without a ninja suit and a set of ropes.

"When I went to school here there was a terrifying woman who manned the doors," I reminisced. "We all called her *Le Dragon*." She never opened the door a millisecond before she had to, especially for me."

"Maybe *Le Dragon* is still the one on door duty," Franck said.

"No way," I said, quaking nevertheless at the thought. "That was fourteen years ago. She was ancient then. She must to be dead by now." I remembered her hair, which was iron colored and shellacked to her skull like a helmet.

When I arrived freshly off the plane with my high school diploma as a Rotary Exchange student representing Canada in Beaune, I was dumbfounded to discover that my new school was in fact an old nunnery. The first time I saw a nun in a full habit and a massive wooden cross wandering around the school's' hallways I could hardly believe my eyes. Even more shocking than the nuns, though, was The Dragon and her insistence that I was not to be allowed out of the medieval school enclosure during the school day.

I cracked my knuckles with my thumb. "Whoever is not opening up the door is going to die if I can't get to my girls in the next few minutes."

Back when I was seventeen I had been as eager to escape the school walls as I now was to get inside. I earned my driver's license the day I turned sixteen, even though I almost failed because I nearly ran over a woman. I suspect the instructor only gave it to me because I cried. I was used to roaming around my Canadian hometown in one of my parents' beat up old cars. I refused to spend my exchange year cooped up behind massive walls with a bunch of nuns.

My stubbornness pitted against The Dragon's tenacity. It wasn't until I got a letter from my family in Canada, a letter from my host family in France, and finally a letter from the President of the Rotary Club of Beaune that she capitulated. She signed my permission card with such a look of hatred in her eye, however, that I knew I had acquired an enemy for life.

Franck knocked against the door but the wood was so thick it sounded little more than a faint thud. "*Allô!*" he yelled. "*Allô, Allô, Allô!* Can you please open the door?"

"So, you are as worried as me," I said, a statement rather than a question.

"Of course. This afternoon it all came back to me."

"What came back to you?"

"The preschool experience in France. I remember in Kindergarten the teacher gave a boy in my class a minus 20 in a test and made him walk around all day with it taped to his back."

Aghast, I pressed my ear up against the door. The gaggles of waiting mothers in chic linen outfits and leather sandals and expensive sunglasses perched on their perfectly disheveled up-dos looked at us askance.

A bead of sweat rolled down my forehead. I had dressed for our day of renovation planning and car shopping in a pair of jeans that were far too hot and a black concert T-shirt with "Rolling Stones – Steel Wheels Tour" emblazoned on the front.

Franck leaned against the door beside me.

Without warning it gave way from the other side, opened by a woman with a pinched mouth and daggers in her eyes.

"*Monsieur?*" she confronted my husband who had almost toppled on top of her. "Do you have a problem?"

Before Franck could answer her gaze shifted to me. It had been almost fifteen years, there was no way she would-

"*Vous!*" she gasped.

Le Dragon. She did not appear to have aged a day.

"*La Canadienne!* What are you doing back here begging to get back inside my door? If I remember correctly - and I'm sure I do - all *you* ever wanted was to get out."

"I'm a mother now," I said.

She narrowed her eyes at me in disbelief.

"My daughters are inside there, in the preschool. It's their first day."

"You came back?"

"Yes," I said. "With my husband." I gestured to Franck who graced her with his most charming smile. Instead of melting, she sneered. Actually *sneered*.

More than anything I wanted to tell her off. I wanted to tell her how much she had terrified me when I was only seventeen and newly arrived in Burgundy and didn't speak a word of French. I might have done so too except I couldn't slay this dragon; she held my children hostage.

"I missed Saint Coeur when I was in Canada," I said, instead.

The scowl didn't leave her face but she stood aside to let us pass.

"Camille is a darling little girl," the young teacher named Séverine told me. She had a gamine haircut that suited her delicate bone structure and wore a metal cross around her neck that looked weighty enough to give her lumbago. "She did very well."

"Did she speak any French?" I asked. We divided to conquer. Franck ran to get Charlotte while I fetched Camille. We couldn't bear thinking that either of our girls would think we abandoned them in the Gaza Strip of the Saint Coeur preschool playground.

"Well no…"

"I suppose it's normal that she speaks English at first."

"Actually, I didn't hear the sound of her voice all day. Have you ever had her hearing tested?"

I almost dropped the thick sheaf of forms in my hand. Camille had never in her life been described as quiet. She screamed from the time she was born until she turned two at which point she switched to talking non-stop.

Séverine patted me on the shoulder. "I'm sure she will begin to talk soon. This is an enormous change for her. Children need time."

I clasped Camille's little hand in mine. Before having children, I began to feel like I was getting a handle on this 'life' thing. From the minute I had Charlotte, I felt like a newborn again myself. I had no idea how to be a mother or if I was doing it well. Most of the time, like right now, for instance, I was certain that I was doing this whole parenthood thing badly. *I needed to be a better mother.* I needed to be more patient, less impulsive, more domestic, less messy, more devoted and far-seeing…less egocentric.

Camille tugged my hand and I looked down to see utter exhaustion in her big hazel eyes. Charlotte and Franck came up behind us. Charlotte was crying silently and had blood trickling down her leg from a skinned knee. I wanted more than anything to make my girls happy but had no idea how.

The last time Franck and I began renovations on a vacation rental we were newlyweds. I had an Oxford law degree, but yearned to escape the legal career that was traced out in front of me. In these past few months of packing boxes and filling out tax forms and saying our good-byes, neither Franck nor I ever considered that we weren't embarking on this adventure with just the two of us, we were dragging our innocent children behind us in our wake.

Somehow, I hoped this move to France would not only allow us to renovate an ancient winemaker's cottage, but to renovate our family life as well. There was a lot of joy since the girls were born, but it also felt that we hadn't yet found our groove as a family of four. I held my little girls' hands as they stumbled through the parking lot, exhausted, and marveled at our folly.

CHAPTER 3

I thought we were heading directly to sign the girls up for judo but Franck squealed out of the parking lot in the opposite direction.

"Where are we going?" I asked.

"I phoned Stéphanie after lunch. The sign-up isn't until Thursday of next week and Mémé will want to hear about the girls' first day at school." Franck honked and made a rude arm gesture at the driver of the red Peugeot in front of us who couldn't seem to decide on a lane.

When we left the newly renovated *La Maison des Deux Clochers* to return to Canada six years previously Mémé, Franck's ninety-three year old grandmother, had declared that she would surely be dead by the time we moved back to Burgundy. As it turned out, she was still very much alive and had just moved into a chic little studio apartment in a luxurious retirement home in Beaune called *"Les Primevères"* or "The Primroses".

She had, however, come close to fulfilling her prophecy a few months before our arrival. She suffered a massive heart attack but, like a phoenix, had resurrected herself from the edge of death.

Once we parked and got inside *Les Primevères* we stopped in front of the elevators while the girls weighed themselves on an old-fashioned scale. A local pharmacy donated it to the retirement community, and it probably weighed as much as a baby elephant. Only then did we walk up the three flights of stairs to Mémé's apartment.

She swung her door open and, after swooping her elegant gray and blue shawl over her shoulder, gave us all a resounding kiss, as fresh as a proverbial primrose.

"I knew you would come!" She clapped her hands. "I was thinking about the girls all day today. How did they like their first day at school?"

Camille was busy rubbing Mémé's kiss off her cheek but Charlotte gave a quivering smile and an equivocal "*ça va.*"

"Aren't you brave!" Mémé swept them over to the round table ideally placed for entertaining in the center of her room. "I think you've both earned a treat, don't you?" She took out a package of *Pétit Prince* brand chocolate biscuits that always resided in her kitchen cabinet.

While the girls happily munched on their snack she served Franck and I glasses of *kir* and proceeded to instruct Franck on exactly how to hang several framed sunflower photos on her wall.

"They go perfectly with the rest of my *décor*," she said.

The studio was decorated in cheerful tones of yellow and blue and the bright sunflower photos were the perfect final touch.

Mémé was a formidable maternal presence in Franck's family like my own mother was in mine. From the time Charlotte was born my mother swept in and helped us with everything from childcare to grocery shopping to cooking to soothing crying babies. To me, she still felt very much the mother and I still felt very much the child. I wondered if Franck's mother had ever wondered, like me, how to own one's own identity as a mother when your mother had you trumped on pretty much every domestic front.

"Just think!" Mémé said. "Everyone was ready to bury me a few months ago." She laughed.

"How do you feel now?" Franck asked.

"Wonderful." Mémé tossed her head, not unlike a frisky foal. "I did almost die though. They weren't wrong about that."

"*Vraiment?*" Franck said.

"Oh yes. I was giving up, you know. The night I was admitted to the hospital the doctors told the family I was slipping away. It is strangely easy to give up – that surprised me. The doctors instructed Jacqueline and your mother and Renée to go back home and collect my clothes to be buried in and to return early in the morning to say good-bye."

"What happened?" Franck asked.

"I was lying in bed in the morning, feeling so old and tired that I was eager for death to come and claim me. Then the door to my room opened up and I could hear the click of heels and the curtains were whisked back. I blinked in the sunlight, wondering who would dare disturb an old woman on her deathbed. It was my nurse. She was perfectly coiffed, you know, with an elegant chignon." Mémé threw her shoulders back and imitated the confident stature of her nurse. "She was a large woman, neat as a pin in her uniform.

"There I was in bed, my hair like a bird's nest and wearing only a stained hospital gown. Something about her made me feel embarrassed about being so unkempt, even though I was, *vous savez*, dying." She shrugged.

"The nurse turned from the window and said to me '*Alors* Madame Menneveau, what is this *laissez-allez*? Have you decided to give up on yourself? Look at your *coiffure*, it's a disgrace! If you have made up your mind to go and die – even though I think that is lamentably weak-spirited – the least you can do is make yourself *élégante* for your passing'."

"Did you tell her off?" Franck asked.

"Heavens no!" Mémé declared. "I got angry, first at her, then at myself. She saved my life."

"What did you do?" I asked, spellbound as always by Mémé's stories.

"I sat up in my hospital bed and demanded she find a comb and do up my hair properly as well as fetch a bit of rouge for my cheeks and lips. I told her to pass me my dressing gown and my scarf and I put those on– there wasn't much I could do about my hospital gown but at least I could cover it up. When that was done and I was looking respectable once again I ordered a large breakfast and polished off the entire thing. That nurse reminded me that I was Germaine Menneveau, and I was not someone who let myself go!"

"When the family arrived my daughters were carrying my funeral outfit and all hunched over and clinging to each other, sniveling. I told them that they had chosen the completely wrong outfit and that, besides, I wasn't dead yet so they would have to wait a while to put it to use."

Franck burst out laughing. "My mother left out that part of the story."

Mémé shrugged, "I think they were all embarrassed that they had taken me for dead, although truth be told it could have easily gone that way if not for that nurse. Anyway, when I die is already *écrit dans le grand livre* – written in the Big Book. No point in any of us fretting about it. Our job is to live, not to worry about when we're going to die."

"Is that why you decided to move in here?" I asked.

Mémé gave another one of her evocative shrugs. "When I was released from the hospital and Renée told me about the lovely apartment she had rented here I was intrigued. I had never had a home that was completely my own to decorate just the way I wanted. I knew this would be the right choice for the next chapter in my life. Nobody is ever too old for a new adventure you know – even at ninety-three."

I let that sink in. No "*laissez-aller*". We all had to at least try to do our best to make a new life here in Burgundy, despite Dragons at school gates, miniature delinquents in my daughters' schoolyard, and the fact that I had to learn how to drive a stick shift. Maybe this was my chance to become *formidable* like Mémé and my mom.

We chatted a few minutes more and invited her to Sunday lunch two weeks from then. If Mémé could change her life in her ninth decade, we had no excuse.

We found a house to rent in the village of Savigny-les-Beaune until Christmas. We didn't have much, but luckily the house, actually more of a mini chateau, was furnished, albeit in a highly eccentric fashion.

"The estate agent is meeting us here in ten minutes to do the inventory." Franck maneuvered the car like a Formula 1 driver through the unbelievably narrow stone gates that led into the courtyard of our temporary abode.

Inventory? At our vacation rental in Magny we never did inventory. I couldn't imagine the administrative nightmare of trying to go through our house's contents with every guest. Also, I trusted people. Franck was always getting mad at me for leaving our car doors unlocked and windows wide open in Canada but nothing could shake my belief that most people were good and that those who wanted to rob me were few and far between.

Franck was always amazed in Canada at things like the roadside stands that popped up in the Spring with beautiful bouquets of wildflowers or freshly picked vegetables and a little tin for people to pay for what they took. "In France," he said. "Within an hour somebody would have stolen the flowers, the vegetables, the money can, *and* the stand."

"The house is so huge and full of stuff," I said to Franck as we got out of the car. "It's going to take days to do a complete inventory."

Franck shrugged as he unbuckled Camille from her car seat. "I'm hoping this guy knows what he's doing. He must do these all the time."

Charlotte ran around to Camille's side of the car. "Let's go play in the upstairs! We can find the loose tiles!"

The girls felt that our rental was the lap of luxury, not because it was most likely over two hundred years old and had about eight bedrooms, but because it had an *upstairs*. Our house back in Canada was a little 1950s beachside bungalow that measured about one thousand square feet so they had never had the heady experience of living in a house with an "upstairs."

Their favorite pastime, besides exploring all the nooks and crannies, was jumping from one loose tile to another on the landing of the third floor. These tiles, called *tomettes*, were the ancient hand fired terra cotta hexagonal tiles that were found in old houses all over Burgundy. This game, happily, seemed to keep them busy for hours.

I was in the kitchen when, half an hour later, I heard a clamor of honking outside our pillars.

"I think the Estate Agent is here," I called to Franck.

The house was situated on one of the narrowest streets of Savigny-les-Beaune, a village known in the area for its extremely narrow streets and fast drivers. As we found out on our first foray out of the house, maneuvering to get in the gates resulted in an immediate line of twenty irate drivers all honking their horns and gesticulating wildly to get past.

Not only did I have to learn how to drive standard, but sooner or later I would have to squeeze our car through those gates. Better not to think of that right now.

A green Renault rumbled across the gravel. I went out the kitchen way, and watched as the estate agent, young and wearing a stylish thinlapelled suit but red-faced, climbed out of the car and tried to regain his composure.

"I hate driving in Savigny-les-Beaune," he said. "What idiot made such narrow streets that all run into one another? And your gates! How are you actually expected to squeeze in here?"

Franck fought back a smile. "You'll have to ask the owner. You're the one who communicates with her, remember?"

Normally we couldn't afford a rental like this, but the owner was apparently desperate. It was a family home on her husband's side, and he passed away a few months before. She was mired deep in the horrendous muck of French succession law, and needed to earn a little extra money to buy herself some time. She wanted to rent it to us for a year, but Franck was adamant – we had to find another place to live before Christmas. "Can you even imagine what the heating bills for this place would be in the winter?" Franck had explained when I argued for staying until at least after Christmas. "We'd put ourselves in the poorhouse within a week."

We never planned to live in the cottage we moved over to France to renovate. It was too small for our family of four, not to mention the fact that it would be ripped apart over the next several months. Our vacation rental in Magny-les-Villers was renting so well that we didn't want to give up our rental income to live there either. The plan was to buy another place of our own, something cheap but livable that we could eventually turn into a third vacation rental. Truth be told the chief proponent of this particular plan was *moi*.

"The owner is a *vieille folle*." The estate agent straightened his tie. I wasn't that conversant in the manners of estate agents in France but I wondered about the ethics of calling your client a crazy old woman.

"Would you like a café?" Franck asked when our visitor put his briefcase down on the kitchen table and removed an imposing wad of paper from it. The estate agent hesitated.

"A *kir*?"Franck asked.

"That would be most welcome," the estate agent agreed. Franck poured one for each of us.

"Where should we start?" Franck asked once we had done the obligatory cheer of *santé* and clinked our glasses together.

The estate agent began rifling through his papers with a growing look of despair. "*Mon dieu.* She wants me to inventory every fork and glass in this place. You are her first renters, *vous savez*. She is convinced you're going to steal everything." Ah. So my husband wasn't the only French person who secretly believed everyone was a thief at heart.

"We weren't planning on it," I said. "But now that you mention…"

Franck stepped meaningfully on my foot.

"It's not even like she knows what she has in here," the man said. "Usually the inventory is a checklist. She actually expects me to go through the entire house and mark everything down inside?" I assumed this was a rhetorical question.

I could hear Charlotte and Camille as they clattered down the servants' staircase. "We'd better get started," I said. "Our daughters are going to want dinner soon."

The estate agent gave one look at the papers with a sigh and said. "*D'accord*. I guess we could start with the cutlery."

I lead him to the mammoth wooden buffet that sat to one side of the kitchen and contained four enormous drawers. I pulled open the drawer where I had discovered the cutlery. It contained about two hundred mismatched forks, spoons, knives, and even some *escargot* tongs.

"*Ce n'est pas vrai*," the estate agent gasped. "How are we supposed to count all that?"

Franck was the only one of us that wasn't overwhelmed by a sudden wave of despair.

Forty-five minutes later we had counted all the cutlery in the drawer, although we had given up early on trying to sort them into sets. There didn't appear to be a complete set of anything.

The estate agent went outside for a cigarette while Franck refreshed our glasses.

"Maybe we should do inventory for our rentals every time a new guest arrives," Franck mused.

"What?!"

"Kidding."

The estate agent came back in, fortified by nicotine. "All right," he said, "Let's see what is in these other drawers." He pulled one open, only to reveal that it was about twice as full of cutlery as the one we just inventoried.

Panic in his eyes, he pulled out the third drawer and then the fourth – all were filled with silverware, some of it solid silver – all mismatched and jumbled in the drawers. He appeared too stunned for speech.

"What about this," Franck finally suggested. "How about we promise to take care of everything in the house and you promise to come back at the end of our tenancy and sign your papers saying that we haven't damaged or stolen a thing?"

The estate agent turned to Franck, gratitude in his eyes. "That is an excellent suggestion."

"Shall we drink on it?" I asked, and raised my glass. We all clinked to our secret and exhaled.

I woke up the next morning with a minor problem – I was unable to breathe. Since we moved here two days before, sleep had been fractured and almost non-existent. What felt like needles poked me through the mattress, which was lumpy and hard to boot.

Franck, who had never been known to have an allergy in his life, sneezed.

"What the hell is going on with these beds?" He leapt up and stripped the mattress cover off his side of the mattress, releasing a cloud of noxious brown dust.

I began to wheeze and stumbled towards the bathroom in search of my inhaler.

"Put the mattress cover back on!" I shouted out him, invigorated by a few hits of Ventolin. "What in God's name is under there?"

Franck was inspecting the mattress. "You're not going to believe what this is made out of," he said, without looking up.

I stayed at a safe distance. The mattress was covered with gray, brown and yellow stains. "Desiccated cats?"

"Close," he held up a very dusty clump of hairs that had been poking out a hole on his side of the bed. "Horsehair."

I drew closer and sneezed again. "So that's what was poking me all night long? Revolting."

We both stared down at our bed, repelled yet fascinated.

"Just think of all the people who have had sex on this mattress," I said. "Maybe some babies were even born here. Maybe some people even died on here...I'd definitely bet some people died here."

"I don't care so much about that, but it must be crawling with dust mites and bed bugs and who knows what other little beasts. Can you imagine having a beautiful house like this and then sleeping on such godawful..."

I interrupted him with an uncontrollable sneezing fit. "We have to get new mattresses," I said once I caught my breath.

"Agreed," he said grimly. "But first we have to get the girls off to school."

Franck found me in the cellar when he returned from Beaune, wrestling with the laundry machine. The drum was a top loader and mounted sideways compared to a North American machine. It had to be unlatched at the end of the cycle but this one wouldn't budge.

"Did the girls do OK?" I asked Franck as he picked his way past teetering piles of terra cotta roof tiles and bicycle wheels over to me. Guilt sat uncomfortably in my stomach that I hadn't gone along for drop-off but I honestly wasn't sure I could leave my girls at that place a second time.

"They got into their classrooms without suffering bodily harm. I consider that a success."

I grimaced. Our definition of parenting success had been drastically downgraded since moving to France.

Franck stood close to me and I caught his familiar whiff of *savon de Marseille* and apples. I felt strangely shy at his proximity. We barely shared a minute alone in the past two months. We worked fiendishly to move ourselves and Camille and Charlotte out of our little beach bungalow in Victoria and over here to France. Since arriving in Burgundy we dragged Charlotte and Camille around with us as we obtained medical cards for the family, bought cell phones, and set up school insurance. Our downtime was mainly spent bribing the girls with merry-go-round rides on the Place Carnot. For the thousandth time since Charlotte was born I wondered how Franck and I were supposed to pull off the magic trick of being both a romantic couple and the parents of two young children.

I pushed and pulled at the latch of the metal drum inside the laundry machine. It didn't open. Not only did I not feel like a grown woman or competent mother in France, I actually felt like a child again most of the time, unable to accomplish the most basic tasks. I couldn't drive until I learned to drive a stick shift, this morning I couldn't figure out how to light the gas elements to heat up the milk, and now I couldn't even open the washing machine to do a load of laundry. I kicked the machine and swore in English, then in French for good measure.

"Here, let me." Franck clicked the latch open with a flick of his fingers.

"How did you do that?" I demanded.

"You have to press it in before pulling on it to unlatch."

With Franck and me there was always a certain element of inequality in our relationship. When we were back in Canada I was the one who knew how everything worked from things like avoiding conflict at dinner parties to applying for a Visa card. In the past few years I hadn't always been overly sympathetic of Franck's feelings of isolation and alienation in a foreign culture. Were things like this washing machine in fact karma giving me a long overdue slice of humble pie?

"We have a lot to do today." I kicked the machine one last time. "What should we start with?" The list went on and on - starting to search for a house to move into before Christmas, getting the tradesmen to come by the cottage we were renovating to begin giving us quotes, signing me up for driving lessons, new mattresses...

Franck pushed me against the washing machine for a deep kiss. "We haven't explored the house yet," he murmured against my lips after some time. "There must be at least a dozen beds."

I felt like we should talk first to reconnect after so much business. As usual though, there was no time for that. "Do you think any of them have better mattresses than the ones we slept on last night?"

Franck began to stuff the pile of clothes on the floor into the washing machine. "Let's find out."

By the time we got to the eighth bedroom in the house, under the eaves and with a wet patch on the ceiling but a spectacular view out to Savigny's vineyards, we had to conclude that our mattress was, tragically, the best of the lot.

We couldn't lie down on any of them for more than five seconds before we both fell into a violent sneezing fit.

Franck checked his watch. "I hate to admit defeat, unless…there's the pool table down in the games room…"

"It looked ancient and not very sturdy," I said, regretfully.

Franck sighed deeply. "Let's go down to Beaune and try to find some new mattresses. We have to pick the girls up in about an hour anyway."

We found four cheap mattresses at a discount store, which briefly buoyed our spirits. I tried not to be disturbed about what constituted fun for Franck and I these days. However, when we picked up the girls for lunch at school, Camille's teacher informed us that our previously talkative daughter had still not said a word. At recess, Séverine said, Camille sat at the base of the Virgin Mary statue singing to herself until the children were called back into the classroom.

Charlotte's teacher said that our daughter was speaking, but the *maitresse* confessed to me that she had grave concerns over my eldest daughter's hand-eye coordination.

"What do you mean?" I asked, confused.

"Charlotte doesn't hold her scissors properly. It means she will not be able to handwrite properly when she is older."

"She'll just get the hang of it. It doesn't worry me too much." I had a nostalgic thought of Charlotte's "learn through play" preschool back in Canada where not cutting off your own fingers or your best friend's hair qualified as superlative scissor skills.

Charlotte's teacher looked at me, astonished. "Her cursive writing may never be as it should be, you know. I have seen this scissor problem with other students in the past."

"Is there anything we can do about it?"

"I can try to teach her better scissor skills at school and you can reinforce them at home, but this problem is usually impossible to fix."

"Luckily we live in the computer age!" I laughed.

The teacher looked at me askance and then turned her attention to a child named Maxance who had not buttoned up his cardigan properly.

We hustled off our scissor-challenged and mute daughters back to our house, where I had the temerity to suggest to my husband that we whip up the girls a couple of ham sandwiches on baguettes.

Franck took a casserole out of the large pine armoire in the kitchen pantry. "Laura, this is not North America. We must have a hot lunch."

I sneezed a few more times and searched in vain for a Kleenex or paper towel to blow my nose. "Look Franck, we're both exhausted and...ah..." I took note of Charlotte and Camille looking up at me, listening to every word that came out of my mouth like a couple of attentive owls. "*Frustrated*," I finished euphemistically. "We have to get the girls back to school in another hour and a half. Let's cut ourselves some slack."

Franck cast me a horrified look. "We are back in France now."

"So?"

"That means we can stop living like demented North Americans grazing a few scraps of food at lunch. The girls are given a two hour lunch break because we are supposed to sit down and eat a proper meal as a family."

"Can't we just start doing the hot lunch thing tomorrow?"

"I'm going to make us some chicken in mustard sauce with green beans, and maybe a salad." Franck began clanking the pots and with a lot more noise than was necessary. "I refuse to eat like a savage."

I rolled my eyes, and shooed Camille and Charlotte up to the landing to play their game with the *tomettes*.

I threw the baguette back down on the kitchen counter. "Fine. Knock yourself out. I'm going to hang up the laundry."

"You do that."

I tripped over a pile of empty wine bottles on my way back to the machine. When I was running on empty, all I wanted to do was stop everything and rest. When Franck was out of gas, his way of coping was to just keep pushing himself harder.

It had been a difficult few months – wondering if we were making a huge mistake, emotional good-byes to everyone, plus the sheer logistical nightmare of packing up a house and two young children. By the time I got on that airplane seat to fly to Burgundy I was literally vibrating with anxiety.

A hot lunch? Of course I was too damn tired to make a hot lunch. I took soggy clothes out of the washer and hung them on the drying rack that stood beside the washing machine. *Why couldn't people in France just have dryers?* The clothes were so wet that I had to wring them dry before hanging them. Nothing worked here the way it should, including Franck and me.

I wiped the water pouring from my eyes. Even though I was away from the horsehair mattresses my allergies were getting worse. My nostrils were completely plugged up and I could only breath out of my mouth. There was something about these old houses…I loved them but they didn't always love me back.

Franck opened the door. "Come on Lolo," he said. "*À table.*"

I sneezed for an answer.

CHAPTER 4

I was such a mess by the time we dropped the girls back at school that all I wanted to do was go back home, snort nasal spray, take some heavy duty allergy medication, and collapse on our new mattress. Another appealing option was surgically detaching my nose from my face.

"Can you take them to their classrooms?" I asked when Franck parked on the curb. "I think I'm better off staying in the car."

My eyes were beginning to stream and puff up, so Franck didn't argue. I gave the girls a kiss then rested my head on the back of the car seat and closed my eyes. Maybe if I just stayed like this for a few minutes without moving my nose would unplug.

That hope proved futile. By the time Franck returned to the car I was even more stuffed up.

Franck started the engine. "We must go to the bank. We need to start meeting with bankers about the mortgage…"

"I don't want to go to the bank!" I burst into tears. "I'm a complete mess. Look at me."

"Where do you want to go then?"

"Not anywhere around people."

"Home?"

"My allergies will just get worse." Today, for some reason, everything seemed impossible.

Franck thought for a moment. "I have an idea."

"Good," I said, rested my head back on the car seat and closed my eyes. "Wake me up when we get there."

I didn't fall asleep. My plugged nose and itchy throat wouldn't let me do that. Also, Franck's driving with all of its sudden bursts of speed and abrupt braking could not exactly be described as conducive to slumber.

After about ten minutes we turned a sharp left and then squealed to a stop.

Franck touched my shoulder. "Lolo? Here we are."

I opened my eyes. We were parked in front of a café in a village that I didn't recognize. "Where are we?"

Franck reached over and undid my seatbelt. "The Alps, or the closest thing to it around here. I figured if there was anywhere you would be able to breathe better, it would be here."

Still sniffing, I got out of the car.

Before I left Canada everyone had raved about how I was living out their dream by moving back to France. The bones of my story sounded idyllic indeed - French husband, rolling vineyards, a 17th century ruin to bring back to its former glory. Somehow nobody, especially not me, imagined allergies as part of that picture.

"Are we going for a café?" I asked.

"Later." Franck took my hand and we strolled into the village.

"What village is this?" I admired a late blooming rose that was a color somewhere between fuschia and orange climbing up the stone wall of a house.

"Bouilland. It's completely unlike any other village around here. Look up."

Towering above the village on both sides were soaring cliffs of green trees giving way to white rock. I tried to take a deep breath, but my nostrils were still completely closed up.

"Come on." Franck led me to a stone structure that cleaved the main road of the village in two.

We walked up a mossy stone step and then another to the rectangle of square water in the middle set into the well-worn stone. It was the old village washing house.

I bent over and began to cough uncontrollably, disturbing the timeless tranquility of the spot.

"Franck!" I heard a male voice call my husband's name.

I straightened up to see a tall man in a navy business suit and tie with a cell phone glued to his ear.

"Martial!" Franck went over and shook his hand. "I don't believe it. What are you doing loitering about Bouilland?"

I recognized the man now. It was the suit that had thrown me. Martial had grown up in Magny-les-Villers and had formed part of Franck's pack of village boys who spent their youth making slingshots and riding around on *mobilettes* – the noisier the better.

Martial leaned forward to give me *les bises* and I held my breath so as not to sneeze on him.

"I heard you were coming back to Burgundy." Martial's blue eyes had a way of laughing for him. I was going to answer, but was waylaid by another coughing jag. I dug in my pockets for Kleenex but came up empty. "How are you finding being back in Burgundy so far?" Martial asked as I contemplated my sleeve.

"Laura has allergies," Franck explained. "She's miserable today."

Martial studied me. "Allergic to Burgundy?"

"I feel like it at the moment."

"Why are you looking like you're running for political office?" Franck asked Martial.

"I'm not fixing church bells anymore." Martial pointedly dusted off his impeccable lapel. "I have a new job."

"Modeling menswear?" Franck guessed.

"*Non*, although I am certainly handsome enough. I sell street signs to the mayors of France. *Monsieur le Maire* of Bouilland needs new ones. You can hardly read those old Michelin ones anymore."

"Can we buy you a café and catch up?" Franck asked.

"Normally I would love to, but I'm already running a bit late and as it happens *Monsieur le Maire* of Bouilland does not like to be kept waiting. How about dinner soon?"

"Definitely. Good luck with your signs. We're going to go up to the cliffs."

"Don't fall off like I did," Martial said, holding up his arm. "Twelve metal pins. They'll be there permanently. I'm a bionic man now."

I remembered something else endearing about Martial. He was as accident-prone as he was addicted to extreme sports.

With that, Martial rushed off to his *rendez-vous* and Franck dragged me up the winding roads of the village of Bouilland to the cliffs.

We finally made it up to the top. I was gasping for breath whereas Franck was not even breathing heavier than usual.

I plopped down on an outcropping of rock that overlooked the spectacular valley carved in the rocks towards Beaune. I could actually inhale a thread of air through my nose now.

We soaked up the cooler air and sweet smell of wild grasses while admiring a *buze* – a large local bird –soaring over the treetops and then over the rooftops of the village.

"It's not easy," Franck said, out of the blue.

"The hike up here? Try it with a plugged nose."

"*Non.* That's not what I meant. Moving back here. It's not as easy as I thought it would be."

I turned and watched his pensive hazel eyes. "Even for you? I thought it was just me."

He reached his arms back and stretched out his legs. "Even for me. Those years back in Canada I built up this ideal vision of what life back here would be like. It's not turning out how I had imagined. I mean, of course my family is glad to see us but the reality is that they are all busy with their own lives. Also, I realize how much work we have ahead of us if we are going to build anything even remotely like the dream we had in our minds. It's going to take time."

I lay back beside him, relief washing through my bones. "I can't drive, I can't understand the cultural undercurrents of what is going on most of the time, I can't even do anything concrete to help us get in and start renovating the cottage quickly. I hate feeling so useless."

Franck picked a long stalk of dried yellow grass from the clump that sprouted up beside us and stuck it between his teeth. "You've been renting out the cottage for us," he reminded me.

I gazed up at the sky. "Is that really a help?" I wondered aloud. "Or does it just add more stress to our lives that we have an absolute deadline?"

"I guess that remains to be seen."

The clouds floated above us, small fluffy dots in an azure sky. How peaceful and far away from everything I felt up here.

"I feel like just another extra burden for you," I finally admitted. "I think I hate that the most of all."

Franck tickled my ear with his stalk of grass. "You could never be a burden to me."

I batted the grass away and found the perfect spot to nestle my head in the crook between his shoulder and his neck. "Camille not talking is worrying me. It's so unlike her. Do you think the other kids are bullying her? Not knowing what is going on makes her vulnerable."

"I think she understands more than she lets on."

I didn't agree. If Camille did understand the French spoken at school, what was she waiting for? Before moving here I had never worried about the girls' integration into French life. Maybe the fact that I didn't meant I was a negligent parent.

Charlotte had been a Buddha baby who basically just smiled and gurgled at the world. Franck and I did a significant amount of patting ourselves on the back about that, quickly concluding that our firstborn was so easy because we were such amazing parents.

Camille's arrival rid us of that illusion. She emerged from my body hollering and didn't stop. She screamed during the day. She screamed during the night. She screamed as though she was being stabbed to death. The doctors said it would pass, except it didn't.

Franck and I were catatonic with exhaustion. My panic attacks came back with a vengeance. Then, magically, as soon as she could start forming short sentences, Camille's screaming stopped. It only dawned on me then that Camille's discontent was not colic or a dislocated shoulder, but rather that she hated being a baby. When she began talking she transformed into the most competent, independent child I had ever known, sort of like a mini Martha Stewart.

The wheat smell of grasses wafted around us. The sun touched the treetops on the opposite cliff top. In the few months before we moved to Burgundy, Camille had been contented for the first time in her life. Had we upset that balance in moving here? Had we traumatized our daughter for life? Now that she had stopped talking at school, would the screaming begin again?

Franck and I spent the entire afternoon on the cliffs, descending to real life just in time to have a strong black espresso under the *tilleuls* of the village café before going to pick up the girls from school. It was strange how there could be moments that were idyllic in the midst of the chaos and confusion of creating a new life here in France. When we had imagined all the ideal images before we moved here we were seeing just a sliver of the whole picture.

When we arrived at Saint Coeur, Franck went to Charlotte's classroom while I made my way to Camille's, dreading to see my traumatized little raven-haired girl.

Camille sat at the end of a row of children on a bench by the door of the classroom. She was looking pensive and clutched her bag of school slippers to take home for the weekend. My heart contracted with guilt. I heard Franck and Charlotte arrive behind me.

Camille's teacher was helping a crying child do up her zipper and had her back turned. A blond headed boy who didn't have a coveted spot on the bench took advantage of this fact and squeezed himself between Camille and the next child on the bench. I watched as he, with a strategically placed elbow, shoved Camille off the bench and sent her tumbling to the ground.

Before I could surge forward past the crowd of parents to pick my daughter up off the floor and dry her tears, Camille sprung up and dusted off her denim jumper. Camille narrowed her hazel eyes at the little boy with a look of calculated vengeance.

She inserted herself beside him again so now he risked teetering off the end of the bench.

The little boy began to whine to the teacher that Camille was pushing him. Camille took a cursory glance at her *maitresse* to ensure that she was still preoccupied with the other child's zipper dilemma. Safe in this knowledge, Camille pivoted herself, raised one leg and gave the wingeing boy such a decisive kick in his ribs that he flew airborne.

By the time the *maitresse* turned to discover why the little boy was sprawled, sniveling, on the floor, Camille was sitting with her knees together and her hands folded in her lap, the perfect angel.

I felt Franck's hand on my shoulder. "I think Camille is going to be just fine," he murmured in my ear.

CHAPTER 5

The next week's "To Do" list was daunting to say the least:

1. Find a house to buy for ourselves.
2. Meet with our banker to get a mortgage for *La Maison de la Vieille Vigne.*
3. Figure out what we need to do as far as renovations to ready the cottage by July 12th and start doing it. Fast.
4. Teach Laura to drive stick shift.

Of all the items on the list, the last one intimidated me the most. Unfortunately, it was the first item we tackled. I was booked in on Monday morning for my first driving lesson.

We dropped the girls off at school under a rumbling sky. The humidity of the past few days was fast blossoming into a thunderstorm. By the time Franck turned into the "*ABC École de Conduite*" off the ring road in Beaune fork lightning was flashing overhead.

Franck glanced up at the sky. "This could get interesting."

I had a flashback to my driver's test, taken like every good North American child of my generation the day I turned sixteen.

It had begun auspiciously. I was appointed a cute examiner who was probably only a few years older than myself. I executed a flawless parallel parking maneuver and merged like a pro. I must have become overconfident. That was the only explanation for not seeing the old lady with the walker crossing the sidewalk. As Franck and I got out of our car fat raindrops started to fall from the sky. We hurried inside where two well-cured specimens were smoking cigarettes and drinking espressos with their feet up on the counter.

"*Bonjour*," said one of them. "If you're my nine o'clock, you're early. You'll have to wait until I finish this cigarette."

Franck nudged me forward. "I'm Laura Germain," I said. "And, trust me, I'm in no hurry."

After I had almost run over the old lady on my sixteenth birthday, the instructor turned on me, sweat beading on his forehead. "Didn't you see her? You almost killed that woman! Get out. I'm driving back."

I spent the rest of the short drive back to the Motor Vehicle Center in agony. I was guilty of daydreaming when I almost flattened that woman. I pictured myself walking in the door of my house and showing everyone my license. Stupid. Stupid. Stupid.

When the instructor pulled us into one of the parking spots at the testing center he scribbled furiously on the paper attached to his clipboard. I couldn't remember ever feeling so mortified.

"Mme Germain!" the skinnier man with the longest, boniest fingers I have ever seen and who seemed to be my instructor snapped me out of my memories. "I have a very important question to ask you."

"*Oui?*"

"Do you mind me smoking in the car?"

Of course I minded. My allergies were only slightly minimized by the heavy doses of antihistamines and my asthma was acting up. Still, maybe a little discomfort was worth it to stay on my instructor's good side.

"*Non*," I answered. "It doesn't bother me at all."

Thunder boomed overhead. I held to a faint hope that my lesson would be cancelled.

"*D'accord* Madame Germain." The man stubbed out his cigarette and stood up, dashing that idea. "I will teach you how to drive. My name is Cyril."

"Call me Laura." I shook his hand, which I noticed was stained yellow from tobacco.

"I will address you as Madame Germain," he said.

"It's not necessary."

"Yes it is Madame Germain. Are you ready?"

"*Oui*," I lied.

He beckoned us outside where there was a little red car. The rain was banging down on its roof and everywhere else. Surely he was going to drive to begin with, especially in this terrible weather.

"*Allez-y*," he opened the driver's side and gestured at me to get in.

"I've never driven a standard before," I said, just to clarify.

"That's why you're here, *n'est-ce pas*? Cyril ground his cigarette out with his heel and promptly lit another one. "Please get in and make yourself comfortable." He winked at Franck. "Monsieur Germain, can you pick your wife up in an hour?"

"*Oui*." I could tell Franck was fighting back a smile. "*Bonne chance*." He gave my shoulder a departing pat as I adjusted my seat. "I'm going to go and make that appointment at the bank about the mortgage."

I watched as he climbed up the extremely steep driveway leading to the ring road, abandoning me. It dawned on me for the first time that the only way out of this parking lot was for me to drive the car up the very steep hill that lead directly into three lanes of impatient French drivers speeding around the ring road like it was a Formula 1 racetrack. I froze. There was no way in hell I could do this.

"How am I supposed to get the car up that hill?" I asked Cyril once he settled beside me in the passenger seat.

"Put the car in first gear and then push your foot on the accelerator while you ease your other foot off the clutch."

"I have no idea what you just said."

Cyril gave me a very brief lesson on the gears and the clutch between deep sucks on his cigarette. He nestled back into his seat when he was done. "Go ahead. Get us out of here."

I turned the key in the ignition, tried to coordinate pushing on the accelerator while easing off the clutch. The car stalled with a massive lurch.

"Try again." Cyril seemed to be taking all of this very lightly. Did he have a death wish?

I stalled about fifty times trying to make the car go up the hill. Once I finally got half way up, I started rolling backwards every time I stalled. I wiped my nose on the back of my hand, beyond caring about social niceties.

"Why does this car roll backwards?" I demanded after a few minutes. My heart was pounding. "Automatic cars don't roll backwards. Standard cars are *stupide*. Why make something more difficult than it needs to be?"

I was sweating and unnervingly close to crying. I was a small child again, learning to ride a bike or tie my shoes and it all seemed impossibly difficult and frustrating.

Cyril took a deep drag, nonplussed. "Now that is a complex question, is it not? But for now you need to get this car out onto the *boulevard*. I may be mistaken, but I don't think philosophical questions are going to help."

Anger made me slam the accelerator to the floor while pressing down the clutch. The car flew out onto the ring road - by some miracle not plowing into any other cars. I was so confounded by the clutch that I had no attention left to pay attention to steering.

I stalled again. My car was horizontal across the two lanes of the ring road. A quick glance to my left confirmed that cars were bearing down on me.

"I would try to start the engine again if I were you," Cyril observed.

I'm still not entirely sure how I got out of there. Cars were honking, my heart was pounding so hard that I was sure I was going to pass out, and instead of helping me Cyril was leisurely blowing smoke out his window. I must have tapped deep inside the cavewomanpart of me that remembered how to escape the wooly mammoth. In a massive burst of adrenaline I swerved the car around and managed to park it on the gravel shoulder of the main road. I could barely see out the windshield for the rain. I lowered my head to the steering wheel and tried to start breathing again.

"*Putain de merde*," I muttered. Those were bad French words. The kind of bad French words I told our girls never to say. Yet here I was, saying them in front of my new driving instructor.

"My sentiments exactly," Cyril agreed. "Let's just take a moment and appreciate being alive, *n'est-ce pas?*"

"Let's," I said with some asperity.

At the end of the lesson all I had managed to do was to make one circuit of Beaune's ring road. No laudable feat seeing as under normal circumstances it only took about five minutes to circumnavigate. I stalled roughly a hundred times, often almost killing us in the process.

Cyril studied me as I pulled up the parking break. "That went well," he said finally.

"Are you serious? It was awful!"

"The only way to truly learn things is by doing them," he said, holding his hands out for the keys that I gladly bequeathed.

I rolled my eyes. I had abandoned any pretext of manners quite some time ago.

"You can roll your eyes at me, but it's true," he said. "Learning new things is hard. It's not supposed to be easy."

"Well, rest assured, it's not."

"That's the problem with us adults. We get too used to knowing how to do everything. Learning new things is good for the soul."

"If that's the case, my soul should be shining by now."

"I believe it is." Cyril slammed his door shut and pulled his jacket over his head to protect himself from the rain. "You are glowing."

"That's sweat."

Franck was waiting for me, chatting with the other man behind the counter who had not moved since we left.

"You're still alive?" Franck directed his question at Cyril, not me.

Cyril made a show of checking all of his limbs were present and accounted for. "It appears so," he finally concluded. "Until Madame Germain's next lesson, at least."

Franck booked several more lessons, despite my protests. Thankfully, however, Cyril was leaving *en vacances* for a few weeks so I had a temporary breather.

"I'm never, ever going to do that again," I vowed as Franck and I left the *ABC Auto-École*. "We'll need to return the car we bought and find an automatic instead." I couldn't remember ever feeling so humiliated.

"Automatics are as easy to find over here as snowflakes in the Sahara. Besides, they are obscenely expensive." He grabbed my arm and lifted it up to check the time on my watch as we walked - me with jelly legs – back to our car. "We have an appointment at the bank in about ten minutes."

I groaned. I knew we needed to figure out the financing of our little cottage quickly so that we could begin the renovations. Still, I felt so shaky that I was certain I would require several Diazepams washed down with a large bottle of *Côte de Nuits* before I could conduct any sort of rational conversation about amortizations tables and interest rates.

We were greeted by our French banker, Monsieur Deloire, who had set up our mortgage for *La Maison des Deux Clochers* and who I knew loved taking long walks in the vineyards with his wife and was counting down the seconds until his imminent retirement.

"What is this I hear? You two have bought another house?" he asked us as he sat down behind his desk after the formal greetings. "Isn't one enough?"

Franck clasped his hands together on his lap and smiled. "The vacation rental idea went far better than either of us had imagined."

Monsieur Deloire ran a hand through his pure white hair. "You young people…all this ambition! I'll never understand it."

Ambition? I didn't know if it was ambition as much as kismet. My crazy idea for renting out *La Maison des Deux Clochers* when we weren't using it had evolved into a successful business. Franck and I were a great team. He had the local connections and experience and, unlike me, he paid attention to details which made him a great manager of the day-to-day operations of the rental. I, on the other hand, possessed a knack for marketing and communicating with our guests.

Our little venture was so successful, in fact, that when the opportunity to buy the cottage sprung up my father and sisters wanted Franck and me to buy it on behalf of my family's real estate company. It sounded like a great investment, they said.

The cottage was purchased with the company's money and in the company's name. The full ramifications of this hasty decision only dawned on me now. Unlike our previous renovation of *La Maison des Deux Clochers* this time the risk we were taking on didn't just involve Franck and I, but my family as well. The pressure to make this one a success was thus far greater.

Monsieur Deloire looked rather mystified by us, but said, "So tell me about this new property."

Franck went on to give him a brief description, strategically glossing over the multitude of problems.

Monsieur Deloire steepled his fingers, nodding. "I don't foresee too much of a problem getting another mortgage for you and Madame Germain. Let us begin a *dossier* for you right now." He flicked on his computer and began pressing keys.

"There's one minor difference this time," Franck said, as an afterthought. "This house is actually not being bought in the name of my wife and I. It is being bought by the company of my wife's family."

Monsieur Deloire paused. "A *French* company?"

"No," I said. "It's a Canadian company."

Our banker lifted his hands up from the keyboard and sat back in his chair. "*Impossible*. We cannot lend money to a foreign company. It is simply not done."

I frowned. "What about international commerce and all that?"

"International commerce has not yet come to Burgundy."

"Surely there must be a way," I insisted. My innate stubbornness was fast overtaking my shakiness.

"I know I cannot lend money to a foreign company. My hands are tied. The risk is too great for the bank."

"The cottage wasn't very expensive. It is a very small amount, comparatively speaking," I said.

"The amount is irrelevant."

"We are a third generation wholly owned family company," I added. "We have assets and excellent credit."

"That is irrelevant too."

"In Canada a foreign company can borrow money from the banks. I've seen it done my whole life," I insisted.

Monsieur Deloire raised his thin white brows at me. "In case you haven't noticed yet, Madame Germain, this is not Canada."

I thought back to my driving lesson. "I've noticed."

"French banking rules are unique."

I knew that in a vague way, of course, but the words "nothing can be done" sparked rebellion in my soul. It would be a small amount loaned to a very reputable company. There was *always* something that could be done. The man across from me was simply focused on his retirement and too lazy to create any more work for himself.

I refused to contemplate going back to my family with my tail between my legs, saying we couldn't find a way to finance the property in France. Franck and I had sold everyone on this cottage idea. Now it was up to us to make it work.

The perfect idea flashed in my mind. "What about a trust?"

"A what?" Monsieur Deloire asked.

"A trust," I repeated, thinking to myself *what banker has never heard of a trust?* "We finance the property in our names, but on behalf of the company." Ah-hah! So my Oxford law degree hadn't been for naught. As it happened, trusts had been my best subject.

Monsieur Deloire leaned forward over steepled fingers. "I have never heard of that concept Madame Germain. I don't think such a thing exists in France."

"That's impossible," I protested. "Trusts exist all over the world."

Franck placed a stilling hand on my shoulder. "Don't be so sure," he said. "It's time to pick up the girls."

I looked at my watch in disbelief. This whole two hour French lunch thing every day was wonderful when we were here on vacation, but when we had so much to do…picking up my girls and going back home to Savigny to whip up everyone a hot sit down lunch was not exactly what I felt like doing at this particular juncture. What I felt like doing was finding a mortgage for the cottage.

As it turned out Franck was also shocked over the unforeseen mortgage dilemma. So much so that, for once, he was also feeling uninspired on the cooking front. Lunch was a slice of *jambon blanc* each, Mousseline *purée* from a box, and a big green salad. However, the ham was from Bayonne, the mashed potatoes were spiked with Dijon mustard, and the vinaigrette I made for the lovely green lettuce was flavored with diced shallottes from Provence and mopped up with fresh slices of baguette. Simple was somehow light-years better in France than in North America.

When Franck returned from dropping the girls back at school we sat down to phone our familiar yet incompetent notary, Maître Lefebvre. Amongst its other oddities our rental came equipped with two old-fashioned phones equipped with an extra earpiece, or *écouteur*, attached to the back so I could eavesdrop on the conversation.

Of course our notary was still out for his lunch, which we knew from past experience always extended well beyond the traditional two hours (as well as far beyond the traditional two bottles of wine, for that matter). Franck was more than satisfied, however, to direct my questions about trusts to Maître Lefebvre's secretary who, as we learned during our purchase of *La Maison des Deux Clochers*, was light-years more competent than her wayward *patron*.

"The banker, unfortunately, was correct," she answered in her usual efficient tones. "I am familiar with trusts – they are used in England, for example, but they are not legally recognized by the French civil code. They cannot be used here in France. You must find another way."

"What do you suggest?" Franck asked.

"It's going to be very difficult, if not impossible," she warned.

"I was afraid you were going to say that," said Franck.

"Find another banker," she suggested. "That's what I would try to do. Then if they say no try another and another and another…"

"*Merci*," Franck said.

"*De rien Monsieur Germain*," she said. "*Bon courage* to you and Madame Germain. You'll need it."

Franck hung up the phone and turned to me. "Is there any solution that doesn't require getting a mortgage on the property to do the renovations?"

"No," I said. "We have to leverage it. That's the only way to get a decent return on the company's investment. That is what we promised my family we would do."

"I guess we'll just have to meet with more bankers then." Franck put on his jacket.

"Now?"

"*Non*. We have to go and meet Luc at the cottage now."

"But we can't start on the renovation work until we get the financing," I protested.

"Look, Luc is fantastic. If we don't start using him right away someone else is going to snap him up and we can't afford *that* happening. I'll make appointments with every other banker in Beaune tomorrow."

We quickly sped off up through the vineyards and past the *cabottes* to Villers-la-Faye, both of our minds reeling at how complicated things had become in the space of a few hours.

Luc was waiting for us in his white *camionette* smoking a cigarette and powdered white with drywall dust, *comme d'habitude.*

"Sorry we're always late," I apologized. "It's hard with the kids going back and forth to school…"

"I know," he said. "I've got two."

"Boys or girls?"

"Boys," he said. "Hellions. They're terrifying. You?"

"Girls. They can be surprisingly terrifying too."

Franck unlocked the shutters then the front door and we ventured inside.

Luc coughed. "I have to ask you a question."

"*Quoi?*" Franck turned towards Luc.

"Why this house?" Luc asked. "Why don't you just build a new house?"

Franck eyes widened as though considering this question for the first time.

I answered instead. "I love this wall." I lay my hand on the piled stonewall of the living room that had been built sometime around the mid 1600's.

Luc looked at Franck, confused.

Franck shrugged. "History, I guess," he said. "That's why it has to be this house."

"I love old houses," I admitted.

"There's family history here too," Franck said. "When I was born in Dijon my grandparents were over here having a drink with the old couple who lived here. The woman who manned the only phone in the village – Geneviève I think her name was – ran down here to announce to them that my mother had a boy and that they had a grandson."

"I never knew that! " I punched his shoulder lightly. "Who lived there then?"

"They were winemakers. I can't remember their names, but I do remember what this cottage was like. It had dirt floors and chickens pecking around underneath the kitchen table. There was only one sink for water and it ran outside. They always had a roaring fire going in that hearth." Franck nodded over to the traditional stone Burgundian fireplace against the far wall. "Winter and summer. I don't know if it was to keep the chickens warm or them."

I turned to Luc. "It's hard to explain and it makes no practical sense, but I just feel that this cottage was meant for us." We were destined to make it into the perfect place for people to come and live like the French. The renovation of *La Maison de la Vieille Vigne* and the new start for our family here in France had been inextricably intertwined since Franck and I had begun to contemplate this move. I wasn't sure why, but one couldn't seem to exist without the other for me.

Luc frowned.

"I know I sound crazy."

"A bit," he admitted. "But that's not entirely a bad thing. I've learned that to get through a renovation of an old house it helps to be a bit crazy."

Franck was inspecting the solidity of the fake oak beams between the kitchen area and the rest of the main area. "This all needs to come down," he said, as if making a mental note.

"How have you been doing with the building permits?" Luc asked him.

"The Mayor's office is closed every time I go."

"I would get started on that if I were you," Luc gave the partition Franck was inspecting a solid kick and made a hole in the wallpapered bottom section. "You know…French administration."

"I'll take care of it," Franck said, but I could tell he was already preoccupied by the idea of demolishing the partition. He had always loved the demolition phase of renovations.

Luc was similarly transfixed. "It would only take a small sledgehammer. I bet we could get this monstrosity down in an hour."

"Half an hour," Franck countered.

"I'm sure you could," I interrupted them. "But we need to figure out first what order do the renovations have to be done in. What is our first priority?"

Luc snapped out of his demolition daydreams. "Definitely the roof.

Nothing can be done before that is taken care of. You mentioned skylights, right?"

"Yes," I pointed up to the ceiling beyond the mezzanine and the huge oak beams. "I think three would be perfect. That would fill this room with natural light. "

"They would," Luc agreed. "But you know that the Architect of French Monuments doesn't like skylights, don't you?"

"The who?" I asked.

"The Architect of French Monuments. Any renovation work that is done in this village has to be run past him. So far I have lucked out and not had any direct dealings with him, but I've heard he's not a very friendly person."

"There must be a mistake," I said. "We never ran anything by him in Magny-les-Villers when we did *La Maison des Deux Clochers*. Our house could not be more in the center of the village and I painted the shutters lavender for god's sake. Nobody said anything." Well, they probably did, but not to our faces.

Luc had taken out his measuring tape and was measuring the fireplace. "The difference is that Magny doesn't have any classed historical monuments that are protected by the state. Villers-la-Faye had two."

"*La Maison des Deux Clochers* is right across the street from the twelfth century Roman church!"

Franck clicked his tongue. "It sounds like you are expecting there to be logic behind these things Laura."

"What historical monuments are protected in Villers-la-Faye?" I demanded.

Luc began jotting down his measurements on his clipboard. "The village *chateau*," he said, as though everyone knew that. On second thought, maybe everyone did besides me.

"That's on the other side of the village," I said.

Luc nodded.

"What else?" I asked.

"The chapel on top of the Mont Saint Victor."

The chapel on top of the Mont Saint Victor dated from the 12th century and, granted, the top of the Mont was used as a gathering place from Neolithic times. Still the Mont Saint Victor was covered with trees and there was no way even with a long-range telescope that you could see our cottage from the chapel.

"That's insane," I grumbled.

"It is," Luc agreed. "Yet unavoidable."

"What do we have to do to get permission from this guy?"

"The mayor's office will have the forms, but it won't be easy."

When we had said somewhat depressed *au-revoirs* to Luc and got back in the car, Franck took a right turn in front of the Villers-la-Faye's *Salle des fêtes* instead of going in the direction of Savigny.

"Where are we going?"

"I want to show you something." Franck turned right at the old wine press that was placed for decoration on the next street corner.

He stopped the car in front of an ugly cinder block wall that looked like it belonged on Alcatraz.

"This is the only house for sale in the village," Franck said. "I checked."

We got out of the car and walked over to the rotting wooden fence that was kept shut by a heavy chain linked around the two sides. The yard was a jungle of waist-high weeds. An ugly brick terrace that wrapped around the front broke off suddenly and led to another expanse of unfinished concrete.

The unloved feel of the place gave me the shivers. "It looks like it's never been finished."

"It wasn't. Still, it's been used as a yearly rental and before that it was the village tobacco shop. I used to come here to buy my *gitanes*, along with everyone else in the village."

Franck began to unwind the metal chain around the fence and ease it open.

"We shouldn't..." I began.

"Trust me. There's nobody here. This place has been for sale forever."

No wonder. Clearly the concept of home staging had not yet arrived in Villers-la-Faye.

I followed Franck gingerly through the tall grasses. I'd never been afraid of snakes, but there were little ones here in Burgundy called "vipers" that were extremely poisonous and hung out in neglected places such as this. I breathed a sigh of relief when we stepped up onto the half-tiled terrace.

Franck took my hand. "I know it looks awful. But come here and see." He drew me around to the side terrace where the wall consisted of a winning combination of more unfinished concrete blocks and rotting wood rails.

Franck put his hand under my chin and tilted my head so that my field of vision was suddenly filled with the Mont Saint Victor.

"I love this view of *le Mont*," Franck said, referring to the village "mountain" in the shorthand that all the locals used. "This house probably has the best view of it in the whole village."

If you weren't from Villers-la-Faye or Magny-les-Villers it would be hard to fathom the symbolic importance of the Mont Saint-Victor, that large wooded hill that dominated the landscape of the two villages. Not only was the Mont, according to the historians, the genesis of Villers-la-Faye and the site of encampments well before Roman times, back all the way to the druids, but also generation upon generation of Franck's family and his fellow villagers' families were buried in the cemetery at the very top. The history of Villers-la-Faye was not only found in its streets and vineyards, but most importantly, at the summit of the Mont Saint Victor.

"It's a good view," I conceded.

When I turned away from the Mont I saw that the terrace looked out over the rooftops of Villers-la-Faye, including the remaining tower of the 12th century castle that was partly responsible for us having to wade through French administration to get our skylights approved for the cottage. Beyond that there were fields and vineyards. In the distance I could see Magny-les-Villers, and even the church tower across from *La Maison des Deux Clochers*.

"It's a great view," I corrected myself.

I turned back to the house where there was one French door covered by a set of full-length wooden shutters.

"I wonder why they didn't put a window on this side," I said, pointing to the wall just behind where we stood. "That way it would be balanced, and a pair of French doors here would look right out onto

48

the church in Magny." Uh oh. When I started mentally fixing things in a property I knew from past experience that I teetered on the edge of the rabbit hole.

"There is a lot to do here. It's definitely a project." Franck tucked a stray bit of hair that had escaped my ponytail behind my ear. His fingers lingered on my neck.

"Do we have it in us to take on *another* project right now?" The mere idea was demented, especially considering that with the cottage we had clearly bitten off more than we could chew.

"Do we have a choice?" Franck said. "The house we are in now is only available until December and, trust me, with only electric heat and that many rooms we will want to be out of there well before then. We could rent-"

"No." I had been brought up to believe that the idea of paying someone else rent when we could be paying down our mortgage was ludicrous. I had been taught in my real estate family that buying then living in lousy places until you fixed them up was how a person created a real estate portfolio. Franck and I were by no means rolling in extra cash, but seeing as we had to pay a rent or mortgage anyway, I definitely preferred a mortgage. A rental would be more comfortable in the short term, definitely, but short-term pain for long-term gain had been drilled into my head from an early age. We just needed to find a place to buy that was livable enough until the renovations at the cottage were finished.

"I'd thought maybe we could look in Beaune, you know, near the girls' school," I suggested

A cloud covered the sun and Franck took me by the shoulders. "Laura, I didn't come back to Burgundy to live in Beaune. I want our girls to live in my village, to wake up every day and see the Mont Saint Victor, to lay down in the grass on Les Chaumes on the warm summer evenings and look at the stars."

"And this is the only house for sale in Villers-la-Faye? You're sure?"

"*Oui.*"

I sighed. Franck and I attracted messy and unwieldy projects with what seemed like an irresistible magnetic force. "I guess we better make an appointment to see the inside."

Franck smiled. "I'll call the notary as soon as we get back to Savigny."

CHAPTER 6

It had been a grueling week of adjustment and trouble-shooting. We knew we had so much to do, but what we needed most of all was a little break. For once, Franck seemed to be exhausted enough to be on the same page.

We all slept in late on Saturday morning. At nine o'clock the girls woke up and after breakfast set to exploring the odd old toys in the grand playroom, or "Salle de Jeu". I took my time eating breakfast while reading a fascinating article in the local newspaper about a wild boar who had fallen in to someone's outdoor pool in Gerland. The girls pulled in a stuffed pony to show me. It was mounted on four wheels and looked like it suffered the mange. This was followed by an ancient doll with a decaying orange silk dress. Last was a complete set of *pétanque* balls in a leather case. It took both of them to lug it over to the kitchen table.

Franck examined the set. "Would you like me to teach you how to play girls?" The courtyard outside was pea gravel like most French courtyards, perfect for playing *pétanque*.

The morning was warm so Franck and I and the girls went outside in our pajamas and slippers. I brought my *café au lait* with me and Franck did the same.

He gave the tiny metal ball to Charlotte. "That's called the '*cochonnet*'. Throw it as far as you can."

She did, demonstrating fine form and a good arm in her pink Disney princess nightie.

"All right," Franck said, giving Charlotte and Camille each a well-scuffed *pétanque* ball, large and heavy. "Now what you have to try to do is throw your ball as close as you can to the little one. You can also knock out someone's ball."

"Can I go first?" asked Charlotte.

"Yes. *Vas-y.*"

Camille began to protest that she wanted to go first, but I distracted her by getting her to pick a ball for me out of the case.

Charlotte lobbed her ball overhand before Franck could show her the proper form of the underhanded toss. It went far though, a good foot past the *cochonnet*. Charlotte ran to inspect where it landed and before I realized it Camille launched her ball and the lead ball only missed Charlotte's skull by a few millimeters.

"Camille!" Adrenaline coursed through my veins. "Why did you throw your ball? Didn't you see Charlotte? And Charlotte – when you play *pétanque* you must never run out in front of where people will be throwing balls."

Why, with young children could a seemingly innocuous activity turn into a death-defying moment on the turn of a dime? It was one of the aspects of becoming a parent that I struggled with the most. Some days, I felt like all I did from dawn until dusk was keep my two girls alive.

We played a few more games, enough time for my heartbeat to return to normal. Both girls had the tendency to run out in front of the path where the balls were being thrown, so Franck and I devised a system where we held them back in a modified headlock until it was their turn or the coast was clear. Franck was the clear winner, even though the girls and I got in some nice shots.

"I'm bored," Camille said eventually. "What can we do now?"

"Let's go for a family walk."

This suggestion was met with groans, so I rephrased my suggestion.

"Do you want to go and see a real castle?"

This was met with jumping and clapping. It took more than an hour, but eventually Franck and I and the girls were all dressed and standing out in the courtyard in the warm fall sunshine. Charlotte and Camille had adorned themselves with plastic tiaras that they had brought in their carry-on bags from Canada.

"There are real princesses there, right?" Charlotte adjusted her crown.

"Not any more, but I'm sure there used to be."

We walked out past our huge stone pillars and down the winding narrow path between two large houses that lead to the village church. We turned into a slightly wider passageway and stopped, astounded.

"Wow," Charlotte murmured.

The sight was incredible. We were at the beginning of a tunnel made of roses. Row after row of trellises arched over the passage and on each one grew a different colored climbing rose. Even though it was September the plants were still full of blooms. The perfume in the air was sublime.

"We must be getting close," Charlotte said. "It smells like princesses."

"Somebody from the village does this," Franck whispered to me. "Every year all season long this passageway is covered in roses."

Camille and Charlotte surveyed the beauty above them, then after a few minutes Camille tugged at our hands. "I want to go and see the princess now."

The rose passageway led to Savigny's impressive village *chateau*. It rose up like something out of a Grimm's Fairy Tale. Its blond stone walls were punctuated by four chubby medieval turrets – one on each corner. There was a ditch in the grass around the castle where there once had been a moat and a real drawbridge. Camille and Charlotte stared.

"Is it real Mom, or am I dreaming?" Charlotte asked, finally.

"It's a real castle." I put my arm around her.

"I want to see princesses!" Camille exclaimed. She had always possessed a one-track mind.

"No princesses live here anymore," I admitted. In fact, the owner of the castle was an eccentric Count who had an extensive and motley collection of motorcycles, racecars, and old fighter jets which cluttered the back park of the *château*, but I wasn't sure how to explain this travesty to the girls.

The girls moaned with disappointment.

"*Maman* is wrong. That will happen here in France quite a bit because she is Canadian, you know," Franck said to our daughters. "There is indeed a princess who lives here, but she must have stepped out for a moment."

"Where did she go?" Charlotte asked, bouncing on her toes.

Franck thought about this for a moment. The girls didn't even look to me for an answer - clearly Franck had appointed himself the princess expert. "She must have gone out for a walk in the vineyards. Do you think we should go find her?"

"Yes!" the girls shouted in unison, and they followed Franck back through the winding passageways and cobble streets of the village again until we popped out onto a sloping hill of vineyards for as far as the eye could see. The leaves were bright green and the grapes a dusky purple, so dark that some bunches almost appeared black.

Tractors roared to and fro and the vineyard ahead of us was dotted with workers stationed up and down the rows.

Franck covered his eyes so he could see in the bright sunlight. "The harvest must have started. We were so wrapped up in work this week that I didn't even realize *les vendanges* were close."

Nobody could predict the harvest dates from year to year. Tradition decreed that the grapes be picked one hundred days after the blossoming of the flowers on the grape vines, but winemaking in Burgundy was far more an art than an exact science. So much depended on the weather, especially in the weeks and days leading up to the actual commencement of the harvest.

Before the harvest was declared, the winemakers went out to their vines and tasted their grapes every day, often several times a day, waiting for that perfect concentration and balance of sweetness and acidity. If they harvested too soon the wine would be flat and without character. If they waited too long a downpour could cause rot or worse yet, a bad hailstorm could obliterate their entire crop. I always admired the nerves of winemakers – they played chicken with Mother Nature year after year.

We walked through the vineyards past one of the little round huts built of piled stones. Savigny was known for having many of these beautifully preserved *"cabottes"* dotted through its surrounding vineyards. They were traditionally used by winemakers to store their tools and for shelter during Burgundy's violent storms.

"Is this house for elves?" Charlotte asked. She and Camille played in and around it while Franck and I examined the grapes in the vines near us. The dark green leaves were beginning to take on a touch of scarlet. I popped one of the grapes off the tight bunch. The skin was tough, but once it gave way it was an explosion of deep, tart flavor.

"I think it's going to be a good year," I said to Franck. Despite the unrelenting chunks of bad news thrown at our heads during the past week, I felt optimistic as I watched my girls play in the Burgundy vineyards that were their birthright. This is what we had come here for, after all. Maybe we really could somehow achieve a new, improved family life in France despite all the crises we still needed to resolve.

Franck pressed me back against the curved rocks of the *cabotte*. The sun-soaked stones warmed me through my linen shirt. He took my face in his hands. His thumbs ran down my jawbone as he kissed me.

"I think so too," he agreed. His weekend stubble brushed over my skin. I melted into him. Family life had a constant domino effect. When one of us was happy it made everyone else happy and when one of us was miserable it reverberated as well, affecting all of us. The four of us were tied together for better or for worse.

"I wasn't just talking about this year's wine vintage," I clarified.

"I know." Franck smiled against my lips and we stayed like that for a long time. How could life be filled with so many extreme ups and downs? Having children just seemed to deepen this paradox. Still, today any problems we faced seemed to shrivel up in the warmth of the sun and the stone.

A gagging sound snapped me out of my reverie.

Both of my girls had the tendency to pop anything that looked remotely intriguing into their mouths, including but not limited to cigarette butts, worms, poisonous berries, and dog food. They also made a habit of choking on things so I was finely attuned to gagging sounds.

I looked over Franck's shoulder and breathed a sigh of relief. Charlotte was sticking her fingers down her throat. "Gross," she said to Camille and made the gagging sound again. "They're kissing."

"That's boring," said Camille, and came over to pull at my shirt. "I want to go over there." She pointed to where the harvesters were laughing a few rows over.

"*D'accord*," Franck said. "Lead the way."

Hand in hand, with the girls skipping in front of us, casting up the ochre vineyard dust, we made our way over to the harvesters. They were a motley crew, dressed in filthy clothes, with T-shirts or shorts tied around their heads to protect them from sunstroke. I knew that some of them were probably doctors and lawyers or other well-heeled friends of the winemaker who came and did the harvest every year, picking side by side with backpacking teenagers and unemployed youth. Harvesting was the great equalizer and they would all be complaining about the heat of the beating sun and sore backs from kneeling down in the dirt all day long.

Unlabeled bottles of wine were being passed up and down the rows. Charlotte and Camille stood at the head of the row, wide-eyed and tiaras askew.

"Do you want to try to harvest some grapes?" A man with an impressive girth and a pink t-shirt wrapped around his head came over and kneeled down beside the girls. He held out his wickedly sharp shears.

"Go ahead," I said, while Franck began chatting with another bare-chested man wearing a fraying straw hat. Franck and he seemed to vaguely know each other. I watched as the pink T-shirt man took Camille and Charlotte half way down the row and showed them how to separate the grape bunches from one another and where to cut the grapes off the vine. They cut off several bunches each until the man's bucket was full.

He kept up a constant stream of chatter and the girls occasionally nodded yes or no and Charlotte even squeaked out an occasional *oui*. When he asked them if they were from Savigny the girls shook their heads and Charlotte whispered, "*Non. Nous sommes canadiennes.*"

"Canada!" he exclaimed, then stood up and shouted out to his fellow harvesters, "We have little girls here that have come all the way from Canada to help us with the harvest. Everybody say *bonjour* to *les petites canadiennes!*"

Everyone shouted *bonjour* and Charlotte and Camille were immediately swept into the team of harvesters. My girls snipped off grapes, helped haul buckets to the tractor and then, when that was full, they were invited to ride on the tractor that was festooned with grape vines.

Franck and I followed behind on foot through the vineyards.

"Did you know that guy you were talking too?" I asked.

"Vaguely. Turns out he's a distant cousin, maybe second or third cousin. We couldn't really figure it out." This happened often since we had arrived in Burgundy. Sometimes I wondered whether Franck wasn't related in one way or another to most of the people here.

The tractor wove through the village and into the *cuverie* at a local winemaker's family *Domaine* where the grapes were dumped out on the sorting table. We were all given a glass of freshly pressed grape juice to sip, although our new friend used imaginative miming to explain to the girls that they had to be careful not to drink too much or else they would get an explosive case of diarrhea.

About two hours later we all wandered out of the massive *cuverie*, Camille and Charlotte both wearing crowns of grape leaves and vines laid over their tiaras. They were smiling from ear to ear.

Back at home where we enjoyed a very late lunch outside in the courtyard, Camille gasped. "We never found the princess!"

"I think I saw a glimpse of her gown between the rows of vines when you two were riding on the tractor," Franck said. "We'll just have to keep looking

On Sunday morning we watched a *pétanque* tournament that was being fiercely fought in the village lane. At lunch we went to Mémé 's tiny studio apartment and were treated to a lunch of *blanquette de veau* and floating islands – egg whites that had been whipped up until they were stiff and then poached in vanilla sugar water to make a dessert that was as diaphanous as it was delectable. The egg islands floated in a homemade *crème anglaise* that was one of Mémé's specialties. It was a delicate sauce of eggs, butter, vanilla and milk. *Crème anglaise* separated easily and was recognized amongst French chefs as a tricky culinary undertaking but it was something that Mémé's skill triumphed over time after time. Her finishing touch was a latticework of homemade caramel drizzled over the islands, adding a satisfying crunch. The girls gobbled it up just as enthusiastically as Franck and I and declared that they had found yet another "new favorite" dessert.

On the way home that afternoon we stopped by an outdoor *brocante* in the village of Pernand-Vergelesses and I found a beautiful red old-fashioned hand grinder for coffee like Mémé used to use every day. It would be perfect for *La Maison de la Vieille Vigne*, which – like our new life here in Burgundy - was taking shape in my mind's eye, even though reality was light-years from that vision.

On Monday we began the week with renewed vigor. True to his word, Franck had managed to make appointments with what seemed like every banker in Beaune. We started out Monday morning at the *Banque Nationale de France* on the Place Carnot. The dapper young banker listened to us indulgently for about five minutes but as soon as we mentioned taking out a mortgage in the name of a Canadian company, a wall slammed down behind his eyes.

He began re-arranging paperwork on his desk. "I'm sorry Monsieur and Madame Germain, but what you are asking for is *impossible*. It is simply not done."

Franck and I protested, but we quickly realized that nothing we could say or do, nor any amount of charm in the world, would sway him.

"The bankers in France are completely xenophobic," I announced, perhaps a tad louder than necessary, as Franck pushed me out the door of the bank. We retreated to the café next door to wait for our next appointment over a few espressos. I hadn't seen the finger in Franck's right hand twitch, a sign that he was dying for a cigarette, in many months, but it was doing the samba now.

"It's so frustrating." I reached out across the table, stilling his hand. "Should we have seen this coming?"

"I'm asking myself the same question." Franck nodded at the waiter who came and set down our espressos and handed him a ten-euro bill.

As I stirred my sugar lump into my espresso, I realized that I had been holding on to the hope that our banker had been a one-off, a relic who didn't want to make an effort because he was so close to retirement. Now I had to face the fact that the problem was far more widespread than that.

"I never even imagined that this would be an issue," I said. "The banks in Canada would be throwing money at us."

Franck frowned. "I blame myself. I think I had forgotten how backwards France is at times. The real problem is that we can't afford to lose Luc, which means we have to pay him. I don't see any option but dipping into our small reserve and then spending night and day figuring out a way to get that mortgage." We couldn't use a trust as they didn't exist in France and if we took the mortgage out in our own names the family company couldn't claim any of the extensive tax deductions for the purchase and renovations of the cottage.

I squeezed his hand. It was a risk - what if we didn't get a mortgage before the reserve ran out? - but I also didn't see any other option.

"I feel a debt to your parents." Franck gulped back his espresso in a couple of swallows. "We have to find a way to finish the cottage and have it ready in time for our renters. We have to find a way to make it work, *c'est tout.*"

"Agreed. I would rather grovel on my knees to a hundred bankers than go back to my family and tell them that we couldn't get the cottage ready for a vacation rental."

Franck squeezed my hand. The situation was *merdique* but it made it easier that we were on exactly the same page.

"So what do we do?"

Franck removed my other hand from around the handle of my espresso cup and took it in his. "Remember when I was trying to emigrate to Canada?"

I nodded. Of course I did. That too had seemed impossible at the time. I remembered long hours spent with him on the payphone at my dorm at McGill, trying to figure out a way for us to be together.

"Everybody told me no," Franck said now. "I did not fit the profile. Canada didn't want me. Do you remember what I did?"

How could I have forgotten? It was one of the most romantic gestures I had ever witnessed. "You went to Paris," I said. "You opened the phone book and phoned every single number that had anything to do with Canada."

"That's right." Franck ran his thumbs over my palms. "I met with as many people as I could and I told them all the same thing, that I wanted to move to Canada so I could be with the woman I loved. Person after person told me that it wasn't even worth their time to give me the forms to fill out. I just kept phoning and setting up appointments until finally one woman at the *Délégation du Québec* said after I had told her our story, 'Of all the reasons for moving to a different country, I honestly can't think of a better one.' She sent me to a friend of hers who could fast track my immigration papers and two months later I got off the plane in Montreal."

I knew this story by heart, of course, but it was good to be reminded that tenacity was the reason we were sitting here, married and with two incredible daughters.

"Remember how I bought you balloons?" I picked up his hands and pressed my lips against his knuckles. "And how I was wearing that black skirt and those long black boots?"

"I'll never forget what you looked like." That had been an unforgettable day, not to mention the night. I fell into fond memories.

After a while the waiter came back to ask if we wanted another coffee.

"So we just need to do the same thing here," I said, at last. "Keep trying until we find that one person who will say yes."

"We'll probably hear a lot of no's," Franck warned. "But we'll keep trying. If we run out of bankers here in Beaune we'll go to Dijon, then Lyon, then Paris."

Optimism coursed through my veins once more. "I'm game."

We both stood up. "*Allons-y*," Franck said. "We don't want to be late for our appointment. Maybe the next one will be the good one."

The only way forward was to believe that every time.

CHAPTER 7

Unfortunately, the next meeting wasn't "the good one", nor was the one after that or the ones he had for the rest of that week and the next. By the time we arrived at my next scheduled driving appointment with Cyril, the power of Franck's pep talk had begun to wane and a nagging possibility that maybe the person who would say *oui* to our mortgage didn't actually exist in France.

"You again?" Cyril said in greeting as I walked in the door of *ABC Auto-École* with Franck.

I sighed. "Unfortunately."

Cyril raised his eyebrows. "Shall we try not to stall in the middle of the *boulevard* this afternoon?"

"We shall try," I said. "But we shall not be making any promises."

Cyril's poker face twitched with a smile. He patted his back pocket. "Just making sure my cigarettes are there," he said. "Something tells me I'm going to need them."

As we walked out to the car I looked over at my nemesis - the very steep, very short hill that led directly on to the ring road. Fear pulsed in my chest.

"Why would you even choose this location for a driving school?" I asked as I climbed in the car. "All new drivers are going to have a hard time getting out of here."

"Not all." Cyril belted himself in beside me and pulled out the ashtray in the dashboard. "Some students succeed the first time they try."

"That makes me feel terrible," I informed him.

"It should Madame Germain. It should."

"That hill is terrifying," I muttered.

"Fear is an excellent teacher," Cyril reached over to turn on the ignition, something I neglected to do.

When I wrenched the gearshift into reverse and backed up without stalling, I was amazed. I pointed the car in the direction of the hill and the ring road.

I shifted gears to what I hoped was first gear and eased my foot on the gas while letting up on the clutch. The car actually started to climb! I had to stop myself from crowing in triumph.

I must have let up my foot too fast from the clutch because half way up the hill the car stalled and began rolling backwards.

"What is this car doing?" My feet tried to find the brake but I my mind had gone blank with panic and I kept pressing on the clutch instead. "These standard cars are just so…" I hit the steering wheel and searched for a sufficiently damning word. "French!" I finished.

Cyril made a little tsk'ing sound under his breath and put the car into first gear. "Try again."

I stalled again, then a second and third time and then a fourth and a fifth. My face was blazing and I blinked back tears."Couldn't you just…you know…drive the car up to the ring road for me?"

"*Non.*"

"I hate this." This raw humiliation was not something that, as a relatively competent adult back in Canada, I was used to feeling. Had I somehow over the years become completely unable to learn new things? Was I living proof of the "old dog, new tricks" adage? I cursed Franck and France and the day we had ever concocted the idea of moving back here. Our recent glorious weekends in Savigny faded in my memory. All I was left with was rage. Rage at myself and my new country and my chain-smoking driving instructor who refused to drive the car up onto the ring road for me.

"Use that anger," Cyril suggested.

The next time I stalled, I slammed the car into first, turned the key and pressed my foot down to the floor on the accelerator. The car flew up the hill and right into the second lane of traffic. Again, no cars were in my way. Franck's guardian angels must be working overtime during my driving lessons. My heart pounding, I turned the car straight with a squeal of rubber on the road and sped onwards.

I glanced nervously at Cyril, whose bloodshot eyes were rounder than I'd ever seen before. "That was a lot of anger," he noted.

"You told me to use it."

"You could have gotten us killed, *bien sûr*. Still…most impressive."

I turned back to the road and noticed a traffic light ahead of me. Of course it turned red. I stalled, of course, and all the cars behind and around me honked.

I began to cry in earnest.

Franck was waiting for me back at the *auto-école*, thumbing through a copy of *Le Bien Publique*.

"How did it go?" he asked, clearly before catching sight of my scarlet, wet face.

"*Difficilement*," said Cyril. "But it will get better, won't it Madame Germain?"

I made a nasty sound at the back of my throat. "I'm never coming back."

"So," Cyril said, putting his cigarette in the ashtray for a moment so that he could flip through the appointment book. "Is next Tuesday at two o'clock all right?"

Franck made the appointment and hurried me out to go and pick up the girls at school. I picked up Charlotte while Franck went to Camille's classroom. When I came back Franck was still talking earnestly with Camille's *maitresse* Severine.

"Is anything wrong?" I asked.

Franck turned to me. "Camille is still not talking."

Sévérine twisted the delicate gold cross she wore around her neck. "She seems quite happy and understands most of what is going on. I expected her not to speak at the beginning, but it's been almost a month now. We went on a field trip today to see the grape harvest. I could tell she was interested but she wouldn't ask or answer any questions."

I kneeled down and took Camille's hand in my own. "Why don't you talk in school Camille?" I asked, in English. "Is anything wrong?"

She examined my face with her large hazel eyes for a moment and then gave me an eloquent one-shoulder shrug. I still had no inkling why she was mute at school, but at least she had the non-verbal part of the French communication down pat.

"What does she do during recess?" Franck asked.

She mainly sings to the Virgin Mary statue or plays with her sister. She doesn't appear upset at all, but…I'm just not sure what else I can do so that she feels at ease. I'm at a loss."

"We'll talk to her at home." I stood up and smiled at Severine. "Thank you for telling us."

"*De rien*," Séverine gave us an apologetic smile and went back into the classroom.

My mind was churning as we walked the girls out of the schoolyard and past the massive wooden doors that were being guarded by *Le Dragon*, who gave me a sour look as usual. Sadness and worry jostled for room in my mind. Was Camille turning into a disturbed child? I felt completely traumatized after the fruitless meetings at the bank and the driving lessons. Were we inflicting a similar trauma on our two and a half year old daughter?

We buckled the girls in their car seats.

"Charlotte, do you talk at school?" I asked, eyeing her in the rear view mirror as Frank pulled out of the parking lot.

"A little bit," she said. "Not much, but more than Camille."

"Are the other kids mean to you?"

She gave a shrug identical to her sister.

I groaned. "What have we done?" I asked Franck.

His mouth was tight. He merely shook his head.

When we got into the vineyards before the turnoff to Savigny, Franck turned the car towards the hillside village of Pernand-Vergelesses. The vineyards around the car were erupting with harvesters. Tractors rumbled in the distance and the loud shouts and laughs from the people rang out.

"Where are we going?" I asked Franck.

"Stéphanie's," Franck said. "It's been a bad day. I think we all need an *apéritif*."

In Canada, I would always call first before dropping by someone's house unannounced, but here in Burgundy spontaneity was not just accepted, it was expected.

"Hey kids." I turned around to the silent twosome in the backseat. "We're going to see Tom and Lola. You can have a play with your cousins." The girls erupted in cheers.

Just as we rounded the bend before entering into Pernand–Vergelesses, I cried out "*Arrêt!*"

Franck slammed on the brakes (without gearing down, I noted, which I wouldn't have noticed prior to my lessons…I suppressed a sudden urge to call Cyril and tell him). He pulled over on the side of the road, now swirling with dust, and stared. "What is it? You're going to give me a heart attack."

"Look." I pointed across the street, where harvesters were picking grapes and putting them in the most unbelievably picturesque wicker baskets.

Franck's annoyance evaporated. "Those are the traditional Burgundian harvesting baskets. People hardly use them anymore. That's what we used to use when I was little and my family did *les vendanges* together."

I took my camera out of my bag. "Let's go have a look and take photos."

Franck pulled the girls out of the car while I dashed across the road and began to snap pictures. The beautiful baskets, filled with deep purple pinot grapes, were piled high on a sort of double tractor. It was nothing short of stunning.

Franck, of course, began to chat with the harvesters and pointed to Camille and Charlotte how the old-fashioned baskets were perfectly shaped to fit when balanced on the shoulder of a harvester.

"It makes me so happy to see *les vendanges* done in the old way," Franck said to the harvester he was chatting with. "Is that why you use the old baskets for the harvest, for tradition?"

"They are very beautiful," the man admitted. "But more than that, the boss," he nodded down the row of vineyards to a tall, thin man who was fingering through the grapes in one of the fully loaded baskets, "Is convinced it makes better tasting wine. He doesn't want his grapes in contact with plastic at any time."

"Amazing," I said. "Thank you for letting me take photos."

The harvester shrugged. "My pleasure, but I'd better get back to work. These baskets, pretty as they are, don't fill themselves."

I got back in the car feeling far more reconciled with life. Every day at the moment felt like an exhilarating yet nauseating roller coaster of joy and despair. Was that life in France or just moving to a new country? Or both?

When we arrived at Steph's we were relieved to see their bright orange Kangoo van was in the driveway. We could get a drink and vent a little.

Charlotte and Camille ran around the back of the house where we could hear the shouts of greeting of their cousins Lola and Tom.

Franck and I sauntered after them, slowly and wordlessly soaking up the calm of the countryside and Stéphanie and Thierry's large garden.

"*Salut!*" We rounded the corner of the house to see Stéphanie get up from a hammock where she had been reading a book. "Thierry!" she yelled in the direction of the house. "Bring us out some glasses and something to drink."

"How was your day?" she asked, beckoning us to the garden table set up on their back deck.

I sat down and dropped my head in my hands. "I'm learning how to drive a stick shift. It's so *hard*. I just don't understand why all cars aren't automatic. I mean, why insist on something being difficult just for the sake of being difficult…"

"I don't find driving a stick shift hard," Steph said. She had that French habit of saying exactly what she thought without first asking herself if it was what I wanted to hear. I could tell she said this not to provoke, but rather to soothe, but her comment missed its mark by a wide margin.

"But you learned on a stick shift. It's different."

"Trust me, it's not that hard once you get the hang of it. You will catch on in no time."

I groaned. "Don't be so sure about that."

"I'm not," Franck quipped. Steph laughed and I cast him a dirty look.

"*Quoi?*" he shrugged. "I'm just being honest."

"You French are always so concerned about speaking the truth…have you ever considered just maybe saying something *nice* instead?"

Franck looked over at his sister and pursed his lips. They both shook their heads.

"*Non*," they answered in unison.

"*Jamais*," Steph added. Never.

I longed for some good old fashioned Canadian diplomacy - compliments and encouragements and condolences. I didn't care if it was insincere. Luckily, Thierry emerged from the house with his hands full of wineglasses and a very promising bottle of wine.

"*Salut*," he said, and gave Franck and me a kiss in greeting before setting everything down on the table. "*Ça va?*"

"I hate my driving lessons." I cracked my knuckles. "They're beyond humiliating."

"This should make you feel better." Thierry turned the bottle around and revealed a coveted "hospice" label. The hospital foundation in Beaune had been gifted vineyards since the late Middle Ages from locals who wanted to buy an express pass through Purgatory and through the pearly gates. The result was that the Beaune Hospices owned a mind-boggling selection of the world's most prestigious and expensive vineyards.

Both Stéphanie and Thierry worked at the hospital, which meant they were each allocated twelve bottles of this coveted stuff every year. The label read "*Corton Grand Cru, Cuvée Docteur Peste*, 2002." I liked Thierry's brand of French diplomacy.

Thierry poured us each a glass and I meditated on the ruby elixir that was backlit by the setting sun of the Indian summer.

"*Santé*," Thierry said and we all echoed that and clinked glasses.

"I'm finding life so much harder over here," I admitted. "We're always running back and forth to Beaune to drop off or pick up the kids from school. It feels like I have to learn everything all over again. We won't have a place to live in six weeks or so, we can't get a mortgage on the cottage...everything feels like a battle."

Steph called out to Tom to stop teasing Lola and Camille then took a sip of her wine. "I find life here slow and relaxing," she said, turning back to me. "I don't see it that way at all." Ick. More truth. Even though I knew she was trying to bolster me up by being positive I still felt a wave of envy.

I drank some wine and thought about it. Stéphanie had a comfortable home, she could drive her car, she had a circle of friends and a secure job as a nurse at the hospital that, although certainly not stress free, didn't require arguing with bankers or having to wade through impenetrable layers of French administration. For heaven's sakes, she was reading and napping in a hammock under her cherry tree when we arrived. Would my life here in France ever resemble what Stéphanie's life looked like now, or were Franck and I just not destined for tranquility? Something in both of us attracted upheaval, both for ourselves and now for our daughters.

I was never sure exactly how it happened. Our various projects always sounded like good ideas at the time. Maybe we should have just contented ourselves with coming back on vacation and staying at *La Maison des Deux Clochers*. Maybe the idea of buying and moving over here with Charlotte and Camille to renovate a second vacation rental was pure folly. Where did ambition cross the line into insanity?

The setting sun tinged the vineyards surrounding Steph's backyard with an orange light. The church bell rang six o'clock.

"Why exactly did you come back?" Steph asked Franck. "Was it just to renovate the vacation rental?"

Franck and I exchanged glances. We had talked about this many times over the past few months. One of the primary reasons we decided to move back was a desire to renovate another property. We loved our time renovating *La Maison des Deux Clochers*, despite all of the ups and downs, and we longed to do it again. More than that though, we saw that if we continued to live in Canada without returning to France for longer than three or four weeks of vacation every summer Charlotte and Camille would grow up without truly appropriating their French family and their French roots.

"The vacation rental is part of it," Franck said, echoing my thoughts. "But also we moved back so the girls could get to know what life is like here and spend time with you and Thierry and *papa* and *maman* and their cousins-"

Franck and I had always spoken French together, but back in Canada when we tried to speak French to the girls they would only answer us back in English. Often when we spoke to them in French they got impatient with us. So learning French was definitely a factor, but more than that we wanted them to know what it was to be a child in France; having two hour lunch breaks, going on fieldtrips to the vineyards during the grape harvest, experiencing those big, slow lunches with family or friends almost every Sunday. If we didn't move back here for at least a year Franck and I were worried they would never truly connect with that French part of them that ran through their blood.

A shriek that I recognized as Charlotte's rang through the air. Tom appeared from behind the cherry tree with Charlotte chasing after him, her fist raised. Apparently, Tom had been pulling Charlotte's hair over by the swing set.

Steph raised her brows. "At least the cousins are getting to know one another."

CHAPTER 8

The next week came and we were still striking out with the banks in Beaune. We couldn't fairly hold Luc off any longer so we gave him the green light to start demolishing the walls inside the cottage. Our appointment to visit the house for sale in Villers-la-Faye was Tuesday afternoon, but first I had to survive another driving lesson with Cyril.

Cyril waved me into the driver's seat as usual. "All right, Jacques Villeneuve," he said as he got in the car. "Show me what you can do."

I was so preoccupied with thoughts of our house visit and worrying about how we would pay Luc that I turned the ignition and eased the car up to the top of the hill before I even had time to think about what I was doing.

Cyril trapped his cigarette between his lips to free both hands and gave me a soft round of applause.

"Don't get too excited," I warned. "That may be the high point."

Cyril smiled.

He directed me half way around the ring road where I only – miracle of miracles – stalled once. Even then, I didn't get overly flustered and simply turned the key in the ignition to restart the car, ignoring the row of honking drivers behind me.

Cyril nodded his approval. "Turn left." I swung the car into a tiny cobblestone street. I held my breath as though that would make the car skinnier so it wouldn't scrape against the stone walls that seemed a hairs breadth away from the car doors. Spatial recognition had never been one of my strong points.

The street connected to one of the main roads of Beaune, the *rue de l'alsace*, which was always crowded with cars and jaywalking pedestrians.

"People really shouldn't lurch into the middle of the street like that," I said as I started the car again after slamming on the brakes to let a nimble grandmother dash across to kiss a friend.

"What if they see a friend at a café across the street?" Cyril asked.

"They should walk a little farther and use the crosswalk."

Cyril snorted as though that was the most absurd notion he'd ever heard in his life. "Drive slowly now," he said. "Slower."

"Are you looking for something?" I asked. "Or someone?"

"No. Just enjoying the view."

We kept driving for a good half an hour. Beaune wasn't very large and Cyril kept directing me through the exact same loops in the town, always ordering me to slow down at the same spots. I got so comfortable with the route that I actually looked up from the road during one of the last loops and noticed that all of the places where Cyril asked me to slow down were lingerie shops.

"You're making me slow down so you can look at ladies' underwear!"

Cyril shrugged, not paying me much attention. He was still preoccupied by an admittedly exquisite lavender lace set of panties, bra and garters that were pinned up in the lingerie store we were currently passing.

"*Je ne crois pas*...you planned our route to go past and slow down in front of all the lingerie stores in Beaune," I accused.

He sucked in his cigarette. "Of course."

"It's not very..." I was going to say politically correct, but I wasn't even sure if a French person knew what that meant. "It's not very polite," I finished off lamely.

"What does politeness have to do with lingerie?" he demanded, genuinely perplexed. "Actually if you want to talk about politeness I think what I'm doing is in fact exceedingly polite. Lingerie stores are there to be admired, just as women are meant to be admired. I think it would be terribly impolite *not* to pay attention."

"A Canadian driving instructor would never do that. It's completely unprofessional."

"What's unprofessional? Lingerie?"

"Of course not." I struggled to find the words. "It's just a Canadian man would never admit that he was actually *looking* at lingerie in a store window."

"I find that very sad," Cyril said. He told me to slow down again as we passed another underwear boutique. I sped up instead, just to be contrary.

"Did you marry a Canadian man?" Cyril asked.

"*Non*," I said. "You know I didn't."

He cackled with satisfaction. "*Vous voyez* Madame Germain, I'm not only teaching you about driving, but about French culture too."

"You mean the lingerie?"

"That, and also you may not have noticed but you have been driving beautifully while arguing with me. That is an essential skill here in France, Madame Germain. I feel great progress is being made."

He was right. I hadn't stalled once in the past ten minutes and he didn't even need to direct me anymore. I was whizzing in and out of the narrow stoned streets and avoiding pedestrians and slowing down in front of lingerie stores and ignoring other drivers like a seasoned pro. I did, actually, feel a little bit like Jacques Villeneuve.

"How can you possibly object to me admiring those window displays Madame Germain?"

I didn't answer. I felt backed into a corner, but not sure how I got myself there.

"Perhaps next time you would prefer if I make you drive in circles around the municipal rubbish heap instead?"

"*Non, merci,*" I said, fighting back a smile despite myself.

"Why look at something ugly when you can look at something beautiful?" He reached over and patted my hand. "You can take us back to the *Auto-École* now. I think you have learned enough for one day."

Cyril told Franck that I had driven like Jacques Villeneuve and that we had taken in some of Beaune's most scenic sights.

I gave my husband a modest smile and gloried in my success all the way back up to Savigny, through our lunch of free-range turkey cutlets in a cream and Dijon mustard sauce with ribbons of fresh tagliatelle and a salad of cubed beets in a punchy vinaigrette studded with freshly cut parsley, and all the way to Villers-la-Faye to visit the house.

Franck had discovered the house was for sale by none other than his family's drunken notary, Maître Lefebvre. The downside was that he was a drunken incompetent and had almost botched the sale of *La Maison des Deux Clochers* for us on more than one occasion. On the upside, he was as a rule of thumb too sauced to be truly dishonest. This was an important point, as before we bought *La Maison des Deux Clochers* we had been epically swindled out of a property in the nearby village of Marey-les-Fussey by a polished but corrupt notary from Beaune.

We got there twenty minutes late and to our shock saw that Maître Lefebvre had already arrived and was unlocking the gate.

"Hath hell frozen over?" I wondered out loud in English. Franck looked at me strangely. Idioms were always the last thing one learned in a foreign language.

"*Monsieur et Madame Germain!*" Maître Lefebvre greeted us like long lost family. "Have you grown out of the house in Magny already?"

"In a way," Franck said. "We have two daughters now, but we'll be keeping the house in Magny as a vacation rental."

"Ah! Real Estate investors!" He waggled dark and bountiful eyebrows.

"I wouldn't say we're quite…"

Franck elbowed me soundly in the ribs. Technically we were real estate investors, albeit small-time ones who were trying to cobble together a network of humble vacation rentals rather than building resorts on the Côte D'Azur.

"This is the perfect family home." Maître Lefebvre waved his hand to encompass the not-quite-finished house and waist high weeds in all its hideous glory as though he was presenting Versailles. If this was his idea of a perfect family home I was tempted to challenge him to move in with his family. I knew for a fact he lived in a stunning bourgeois estate in Ladoix-Serrigny. Lucky for him being a notary in France paid well regardless of competence.

"*Venez.*" Le Maitre waved us forward. "Come and discover the interior." I was pretty sure a palace of marble and gold didn't await us, even though Le Maitre's tone promised such wonders.

"Why is he even here, and on time?" I whispered to Franck as we followed Le Maître through the weeds to the front door. "That's never happened before."

"I have no idea," Franck said. "One thing I'll say for him, he always manages to surprise us."

The Maître unlocked the massive wooden front door to reveal a musty smelling foyer lined with the same ugly shade of terra cotta tile as the front porch.

The whole house was very dark, even after Le Maitre dashed around and opened the shutters. It consisted of three bedrooms and one main living area that would be much improved with the addition of another French door. There was also a bathroom with a separate toilet, common in France, and a full basement with, of course, a wine cellar.

Tons of renovations needed to be done, but once the shutters were open I could see it was feasible to actually live there (although not very comfortably) while we picked away at it bit by bit. The positives were that we could actually afford this house (although not any renovations yet), the wraparound deck was a lovely space (even though it needed to be refinished), and – the most compelling of them all - the commanding view of the Mont Saint Victor.

"Are there any other houses for sale in Villers-la-Faye?" Franck asked, just to confirm.

"None," Le Maitre said, watching for our reaction. "Everyone wants to live in these villages all of a sudden."

So that was another non-negligible point in this house's favor. The frost on the ground the past few mornings had reminded us that winter wasn't very far away and we had to find a place, no matter how simple, for our little family to nest.

Franck went over to the far wall in the living room and ran his fingers along the massive cast iron radiator. "This must heat well," he mused. "An oil furnace...at least we'll be warm."

I wasn't falling in love with this house, but I couldn't think of any other solution to our housing dilemma and I was desperate to knock off at least one item on our list of problems to solve. It wasn't much but in my mind it was still better than paying rent. I knew that we wouldn't have any problem getting a personal mortgage. Until the bankers discovered that *La Maison de la Vieille Vigne* was owned by a

75

Canadian company they had been ready to throw money at us.

"So, what do you think?" Le Maître asked as we wandered back outside and he locked the door behind us.

"We'll let you know," Franck said, and then, perhaps unable to resist, added, "You were here rather early today."

"Yes. I had a quick lunch, you see. My wife has put me on this ridiculous diet and insists I eat lunch at home for a month."

"No restaurants?" I said.

He shook his hound dog head. "*Non.* It is lamentable."

Franck and I exchanged glances. Mystery solved.

"We'll call you," Franck promised.

"I'll be waiting to hear from you," said Le Maître and he shook both our hands.

"For once," Franck said. "I actually believe him

Before going to pick up the girls from school for lunch Franck and I had to stop quickly by *La Maison des Deux Clochers* in Magny to drop off an extra set of towels for our guests staying there.

When we lived in Canada, Franck's parents had taken care of the little errands that came with operating a vacation rental. Now that we were back living in France it became part of our job description. Neither of us minded. It was nice to actually meet the guests I knew only from emails before and to see first-hand how they enjoyed Burgundy. Our guests were mainly Anglophones from North Amercia, New Zealand, Australia, and the UK. There were some Germans and Scandinavians sprinkled into the mix.

Because our guests came from farther afield they tended to stay anywhere from a week (our minimum) to several months. We did everything we could to give them the experience of living like a villager in a distinctly untouristy French village.

"We can take some time to discuss the house after we drop off the girls at school and meet with another banker in Beaune," Franck said, plopping a pile of freshly laundered and folded towels in my arms.

"*Merde.* I'd completely forgotten about that appointment."

"It could be the one," Franck quipped as we got out of the car in front of the church across from *La Maison des Deux Clochers*. That had become more and more of an inside joke between us as the "no's" from the bankers piled up.

"Do you ever lose hope?" I asked Franck.

"Never." He slung his arm around my shoulders as we walked under the Passage Saint Martin underneath the two bedrooms. When we popped through the other side into the courtyard he waved his hand up at the house. "Look. We did this, didn't we? That seemed impossible at the time."

Yes, but without two children and with financing and we didn't need to basically rebuild an entire house.

"Now who are these people?" Franck asked again in a whisper. My husband was wonderful with details, the main exception being people's names.

"Joe and Diana from Albuquerque. They're having friends come and stay for two nights, hence the towels. They sounded nice."

The door of the veranda was wide open as was the door to the house. I knocked on the lavender–painted metal to announce our arrival. Many of our guests, under the influence of delicious food, sublime wine, and the French cult of pleasure, rekindled romance during their stay at *La Maison des Deux Clochers*. It was one of the reasons I loved my job and a good reason to never walk in unannounced.

"Hello!" I called out. Franck took the pile of towels from my arms. I could see into the cool entryway and the ancient ceramic tiles that welcomed guests. I would always have a soft spot for this house. It was the first one Franck and I had ever bought and renovated together and the symbol for me turning my back on a prestigious law career and throwing myself into the uncertainty of life instead.

"Oh *bonjour!* You must be Laura and Franck." A dainty woman with astoundingly large hair bustled over and wrapped me in a warm hug. "I feel like I know you already! Thank you so much for bringing the towels." She hugged Franck and then divested him of his charge.

"Do come in!" Franck and I looked at each other. We didn't have much time – maybe five minutes – before we had to go and get Charlotte and Camille from school.

77

"So you've bought another house you're turning into a vacation rental!" She exclaimed. "I read all about it in Laura's blog."

"Yes," I sat down on the couch in the living room even though I knew we didn't have time to stay.

"And you moved your children here with you," she said in the same tone a person would use to say, *"And you lock your children up in the cellar and beat them."*

I nodded. "They were one of the main reasons we decided to move back here."

She patted her gravity-defying hair. "I'm afraid I can't agree with that," she said. "I grew up in a military family and was forced to move all the time when I was young. I hated it. It traumatized me for life. What children need is stability and *roots*. It is selfish for adults to drag them hither and yon and to not consider how it affects a young child to be ripped from everything he or she knows. I had years of therapy to get over it."

Franck and I were silent, equally stunned.

"I guess I never thought of it that way," I said.

"You should," she said.

It was easy to dismiss our guests as crazy. Her hair provided ample ammunition for that conclusion. The problem was that her opinion hit too closely to the guilt I felt on our bad days. On those days I did feel it had been short-sighted and maybe even cruel to force my children to adapt to a whole new life at such a vulnerable age.

"We must be off to pick up our girls." I tried a nervous laugh to cut through the tension but it fell flat. "I don't want them traumatized any more than necessary."

Franck and I beat a hasty retreat to our car. An uneasy blend of anger at our guest for speaking the thoughts I rarely dared voice and guilt that she was maybe right roiled in my gut.

"Don't listen to her." Franck turned the key in the ignition. "She's insane. I mean, just take a look at that hair. I would have loved to have travelled the world as a child."

I thought back to me when I was four, Charlotte's age. I was a painfully shy bookworm with a speech impediment. I couldn't pronounce either 'L's or 'R's properly and the mere act of having to tell someone my name 'Laura Bradbury' was enough to send me scuttling back to the warm familiarity of my house and my mother for days on end. I wouldn't have relished being taken out of my comfort zone at that point in my life. Had we made a huge mistake?

The next day the girls were off school, and we had to go grocery shopping again. Camille and Charlotte were particularly whiny. Franck and I stopped at the toy store to buy each of them a new Barbie doll before hitting the grocery store, as our boxes still hadn't arrived from Canada. I had actually come to hope that the boxes didn't arrive until we were moved into our house in Villers. The house that we had decided the previous afternoon, in a fit of folly or desperation, to buy. I was still shaking my head over that, but the fact that it was the only house for sale in Villers-la-Faye, that Franck was determined to live in "his" village, and that winter would soon be closing in did make the decision easier. The drawback with still not having our things arrive from Canada was that the girls had no toys to play with except the fragile and probably valuable ones at our Savigny mini-*chateau*.

Camille was thrilled with her doll that was raven haired like her new owner and sported a sparkly purple dress.

"Leave your dolls in the car," I said after we had parked at the grocery store in Beaune. "They'll just get lost in the store."

Camille kicked the back of her seat. "No!" she shouted and clung on to her's for dear life. "No! No! No!"

"Won't you be sad if you lose it?"

"I won't lose it," she asserted. She kicked the back of the seat to emphasize this point.

"Franck?" I needed backup.

"Let her take it," Franck said. "We'll do the groceries quickly and then get home so they can play for a bit."

A pounding headache may have been partly to blame, but in any case I caved. I held my triumphant two-year-old termagant by the hand through the hazardous maze of the parking lot. "Do you want me to put your dolly in my bag?" I tried.

"No," Camille said. I hoisted her up into the seat of the shopping cart and got to work. I was consumed by that frantic feeling that parents know all too well. Grocery shopping with crabby children was like trying to shop with a ticking bomb in your shopping cart. It was impossible for me to be relaxed or even logical about the items I was tossing inside. I threw in a creamy *camembert* from Normandy, an ash covered *Selle-sur-Chère* goat's cheese, and an impressively stinky Époisses. I grabbed a much-needed bottle of Cahors wine from Bordeaux from a stand across from the cheeses.

Franck came whipping around the corner with Charlotte in the seat of his cart, playing with her Barbie, a heavily made up blond.

"You're still here in the cheese aisle?" Franck said. "I need you to choose a *salade*, beets, some *paté*, and some *endives* to braise."

Camille began to climb from her seat into the main space of the shopping cart behind it, except that her legs were too short for this gymnastic feat.

"Stay where you are, Camille." I pushed her back in her seat. "That's dangerous."

She began to cry .I rushed to the fruits and vegetable section and began grabbing the things on our list. I didn't take the time that Franck always did to inspect the produce and squeeze and contemplate the different fruits and vegetables, but he was somewhere in the toilet paper section so I figured he would be none the wiser.

I stuffed a bunch of pale green endives into a plastic bag. When I turned around, Camille was standing up in her seat, rocking the cart back and forth as though it was a surfboard. Adrenaline kicked in like an ice pick to the brain.

"Camille!" I pushed her down again and she squawked in protest. "You could fall out and smash your head on the floor if you do that!" I considered lifting her to the ground, but she was fast and knew no fear – a hair-raising combination. Neither alternative was edifying, but I opted for containment in the cart.

As I turned to put the beets in the cart, she was standing once again.

I pushed her down again, this time with the Vulcan death grip on the back of her neck. She began to scream at the top of her lungs. Why, oh why, don't grocery carts come equipped with straightjackets and muzzles for toddlers and young children? Bone deep exhaustion made me want to curl up on the floor underneath the pile of luscious oranges from Provence and fall asleep.

Thankfully, none of the people in the store looked askance. French people were remarkably sanguine about young children having tantrums. The reasoning seemed to be that they all did it, that it was just part of parenting children, and that it was an *affaire* between the parents and the child. I did receive a few sympathetic looks, for which I was fleetingly grateful.

"Stop it!" I hissed at Camille who was trying to stand up a third time as I threw the last of the vegetables in the cart and took off in search of Franck.

I found him, as expected, in the toilet paper aisle. The surprise was he was chatting with Le Gégé. Charlotte seemed to have taken a subliminal cue from her sister and was also standing, surfing, in Franck's cart. Franck had either not noticed or had decided to ignore her.

But... Le Gégé! We were growing to like Luc more and more, but still no-one could ever replace Gégé ,the previously lovelorn but disaster-loving soul who had been an integral part of our renovations of *La Maison des Deux Clochers*. I gave him an enthusiastic kiss. "We loved your postcard. How was Morocco?" I was pleased to see him tanned and healthy.

Gégé glowed, or maybe blushed. "It was incredible. Laurence and I have decided to travel as much as we can."

"I'm so happy for you." Laurence sounded like the perfect woman for him.

"And you?" he asked. "Franck has been telling me about the cottage."

I groaned. "I warned you we would jump into disaster again, remember?" I keeping an iron grip on Camille's little wrist even thoughts she was twisting away from me and shouting at me to let her go. "It was just a matter of time."

Gégé looked at our red-faced, rebelling daughters. It was definitively not their finest moment. Clearly he didn't think that the cottage was the only disaster Franck and I had jumped into over the past few years.

"No kids for you guys?" I asked, my mouth twisted with a wry smile.

"You are welcome to take one of ours," Franck said. Charlotte was punching Franck's thigh. "On second thought, take both. Our gift to you and Laurence."

"I'll have to turn down that enticing offer," Gégé said. "The cottage sounds like a real mess too..."

"I would stay away if I were you." Franck patted his back. "It is shaping up to be a disaster of such epic proportions that I'm sure you'll want to come work with us if you see it in person." Franck clicked his tongue. "Too tempting for you."

Gégé laughed. "I'm finished with lost causes. Besides, Laurence and I are off to Rome next month. That should keep me out of the way."

We kissed and then said our *au revoirs*. Charlotte and Camille had begun crescendo crying, giving Franck and I the pleasure of their tantrums in stereo.

"We could rent these two out as birth control," Franck said, looking askance at our offspring.

"Can we please go to the cash register now?" I begged. We only had about half the things on our list but I was beyond caring.

"*Allons-y*," he declared and we weaved through the crowds, each dragging a wailing girl behind us, until we caught sight of the massive lines at the cash registers.

"*Merde*," we both whispered in harmony.

"I'll take them for a walk," Franck said. "You keep our place in line. You have the Visa card, right?"

It became apparent after several minutes when I had seen Franck and the girls lap around the cash registers several times, the girls getting louder with each lap, that I had chosen the wrong till. The ruddy, solid couple two people ahead of me had embarked in a vocal argument with the cashier about the price of their numerous cans of duck *confit*.

When it finally came to be my turn the cashier turned blazing eyes on me as she began to throw my items across the scanner.

She picked up my bag of *endives*. "You didn't weigh this!"

Double *merde*. I forgot that in France you had to weigh all your fruits and vegetables in the produce section and put a little sticker on the bag before taking them to the till. I berated myself, not only because the people in line behind me had now turned their furious expressions on me but also because it would have been a brilliant ploy to keep Camille amused and actually sitting in the seat of the shopping cart.

"You'll have to go and weigh your fruit and vegetables," she snapped. "Now."

I looked for Franck but he and the girls were now nowhere to be seen. I sheepishly collected my numerous bags of fruits and veg and skirted past the long line of people who were without an exception glaring at me.

Of course there was a long line-up back in the produce section as well. Two of the three machines weren't working. My breathing had started to become ragged and the fluorescent lights became too harsh. Was I having another panic attack? I thought those were under control.

I was sweating profusely and gasping for breath by the time I got back to the cashier with my now labeled bags of produce.

The cashier practically threw my stuff across the scanner while I waited, trying not to make eye contact with anyone, wondering when the bag boy was going to make an appearance. She made a face at my foreign Visa card but rang it through and made me sign. I avoided eye contact with everyone in line. I could hear them complaining about me – and none too quietly either.

"Where are your bags?" the cashier demanded.

"Bags?" In Canada, the grocery stores always provided bags, as well as someone who politely and expertly packed them.

The cashier looked at me as though I were mentally deficient.

"We don't supply bags," she said. "You need to take your things away so that I can ring through the next customer. *Maintenant.* They have been waiting long enough."

I turned and met the eye of a chic bourgeois woman in line behind me with tight jeans, a large scarf, and dangly earrings. Her lips were pressed tightly together and her eyes shot me death rays of pure hatred.

"*Desolée,*" I muttered, and began throwing the items that the cashier had rung through into my cart, which was much too small for that amount of groceries, but I was beyond caring about that...

Franck found me just as I was trying to steer my unwieldy cart that, piled full, had the maneuverability of the Titanic. I needed to put as much distance as possible between me and the people behind me at the cash register.

"Camille lost her doll," he said.

I bit back the "I-told-you-so" that was lingering on my lips when I saw Camille's swimming hazel eyes.

"There must be a lost and found here somewhere," I said. "I'm sure if someone found it they would return it."

"Don't be too sure about that."

Franck took the bar of the cart while I took Camille's hand.

"Look at this *chantier*!" he began, peering into the cart. You put the milk on top of the *salade*-."

"Don't start," I warned. "Where were you when I discovered they didn't provide bags?"

"They sell them at the cash register. You just have to ask."

"You have to *know* to ask. How was I supposed to know?"

Franck just sighed and handed Camille off to me. He pointed to a desk at the far end of the shopping gallery. "That looks like Customer Service."

Camille and I hurried over. "My daughter has lost her doll while we were grocery shopping," I explained. "Is this the lost and found?"

"We did have a lost and found here," the woman behind the desk said. "But nobody ever returned anything so we don't have one anymore."

"So, no doll has been returned?" I asked. "Dark hair, purple dress…"

"*Non.*"

We walked out to the parking lot, all locked in our own private misery. Camille was inconsolable. Charlotte was upset for Camille. Franck just looked exhausted and I was struggling with rage against grocery stores in France who didn't have lost and founds and didn't even supply *bags*.

I strapped the girls in the car and was climbing in myself when I heard a woman exclaim. "Look what I found on the floor of the store Joséphine! A dolly just for you!"

I turned around and saw a stunning woman in a pencil skirt and lovely coral top across the parking lot give Camille's doll to her daughter who was already leaping around in the backseat of their car.

My mouth opened and I started to get back out.

"Don't." Franck reached out and pulled me back. "It's not the way things work here."

"What!? Not the way things *work*? I'm going to go and tell her…"

But I saw that the woman had already zoomed off in her car, neglecting to buckle up her young daughter.

I was stunned at what I had just witnessed.

I can't believe she took it! That…" I said a very bad French word in front of the girls.

"There's nothing we can do Laura," Franck said. "It's just the culture here. It's Darwinism. Finders, keepers."

The sheer injustice of that rankled me. "It's the culture in France to steal from children?" I demanded. "It's the culture to be dishonest and opportunistic?"

"People here just figure that if you are careless enough to lose something in the first place that the person who finds it deserves to keep it."

I wanted to punch something or someone – notably that thieving bourgeois woman who stole Camille's doll. All the way back to Savigny while Camille howled that she wanted her dolly back I chewed on my thumb and thought of all the terrible things I wanted to do to that woman. Somewhere around the Porte Saint Nicolas anger turned into sadness and a single, fat tear ran down my cheek. I hastily wiped it away. I couldn't believe I was actually crying about this, but there it was.

In that moment, I believed that I had parachuted into a country that had no moral compass. Not only had I parachuted myself, but my daughters as well. Camille's tears gave way to big shuddering gulps and Charlotte had reached over and was patting her hand and saying soothing things to her.

"I'm so sorry *ma Camille*," I turned around and said to her. I wasn't just talking about the doll. "I really am."

CHAPTER 9

The next day was our family Sunday lunch, the last big meal before we moved to Villers-la-Faye.

We decided to cook a ham as we did all the time back in Canada and they were dead easy to prepare. We invited Franck's aunt Réné and Mémé to come early for a visit and to supervise our meal preparation. The mother and daughter were both prodigious cooks. Franck and I were of course late coming back from the last minute shopping and Franck sped into the courtyard of our château so fast that he made pea gravel fly.

His aunt Réné's blue compact car was parked in front of the front door, and she and Mémé were already walking around the perimeter of the courtyard, giving it a thorough inspection.

"Bonjour!" Franck shouted as he leapt out of the car. "We're a little bit *en retard.*"

That was a vast understatement but if anyone was closely acquainted with Franck's time dyslexia, it was his family. Besides, in Mémé's eyes Franck could do no wrong – ever.

Réné flung the dangling corner of her magnificent purple and pink cape over her shoulder. "We haven't been bored," she assured us, and gave Franck and me a sound kisses. "Where are the girls?"

Just then they tumbled out of the backseat and were both thoroughly admired and kissed by Franck's aunt and grandmother.

"Shall we go in?" Franck took an arm of each *dame*. He unlocked the kitchen door.

Mémé clutched the threshold of the kitchen and "Ah! Now that's the way a proper kitchen should smell!" she exclaimed and took in the battered armoire full of pots and pans and the gas stove with pleasure. "A real family kitchen."

"How are you two settling in?" Réné asked. Even though Franck was very close with his family, there had been precious little time for family visits since we arrived. We popped in on Réné, who lived across the hall from Mémé in the retirement community in Beaune a few times but we hadn't actual enjoyed a proper visit yet, which in Burgundy meant a multi-course, multi-hour meal.

"Everything is harder than we had anticipated," I admitted. I still hadn't recovered from the doll incident even though Camille gave every indication that she had moved on.

Réné t'sked. "Don't worry about the big things. Find your *"petits bonheurs du jour."*

I must have looked confused, because Réné grabbed me by the shoulder, something she often did when she was emphasizing a point. "My granddaughters always laugh at me, but I have taught them to do it too. Every day I wake up and I begin to seek out the surprise of what the *"petit bonheur du jour"* will be that day. Will it be a letter from one of my grandchildren? Perhaps a phonecall from a friend? Will it be a sublime glass of wine or a beautiful bouquet of flowers I see in the window of *la fleuriste*? When none of the big things are working out just concentrate on finding your little daily joy. There always is one, and often once you start looking you will find many more."

I felt as though a weight had been lifted off my shoulders. I was focusing on the wrong thing. Maybe if I just focused on the little joys, the big stuff would take care of itself. "That's brilliant," I said, and meant it.

"I know!" Réné squeezed my shoulder again and sailed around the kitchen like a galleon at full mast.

Mémé was opening the cupboards and examining everything. She must have found it up to snuff, as she made no criticisms.

"When are we going to be able to see your new house in Villers-la-Faye?" Réné asked.

"It's nothing like this," Franck warned.

"I know that," Réné laughed. "This house is beautiful to be sure, but would cost a fortune to heat. Can you just imagine?"

"*Alors!*" exclaimed Mémé, lowering herself down on a kitchen chair after finishing her inspection. "I'm feeling a little parched."

"*Moi aussi,*" said Réné. "Pour us a *kir* Franck and let's discuss how we will proceed with our work. We haven't come to just put our feet under the table, *vous savez.*"

Franck heaved the ham and a large bag of potatoes out of the grocery bag. "Can you slice these potatoes for a *dauphinoise* while I put this ham in the oven?"

Mémé and Réné exchanged a worried glance. "Have you brined the ham?" Mémé asked.

"No." Franck inspected the haunch of meat. "We cook hams all the time in Canada. All we need to do is whip up a marinade and put it in the oven to heat up. The ham is smoked already which means it's basically cooked."

"It's not smoked," Mémé said, pulling the ham towards her and poking and sniffing at the meat. "This is a fresh ham. You have to brine it for days, sometimes weeks before you serve it and watch out if there is a thunderstorm! That will spoil a brining ham in a heartbeat."

I looked over to Franck, panic stricken. The ham was supposed to be the main course. We were about to serve lunch to twenty of his nearest and dearest family members in two hours. Not only were the cars not automatic in France, but the hams were not smoked. Where was the *petit bonheur du jour* in all this?

Franck came over beside Mémé and inspected it with her, turning the ham over this way and that. "There must be a way to cook this thing."

"I may have an idea," Mémé said. "I've never done it before, but it is a way of dressing and cooking fresh ham without brining. I read about it in *Vie de Femme* magazine."

"Let's do it!" Réné, never one to back away from a challenge, declared.

"Can we leave you two to it?" Franck asked. "I will take care of the *gratin.* Laura, can you wash the salad and put out the cheeses and find some nice dishes and set the table in the dining room?"

"*Oui, bien sûr,*" I left the ham to the experts and whisked myself off to the dining room, which was beyond the games room and the library.

I opened a polished walnut buffet with a massive old key decorated by a silver silk tassel. Inside, there stood pile upon pile of exquisite china plates –at least four different complete sets – one of them looked like it was bordered with pure gold. My favorite ones were Limoges and had an unfathomably intricate silver filigree pattern all around the dishes. I found a linen tablecloth that was actually big enough to cover the mammoth wooden table that must have been unearthed from a monastery.

I discovered when I first arrived in Burgundy as a seventeen year old exchange student that somehow everything just tasted *better* in France. Part of it was the ingredients and I knew part of it was the care and expertise of French cooks from the humble to the expert. I was sure it came from the fact that many meals in France had a ceremonial component to them. They were enjoyed on centuries old tables on beautiful china. Also, French people didn't eat between meals which meant when you came to the table you did so with hunger and anticipation. Hunger was a way of honoring the food and the chefs.

All I consumed for breakfast was a bowl of café au lait and I felt an anticipatory growl in my stomach as I leaned back in the buffet to find matching glasses. While I was rifling around in the probably priceless crystal someone grabbed me around the waist from behind.

"*Aïe!*" I yelped.

Franck spun me around. "You just yelped in French. That's progress." He gave me a kiss and then turned to admire what I had put on the table so far.

"Why aren't you in the kitchen?" I asked.

"It's a critical juncture for the ham," he explained. "Opinions were diverging and I didn't want to be called on to take sides."

"Wise. What glasses do you think we should use?"

Franck plucked out one that was delicately engraved with a filigree pattern that complimented the plates.

"Nice," I said.

He picked up a glass up by the stem, turning it this way and that. "I can't imagine how much all of this is worth. Does it make you sorry that we've never lived in any place long enough to collect this sort of thing?"

I began to take the glasses out and set them on the table. "Not really. I love using these things - they're beautiful – but I don't know if I'd appreciate them if they were mine. It's fun living someone else's life for a while though."

"Would you like to live in a house like this?" Franck asked. We had actually come rather close to doing exactly that with the first house we made an offer for before buying *La Maison des Deux Clochers*. That house in the village of Marey-les-Fussey was actually more accurately described as a "property" with two complete houses, a well, an enormous chunk of land rolling down to the vineyards as well as numerous outbuildings. The cheating notary from Beaune who went by the name of Maitre Ange, or Maitre Angel, had stolen it out from underneath us.

"If we'd bought the house in Marey, you mean?" I asked Franck. We hadn't talked about that house or that disappointment in a very long time. One lucky trait of my personality was that I never spent mental energy regretting or rehashing things in my past. Using my overactive imagination to constantly project myself into the future was much more my style. I always believed this was why I tended towards anxiety rather than depression.

"*Oui*. That one or something similar."

"No." I rarely thought about the house in Marey and when I did it was with the conviction that it wasn't meant to be. I found some matching champagne flutes for the *crémant* that was a part of every fine meal in Burgundy and started putting them at each place setting. "If we'd bought the house in Marey I doubt we would have started this whole vacation rental thing. Besides, our mortgage would have been so huge that we never would have been able to buy our house in Victoria. How many people want to rent a massive house that sleeps dozens when they come on vacation anyway? I like the idea of having a network of several small houses rather than one huge one."

Franck helped me put the glasses in the right spot above each plate. "I never in a million years thought I would own any real estate in my life."

"Why not?"

"Before I met you I was convinced I wouldn't live past thirty."

I stopped, a flute in each hand. I'd never heard that before. "Really? Why on earth did you think that?"

Franck shrugged. "I almost died after I was born."

I nodded. Franck had been born after far too many hours of labor with the umbilical cord wrapped around his neck. I knew that it has been very touch and go there for the first few days of his life.

"I always figured that I was living on borrowed time. Also, I just didn't see what life had to offer that was very interesting after thirty."

"And now?"

He appeared to think about it for a good long while. He shook his head. "Still nothing."

My hands weren't free, but I managed to kick his shin. He laughed and swept me up in his arms.

"Careful...the flutes," I said. "They're probably from Versailles or something."

"Then I met you and life after thirty suddenly seemed like the best part. I mean, you, the girls, living in different countries, living even in different houses...it's like we've lived so many different lives since we met. I hope we're going to live many more."

"Franck! Where are you?" Mémé called from the kitchen. "Jean and Jacqueline are here."

"I'll be right there!" Franck gave me one last kiss. "The table looks great," he said, and winked at me as he left for the kitchen.

And just like that I stood there, in the middle of our little temporary chateau, savoring my first *petit bonheur du jour* of the day.

The meal we collectively pulled together was delicious. A *salade frisée* with melted goat's cheese to begin, then Franck's succulent *gratin* accompanied Réné and Mémé's delectable freshly cooked ham. *La Vie de Femme* magazine had proved its mettle and gotFranck and I out of a major culinary jam. Next came a mammoth cheese course, then Jacqueline's homemade *mousse au chocolat* and *tuiles* biscuits, lacy confections molded on her wooden rolling pin to give them the same curved shape as the roof tiles in the South of France. Lastly we nibbled on handmade chocolates from Bouché in Beaune, and sipped on our espressos. The stunning crystal glasses held *kir royale*, a few bottles of Chorey-Saint-Denis and then a beautiful decade old Vosne Romanée with the cheese.

I did feel a little bit like a *chatelaine* for the day, even though I knew that feeling would completely evaporate once we had moved into our own house in Villers-la-Faye.

In typical Burgundy style, the meal went from noon until about eight o'clock at night. The table was so huge that it accommodated the twenty-four guests with ease. The cousins played *pétanque* in the courtyard between courses. Nobody seemed overly concerned that one of them would end up with a dented skull, so I tried to adopt the *laissez-faire* attitude the French had towards parenting. The wine helped.

Our cooks were the last to leave and Mémé and then Réné gave us both long, wet kisses on our cheeks.

"You see?" said Réné. "Today was filled with *les petits bonheurs*. I wonder what tomorrow will bring

On our second to last day at our *chateau* in Savigny, Franck insisted that I drive our car to Beaune to pick up our girls from school that day. Alone. "Cyril said you were ready at your last lesson. You just have to bite the bullet and do it by yourself for the first time."

Even though I had been driving by myself since I was sixteen back in Canada, I had never driven on my own in France, not since I travelled to Burgundy as a Rotary Exchange student. Well…there had been that ill-fated escapade during my Rotary year when Franck took me deep into the Burgundian forest to teach me how to drive standard. After making out for quite some time we got his Dad's car stuck in mud. Besides that, though, I had grown comfortable, and in fact relieved, at only being a passenger on the French roads. Driving in Victoria by myself did not faze me at all. People drove slowly, the roads were wide and the cars were automatic. In Burgundy it was the exact opposite.

"What if I stall at the lights?" I asked as Franck pushed me into the courtyard and pressed the keys in my palm.

"You'll turn the ignition again and restart."

"I don't think I'm ready," I said. "French drivers are demented." Still, the alternative was to lose my independence. I wasn't ready for that either. I got in the driver's seat.

"Just stay in the middle of the road until the other person gives way," Franck advised. "You don't want to go over to your side too early and give them too much room or they'll run you off the road. It's like that game…what do you call it?"

"Chicken?"

"That's it."

"You are not helping," I said. I felt like I was heading out to war.

Franck tapped on the roof twice. "You're good. *Vas-y!*"

"What about parking at the school?" The thought had just occurred to me and struck terror in my heart. The parking of Saint-Coeur at pick-up time was a war zone.

"Double park," Franck suggested. "Triple park if necessary."

"I can't do that! I'll block other cars."

"You have plenty of time. I'm sure there will be lots of available spots. Just go to Beaune, get the girls at school, and bring them back. Simple. You can do it."

Simple for him, not so simple for me.

He shut the door, mimicked that I should fasten my seatbelt and gave me a cheery wave and a thumbs-up.

I eased my way out of the courtyard. Those stone pillars were even closer together than I had realized. There was barely an inch on each side to squeeze the car through. The street just outside our house was unspeakably narrow and cars hurtled at me from both directions

I waited until the cars had past, pressed my foot on the gas and spun out on to the street. The car almost stalled but I caught it in time. Maybe all those tortuous driving lessons where I struggled to get the car from the ABC Auto-École parking lot up the hill to the ring road were paying off.

I gritted my teeth, and wove my way slowly toward the school. I stalled twice, both times at stoplights, but despite profuse sweating and a pounding heart I had managed to get the car going again. It was such a strange and terrifying sensation to be doing this on my own with no Cyril and no Franck beside me.

I felt almost confident by time I turned into the school parking lot. I made a silent prayer to God, the Virgin Mary, and any of Franck's guardian angels that the perfect parking spot would open up and I could just slide in.

I drove around but all the parking spaces were full. I checked my watch. What a time for everyone up in heaven to be sleeping on the job. I still had ten minutes before the bell rang and I had to go in and get the girls. If I just drove very slowly around and around the parking lot someone would inevitably leave and give me their spot.

Ten minutes ticked by but nobody left. In that time many parents arrived and blithely double or triple parked in front of other cars, or up on sidewalks or wedged between yellow no parking signs or basically anywhere that parking was not allowed. I was appalled at the utter lawlessness.

Just as the parking lot became a congested maze of parked – or rather illegally parked - cars high school students from the *lycée* next door poured into the maw and began to weave in and out of the cars. The French teenagers did not deign to pay the vehicles any attention or even look where they were going as they lit up their cigarettes and French kissed one another.

How was I going to get the girls if I couldn't park? An image of Charlotte and Camille forlornly waiting for their mother as I circled around the parking lot until well into the night lodged in my head. I wanted to cry again. Why were my damn tears so near the surface these days? Why wasn't anyone leaving? I cursed Franck for making me drive by myself and Cyril for declaring that I was fit to drive on my own when he'd never even given me any lessons about parking in France.

Just when tears had actually begun to prick my eyes and the school bell had rung somebody miraculously pulled out just in front of me. I slid in, wiped my face, and went to find my girls.

Charlotte and Camille thankfully didn't realize they had almost become abandoned orphans and greeted me with a big smile. Séverine told me, as she did every day, that Camille still hadn't talked yet, but she had smiled a lot and had begun to clap her hands during songs. I wasn't sure if that constituted progress or whether Séverine just felt bad for me.

"Is Daddy waiting in the car?" Charlotte asked me as we walked up the path to the big wooden door being guarded by *Le Dragon*, who gave me a look that implied she knew I wasn't capable of driving in France.

"No," I said. "I drove here all by myself. Isn't that exciting?"

"By yourself?" Charlotte demanded, not appearing at all excited by my news. "I didn't know you knew how to drive."

"I drove you all the time in Canada!"

"I meant in France," Charlotte said. "Isn't it dangerous for you to drive here?"

Sometimes children cottoned on to things entirely too well, but I decided there was no point in scaring them.

"Remember how I got lessons? Grown-ups can learn new things too, you know."

Charlotte searched my face, skeptical.

I took the coward's way out and waited with the girls in the car until most of the cars had cleared out of the parking lot. I slid out then, chatting breezily to the girls to cover my nerves, and headed back out on the road.

The girls were quiet in the backseat, paying close attention to my driving.

"I like it better when Daddy drives," Camille said, as we got to the first roundabout. "It's faster."

"I'm driving the speed limit," I protested.

"It's still too slow," Charlotte said, opening the window.

I turned and found myself stuck behind a vineyard tractor going at about ten kilometers an hour. I geared down quickly.

"Pass him Mom!" yelled Camille from the backseat.

The drivers behind appeared to be in agreement with my two year old and began to honk and give me angry arm gestures as they whipped past to get ahead of both the tractor and me. How could they do that? It was impossible to see oncoming traffic and I would have to accelerate and change gears so quickly...what if I stalled? My heart pounded as the honking behind me got louder and more insistent.

"This is embarrassing Mom." In the rear view mirror I saw Charlotte cover her face with her hands and sink lower in her seat.

Just as we neared the castle in the middle of Savigny the vineyard tractor luckily veered into the courtyard of a winemaker's home.

I was now, however, caught up in Savigny's unforgiving narrow maze of streets.

I just needed to turn right at the castle, left at the fountain, then right again at the *boulangerie*, I reminded myself. I had long given up trying to chat with the girls. Anyway, they instinctively knew the critical nature of our present predicament.

Villagers darted across the road with no warning. Honks and rude gestures came from every direction.

"You're not very good at driving in France," Charlotte observed.

I growled. At last, I turned the car onto our street – one of the narrowest in the village but at least we were almost at the finish line.

Franck informed me shortly after moving into the house that the only way to manoeuver the car in and out of the courtyard past our stone pillars was to put the car in reverse and back through them. He made it sound easy, but now as I put my indicator light on and began to back the car into reverse all of a sudden I had about ten irate French drivers backed up on either side of me.

"*Merde!*" I hissed. "*Putain de bordel de merde.*"

"*Putain de bordel de merde!*" Camille parroted with glee.

"NOW you start speaking French?"

I tried to put the car into reverse and stalled it once, then twice, then three times. The space between the stone pillars seemed to shrink with each failed attempt.

"Where's Dad?" I yelled at the girls. "Do you see him in the courtyard? Maybe he could come and help me..." Franck however, was nowhere to be seen.

I didn't know what to do. I was stuck in the middle of the road and I could feel the collective fury of twenty French drivers focused on me. It was more than my Canadian soul could take. I snapped

I gunned on the gas and the car flew somewhat between the pillars. Just when I thought I was through I heard crunching metal and grinding stone.

"Mommy!" I think you're stuck!" said Charlotte, peering out her window.

I could feel it. One side of the car was caught on the stone. I had a choice, venture out and try the maneuver again and make the irate drivers wait some more or just sweat it through and get into the courtyard. Pure adrenaline made me press the accelerator to the floor.

More horrific noise and then all at once the car was free of the pillar and rolled to a stop on the pea gravel.

I snapped my head around. "You OK girls?"

"Why did you do that?" Camille asked.

"I think you broke our new car," Charlotte said.

I dropped my head on the steering wheel. I heard the front door open and shut and out of my peripheral vision saw Franck appear at the driver's window.

"Was that sound what I think it was?"

"Mommy got the car stuck on the pillar!" Charlotte reported.

"The pillar?" Franck went over and inspected it, a worried crease between his eyes. He came back again. "It's okay, it's a teeny bit scraped and has some green paint from the car on it but I can get that off." He walked around to the side of the car and I heard him swear low and long in French under his breath.

"Laura…" he began.

I got out of the car and slammed my door. "Don't even say it! I told you I wasn't ready. Those pillars are so skinny and how is anybody supposed to back up when everyone is getting mad and honking at me-" I looked at the side of the car and there was a massive scratch and a large dent and burst into tears.

"You can't worry about the other drivers," Franck said, wrapping his arm around me. "You just have to learn to ignore them."

"I can't *do* that!" I wailed. "I'm Canadian!"

Franck and I both looked down at the mauled side of our new car. Camille and Charlotte crouched down to get a better look.

"It looks like a smile," Charlotte said, finally. "It looks like the side of the car is smiling."

"You see?" Franck pulled me in closer and dried my tears with his shirt sleeve. "You personalized the car for us."

It was a far cry from *un petit bonheur du jour* but at least it was something.

CHAPTER 10

Two weeks later we hadn't made any progress with the banks or the renovations, but we had moved into our new house on the *route des chaumes* in Villers-la-Faye.

Although the speed of our possession of the house was head spinning, the move was probably one of the least stressful we had ever made. There was nothing to move besides our suitcases and ourselves, a lesson in the benefits of travelling light.

I called my parents in Canada to give them our new phone number and street address for letters or, better yet, care packages.

"There's something wrong with the phone connection," my Mom said after we had spoken for a few minutes. "There's a terrible echo."

I looked around the absolutely bare room and its badly tiled floor. "I don't think that's the phone line. I think it's our house. It's empty."

"You need to get some carpets."

"First we need to get some furniture," I said.

That night we slept on mattresses on the bedroom floor. All we had for light was a single bare bulb screwed into a socket which gave our bedroom all the charms of a Columbian drug lord's torture chamber. In the morning we had our coffee and hot chocolate in bowls, but we had to drink them standing up as we had no table to sit around or chairs to sit on.

"I know what we need to do tonight!" Franck exclaimed in between sips from his Duralex bowl.

"What?"

"Invite Martial and Isabelle over for dinner to baptize the house."

I snorted as I rinsed my bowl. Besides furniture, the house was also glaringly lacking a dishwasher. "Right."

"I'm serious."

I paused and looked at him. "Where are we going to sit? The floor?"

"We'll go furniture scrounging today. I promise you by tonight we'll have a table and chairs. I'm going to go and call Martial, *d'accord?*"

"OK." In Canada I never would have said yes to such an insane proposition but something about the current chaos of our life had led me close to something that felt like surrender, at least at fleeting moments. Besides, as unlikely as it seemed maybe having old friends over for dinner in our unfurnished house was the ticket to my *petit bonheur du jour*. That, or my ticket to disaster, but there was no way of finding out without jumping into the unknown.

Camille and Charlotte slid by the kitchen door, chasing each other in their stocking feet. Their shrieks of excitement bounced off the walls and ceilings.

Franck came back in the kitchen and picked up a towel to help me dry the bowls. "They can come," he said. "Seven o'clock."

"*Géniale*," I said. "Do you think we are ever going to feel settled in this house?" I asked Franck. It was ours (well, more accurately it was mostly owned by the bank for the next several years but I didn't tend to get hung up on such niceties) but it felt so makeshift.

"*Zut*. I forgot to do something important yesterday," Franck said, not answering my question.

"Did you forget to return the key for Savigny to the realtor?"

"*Non*." Before I realized what was happening Franck had whisked me up in his arms and walked out of the house and then turned around on the patio and said, "Girls! Come and watch me carry your mother over the threshold." I was still clutching on to my damp dishtowel.

Charlotte and Camille appeared. "Why are you doing that?" Charlotte laughed.

"It's good luck!"

"I want to do it too!" said Charlotte, so Franck swept her up and carried her over as well, then it was Camille's turn. After that Charlotte had to carry Camille and Camille had to carry Charlotte, then I had to carry both of them over. Eventually Franck tried to carry me while both girls grabbed on to his back and we all ended up in a laughing pile in the front hall.

It felt more like home already. Now, for some chairs...

By that evening Franck's parents had unearthed a round wooden table with lovely curved feet and eight mismatched chairs in the barn across from their house, which I was fast discovering rivaled Ali Baba's cave. We also found a huge trunk of things that we owned the year we had lived in Paris while I studied at the Sorbonne. It was a treasure trove of forks and knives and dinner plates and even a few candlesticks that we had completely forgotten about, as well as many dog-eared tomes of medieval French texts (in their original middle age French) including *Tristan et Yseult* and *Guillaume de Dole*.

I had loved studying medieval French literature so much that I had never been able to bear getting rid of my books. I still couldn't so I took them back to our house with us. We didn't have any bookshelves but we would have the beginnings of an intriguing library. That made me feel light years better.

Franck wanted to attempt a Moroccan chicken tagine so we borrowed Stéphanie's tagine pot and headed to Beaune after a delicious lunch of roasted lamb with *herbes de Provence*, flageolet beans in the most divine garlicky sauce, and a trio of creamy Saint Marcellin cheeses in their ceramic containers at Franck's parents' house. We stocked up on *label rouge* farm bred chicken, onions, brined lemons, olives, and dried apricots.

Back at our kitchen, I set our new/old table with a blue tablecloth adorned with bright red cherries culled from our Paris trunk as well as blue and white dinner plates. The wine glasses were mismatched and had seen better days but we unearthed excellent wine to fill them with – a magnum of 1985 *Savigny-les-Beaune Les Guettes* that had been given to us as a wedding gift by one of Franck's many distant uncles who also happened to be the winemaker.

As I was digging through the trunk in search of napkins there was a knock at the door. There was a doorbell at our new house but it probably hadn't worked in years.

Franck went to welcome Martial and Isabelle and their boys, Gabin and Arthur.

They came with their arms full with gifts. The company Martial worked for was based in the neighboring Jura region so he had brought us a bag filled with fresh Jura cheeses, a huge wedge of *Comté*, two large wodges of *Morbier*, and a rare one that I had never tried called *Bleu de Jax*. He also brought two bottles of wine, one a *Corton Grand Cru* and one an unlabeled (but delicious, he assured us) white from a friend's vineyard near Ladoix-Serrigny. Isabelle was almost hidden by a huge bouquet of flowers and Gabin held in his hands a round box of Haribo candy for Charlotte and Camille. We ushered them in to our new abode.

Martial glanced around our empty home. "I love what you've done with the place."

I took the flowers from Isabelle. We had a good laugh when we realized that I didn't actually own a vase. We eventually found a water jug in my Paris trunk that did the trick and I put them in the middle of the table, the only surface of the house that was available,

Even though we hadn't seen each other in a few years besides my allergy-induced grump fest in Bouilland when we had run into Martial, I remembered them as an easy-going pair. I was longing for friends here. Although we had gone through many adventures already as a family I still had moments of feeling overwhelmingly isolated. We needed friends here. Good friends. I had high hopes that, despite our lack of furniture, this evening could be the start of our social life in France.

"I'm sorry we don't have many toys for boys," I apologized to Isabelle. "We actually don't even have any toys for girls. Our boxes still haven't come from Canada. We're starting to think they may be at the bottom of the Atlantic. Anyway, we bought the kids a few foam balls today and the living room is totally empty.

"They'll figure out a way to have fun," Isabelle said. "Trust me."

Martial and Isabelle sat down at the table in the kitchen while Arthur organized a complicated game that seemed to be combination of rugby, soccer, and basketball in the living room.

Martial eyed the overflowing tagine pot that Franck was filling. "Are you sure you haven't filled that up too high?"

"Is it going to fit in the oven?" I asked.

"Ye of little faith." Franck placed the lid over the overflowing onions and chicken pieces and slid the tagine pot into the oven. It fit, with about a millimeter to spare.

"*Voilà!*" he turned and bowed.

"I hope the oven works," Franck said, as he began to fiddle with the dials. "I guess I should have tried to preheat it first.

We all held our breath until a little red light flicked on and a reassuring sound like something mechanical warming up made us explode in cheers. Martial then led us on a rousing round of "*Le Ban Bourgignon*" which is a traditional song that consists of basically singing "la la la" and clapping and turning your hands. Burgundy was synonymous with pleasure and wine and *Le Ban Bourgignon* was the perfect celebration song for our region of France, everyone said, because it was even possible to remember the words (or "la-la's" more accurately) after drinking significant quantities of the local nectars.

Franck sat down and began cutting up the *saucisson sec* we bought from our favorite *charcuterie* in Beaune. We had filched an ancient wooden cutting board from *La Maison des Deux Clocher's* kitchen.

We started with Martial's mystery white wine from Ladoix, which tasted of dry minerals and restrained fruit. The sheer diversity of wine in the geographically tiny area of Burgundy between Dijon and Beaune produced some of the most expensive and lusted after vintages. A favorite game around the table, that sacred centerpiece of Burgundian life, was guessing the origins and vintage of a mystery bottle. This could be played formally. Franck's *tante* Réné often brought out a set of sock-like things that were slipped over the wine bottles for this very purpose. It also could be played informally like tonight when tasting one of the many bottles of unlabeled wine that exchanged hands between local Burgundian winemakers and locals for a variety of reasons (and only about half of these reasons were illegal).

"*Très bon*," Franck commented as he swirled the wine in his glass. "What are the possibilities?"

"From our side of *La Nationale*, most definitely," said Martial.

La Nationale was the main road that ran through Dijon and Beaune and split the wine coast into two halves. "Our" side included Ladoix-Serrigny, Pernand-Vergelesses, Savigny-les-Beaune, and Aloxe-Corton to name a few.

"Do you know what it is?" I asked Martial after peeling the skin off my circle of *saucisson*, a dried and spiced pork sausage that was one of my favorite things to nibble with wine.

"No," said Martial. "Though I am enjoying the mystery." He took another sip. "I think it could be a Pernand-Vergelesses. If that wine was good enough to be the favorite of Charlemagne, it's good enough for me."

"Me too," I mumbled through a full mouth.

The next hour was spent sipping our wine and catching up with Martial and Isabelle. We had drifted apart in the past few years. We had been in England for the two years when I was completing my law degree at Oxford and then in Canada except for brief stints here when we were working night and day on renovations for *La Maison des Deux Clochers* or on short visits spending all of our limited time with Franck's very large and social family.

The noise level in the next room had been escalating steadily since we sat down.

Isabelle pushed her funky orange plastic glasses up her nose. "*Oh la!*" she yelled to the kids. "*Calmos!*"

"It's not completely their fault," I said. "There's an unbelievable echo in there. Besides, it's not like we have anything quiet for them to play with, not even a TV."

Just then Charlotte came to the kitchen door, clearly in the position of emissary.

"We're hungry," she said. "When's dinner?"

Franck peeked in the oven and frowned. "Dinner isn't ready yet. Come and have some baguette and *saucisson*."

The kids swarmed in like a hoard of locusts and in a few minutes decimated our *apéritif*, leaving us with only a few baguette crumbs and a messy pile of *saucisson* skins.

"*Mon Dieu*," commented Isabelle. "What a bunch of savages. You'd think we starve them."

Another hour went by, with Franck going to check the oven at more and more frequent intervals. We finished off the bottle of white, although we were all too polite to ask how the *tagine* was coming along.

Finally, Franck said, "Maybe I shouldn't have filled the *tagine* so high after all. Should we open the magnum?"

We all agreed. Franck poured us each a glass of the 1985 Savigny from our wedding that he had uncorked some time before.

We all took a sip. The wine was elegant, complex…an explosion of delicate blackcurrant and cherry with an earthy undertone that revealed itself slowly and sensually, like a person doing a very classy striptease. The wine was complex and astounding. It was a work of art and an absolute privilege to taste.

The only sound came from the living room where the ball game was starting up again. We adults had lapsed into reverential silence and were staring at our glasses.

I spoke first. "This wine is sublime."

We all took another sip.

"*La vache*," Martial said in a whisper. "Pure magic."

"Incredible," added Isabelle.

It was a perfect moment, a moment when a group of people is spontaneously and collectively moved by something so beautiful as to be almost otherworldly. I savored the moment as much as the wine, made more incongruous by the unfurnished house and the children playing their ball game in the next room. This was bigger than *un petit bonheur du jour*. I knew that this was one of those transcendent moments that I would remember my entire life. Truly great art like this wine had a way of taking us outside of ourselves for a glorious moment in time.

"Do you know what would go well with this?" Martial said.

"*Tagine?*" Franck smiled.

"Well…"

"Sorry." Franck shook his head. "It's nowhere near ready."

"I was actually thinking of the cheese I brought," said Martial. "How about we do the meal backwards tonight?"

Cheese was *always* served at the end of the main course and before the dessert in Burgundy, but nothing about this evening was turning out routine.

Martial took out the hunks of cheese he had brought from the Jura and placed them out on the cutting board I sponged off. "Do you have a sharp knife?"

By now the incredible wine and lack of food had given me a languorous feeling that had seeped through my limbs. "Sorry, we just have butter knives."

"That'll do."

I nodded. I cut some more bread and we began feasting on the cheese, which turned out to be a perfect counterpart to the strength and finesse of the wine that just improved with every sip.

"I missed this so much in Canada," I said to no one in particular.

"An empty house?" Franck ventured. "An uncooked tagine? Feral children?"

"Cheese," I sighed. "Delicious, smelly, raw, unpasteurized cheese…and incredible wine."

"Welcome back to France then!" Martial raised his glass and we all clinked them together. "*Santé!*"

Some time later Franck finally took the tagine out of the oven and declared it was cooked enough to enjoy. It was about eleven thirty by then, and we had eaten most of the cheese Martial had brought as well as the chocolate meringue *tarte* that I had bought from the *patisserie*. About half way through the magnum we told the kids that they could go ahead and eat the box of candy for dinner. We were all very cheery by that time and greeted the tagine with an even more resounding round of *Le Ban Bourgignon*.

Franck doled out tagine. Although it was strange to be eating it as the final course of our dinner, it smelled a delicious combination of the sweet dried apricots and the savory chicken and brined lemons and we all dug in with gusto.

"I won't fill it as full next time," Franck said.

"It's delicious," I said, chewing appreciatively. Martial and Isabelle both nodded in agreement, their mouths full, which was always a good sign.

We had gone back to the picking off the cheese plate and had begun making inroads on the Corton Grand Cru when Camille came in the kitchen and pulled my sleeve.

"Mommy, I think I'm going to go to bed."

I looked at my watch. It was already 12:30.

"Come on, I'll help you get your pajamas on." I took her hand and we went and found a pair of pajamas in her suitcase. I tucked her into her mattress on the floor and gave her a kiss.

"Sleep tight *chérie*," I said, smoothing her hair back from her brow that seemed a little sweaty. She had probably been running until she dropped. Camille had always operated at full speed from the moment she opened her eyes in the morning until she dropped at night.

I went back in the kitchen where Franck and Martial and Isabelle were debating the merits of twelve versus eighteen month *Comté*.

Unlike Canada, where people would probably be looking at their watches and saying that it was time to get their kids to bed, Martial and Isabelle made no move to go home and I was glad. Another difference was that our conversation turned around food and family and shared memories. We rarely talked about money or work – the main topics at most dinner parties back home. The French, and the pleasure-loving Burgundians in particular, generally considered work as a necessary evil that enabled them to follow their true passions. Most Burgundians considered it a monumentally boring topic of conversation, as work usually had nothing to do with the core of who a person really was and what they really cared about.

As for talking about money, I had learned shortly after meeting Franck that money and rich people were regarded with no small amount of distrust in France. The way the French economy was set up many rich people had gotten that way by playing fast and loose with the law. Besides that though the French regarded the pursuit of wealth as something that was indulged in by intellectually stunted people, people who sadly didn't possess the curiosity and soul to realize that the true pleasures of life had nothing to do with money. These money-obsessed individuals were pitied rather than revered and they certainly were not allowed to monopolize the conversation around a French table.

We laughed and talked for a few more minutes until Charlotte raced into the kitchen with Arthur and Gabin at her heels.

"Camille is throwing up!" they all announced at once, their eyes shining with the thrill of bearing such exciting tidings.

Despite the amount of wine he had consumed Franck was out of his chair and down the hall in an instant.

"*Ma pauvre!*" I heard him exclaim. That didn't bode well.

Martial, Isabelle and I traded rueful looks. I got up to help and Martial and Isabelle did the same.

"No, no," I said. "Sit back down. "Franck and I will handle it."

"Don't be ridiculous," Isabelle scoffed. She followed me to the girls' bedroom.

It was bad. Camille had upchucked several times. Her sheets and pillow were covered in vomit as was her face and hair. Barf had even splattered across the wallpapered world map that was on the wall at the head of her mattress.

"*Regardez!*" Gabin, peering at the mess through his round red eyeglasses and pointing at the wall. "There's candy in it! That's *incroyable* Camille!"

Indeed, Camille's vomit was dotted with barely digested jelly candies like brightly colored jewels in a river of mud.

"Laura, you take Camille and shower her off," Franck said. "I will deal with the room."

I was fully expecting Martial and Isabelle to, like sane people, take their leave at this juncture. Instead, Isabelle started digging through the suitcase on the floor (which thankfully hadn't been in Camille's barf trajectory) for a fresh pair of pajamas.

"Go and start bathing her, I'll bring these in and help," she said.

"You guys can go home," I said. "You really don't need to stay and deal with all this too…"

"Laura!" Isabelle adopted a mock tone of command. "Stop arguing and do as I say!"

Camille was clearly feeling better now that she had gotten rid of all the candies in her tummy. She insisted she didn't want to be carried into the bathroom and could walk in there on her own.

"My poor sweetie," I said. "How does your stomach feel now?"

"Much better," Camille said.

I turned on the water in the eggplant bathtub as hot as it could go. I stripped Camille of her pajamas and piled them in a malodorous pile on the floor. I popped her in the bath and began to soap her up then rinse her off with the telephone handle sprayer. Little partially digested candies were spangled through her dark hair, so I picked those off and threw them in the garbage can before washing her head.

Isabelle came in while I was busy with Camille, who was complaining that she didn't like getting her hair washed.

"You're just going to have to suck it up," I said to her.

When I turned around, Isabelle had Camille's dirty pajamas in the sink and was plucking off the candies that were stuck on them and throwing them in the toilet.

"Those would have completely plugged up your washing machine," she said, finishing up and then depositing them in a plastic bag she had found I-don't-know-where.

"I'm going to take these down to the washing machine," she

said. "Do you want me to get you a towel for Camille first?"

"You didn't need to stay for all this...I mean, I'm so sorry."

She waved a hand, dismissing my protests. "What kind of friends would we be if we didn't stay and help you? We're not just here to drink your *incroyable* wine, you know."

I waffled for a moment, but finally decided to surrender a bit more and accept Isabelle's help. It had always been hard for me to graciously accept assistance. Somewhere along the way I had acquired the belief that accepting help was an admission that I was not good enough. This insecurity was, of course, exacerbated tenfold with my foray into motherhood. I felt like I failed as a mother every day since Charlotte was born – for big things such as not being able to breastfeed to small things like allowing my girls to eat candy, *saucisson*, and cheese for dinner. Still, something about Isabelle's matter-of-fact approach inspired me to just let go of all that self-judgment, at least until we had the vomit situation under control.

"Thank you," I said, from the bottom of my heart. "A towel would be great. There should be a few in their suitcase."

I got Camille out and dried off and into a fresh pair of pajamas. I deposited her in our bed and then went to check on the progress Franck was making in cleaning up the girls' bedroom.

Franck was nowhere to be found, but Martial was cheerfully scrubbing the wall with a sponge and a bucket of water, whistling the French national anthem *"Aux Enfants de la Patrie"*.

"Franck's taken the sheets downstairs to the washing machine," he said. "Do you have any fresh ones?"

"Nope," I said. "I guess we will all be sleeping in our bed tonight."

"How is Camille?"

"The barf machine is clean and warm and sleeping soundly in our bed. Or mattress, more accurately."

I went over and tried to wrest the sponge away from Martial's hand. "I can do that now." He wouldn't let me take it and in fact began to slap me away.

"So can I," he said. "And frankly, I'm very good at wiping vomit off walls. Don't steal my thunder."

I put my hands on my hips. Relief and gratitude warred briefly with the shame of inviting our friends over for dinner only to have them clean up such a mess. Against Martial and Isabelle's kindness, though, my shame didn't stand a chance. "Well...thank you both so much," I said.

Martial shrugged, looking at me with a bemused expression. "Laura, this is what friends do."

CHAPTER 11

Now that we were in our house, the word "settled" couldn't accurately be applied to our situation. We had to make progress with the cottage. It was already November and our first guests were due to arrive at the cottage in less than nine months. We had roughly the time of a pregnancy to turn a derelict cottage into something cozy and beautiful.

Thanks to the utter xenophobia of French banks, we still had no money for any of the renovations. Luc finished with his demolition of the interior walls and pleaded with us to meet him to decide on the location of the new walls. Franck still hadn't been able to locate the papers he needed to fill out so the shadowy figure of the Architect of French Monuments could approve our skylights. We also needed to find a roofer like, yesterday, a plumber, an electrician and a dozen other tradesmen.

One of our problems was that by going back and forth to Beaune to pick up and drop off the girls for lunch, we never had extended chunks of time for work. We would drop off the girls at school at eight-thirty, then pick them up at noon for lunch (which lasted a full two hours), then drive them back down to Beaune at two o'clock, then drive back down at five to pick them up. The trip wasn't long each way, only about ten minutes, but we were finding it difficult to squeeze in work and meetings around their timetable. The two-hour lunch was a wonderful concept for our family on paper but seeing as we were under the gun for getting the cottage ready for our guests, something had to give.

"We'll just put them in the *cantine* for lunch a few days a week, starting tomorrow," Franck said as we raced to pick the girls up for lunch once again.

"The cafeteria?" Memories of my high school cafeteria were not good ones. Officially named "Brown Hall", everyone referred to it as "Brown Hell" and not without reason.

"We can't do that to them," I said as I shut the car door behind me. Franck had parked up on the sidewalk as usual, completely blocking foot traffic but like anyone worthy of a French passport he was unperturbed by this fact.

"What are you talking about? I loved the *cantine* when I was little. I begged my parents to let me go more often."

The dragon at the door nodded curtly at us as we walked through the school doors.

"Come here." Franck took my hand and led me to a sheet that was taped to the preschool door. "Read that."

It was a five-day menu for the school cafeteria. Today was Tuesday so I looked up *mardi*. "*Celeri roumalde* for an *entrée*, a *blanquet* of veal with its sauce for a main course, a selection of cheeses from the Normandy region for the cheese course, then a vanilla *crème brulee* for dessert," I read out loud.

I turned to Franck in astonishment. "*That* is what they serve at the school cafeteria?"

"*Oui.*"

"Are we allowed to eat there?"

Franck shook his head. "I'm afraid not. It's just for the students and the teachers. They post the weekly menu so that at home parents can make meals that harmonize with what the children eat at lunch."

"Where do we sign them up?" I asked, my reservations gone.

However, when we broke the news to Camille and Charlotte that night at dinner that that they would be staying at school and eating at the *cantine* the next day for lunch they burst into tears.

"I don't want to Mommy," said Charlotte. "What if they make me eat spinach?"

"There's no spinach on the menu tomorrow," I said. "I checked."

"What will we be eating then?"

I decided to not mention the beet and couscous salad for the entrée. "*Boeuf Bourgignon* with tagliatelle pasta. You love that! Dessert is chocolate mousse."

Charlotte thought about this but still had reservations. "I won't know where to go."

"Don't worry. We'll talk to your teacher and there's a helper who takes you."

"What about Camille?" Charlotte asked. "She still doesn't talk at school."

I turned to Camille. "Do you understand when people talk to you at school in French?"

Camille just gave me her trademark inscrutable shrug.

"She'll be fine," I said, with confidence I didn't entirely feel. "We'll talk to Séverine and I'll make sure that she helps Camille get to the right place."

Charlotte flung herself in my arms. "I don't want to mommy! I want to come home for lunch with you and Daddy!"

I smoothed her hair. "Sweetie, Daddy and I have to work while you and Camille are in school. We just can't get enough work done when we have to pick you up every day for lunch. Going for lunch at the *cantine* is how you can help us. It's sort of like your job, do you understand?"

Charlotte pondered this for a moment with a quivering bottom lip. "OK. I'll try."

"That's my girl." I gave her a kiss on the top of her head.

The next morning the first thing Charlotte asked when Franck and I sat her and Camille down at the round table and gave them their bowls of chocolate milk was, "Do we still have to go to the *cantine* for lunch today?"

"Yes. That didn't change overnight."

"My tummy hurts." She frowned down at her breakfast. "I'm not hungry."

Camille also pushed away her bowl. "No *cantine*."

Oh wonderful. A hunger strike.

Guilt pulsated through my veins and Franck must have seen that I was in danger of caving as he pushed me gently out of the kitchen. "Go have your shower. I'll get the girls ready and drive them down to school."

"Mommy!" Camille held her hands up to me and began to cry. I couldn't seem to move, like a deer caught in headlights. "*Allez!*" Franck waved me out of the room.

Franck was much better about sticking with parental decisions than me. I could usually be swayed by some half-hearted pleading and a few fat tears.

I stepped into the bath, reminding myself of the fresh tagliatelle and chocolate mousse. I had no idea yet what Franck and I would be eating for lunch but I doubted it would be as good.

I shivered. We needed to fire up the huge octopus of an oil furnace in the basement and turn on the heat. The leaves on the vineyards had already turned fiery shades of yellow and red and orange and begun to fall off. Fall had unequivocally arrived.

Our house had one of the asinine French set-ups whereby to "shower" I had to kneel down in the freezing iron bathtub and wash myself with a shower nozzle that was attached to the tap with a long twisty metal cord.

When we had installed our wall-mounted showerhead at *La Maison des Deux Clochers* I had vowed, Scarlett O'Hara style, that I would never put up with a kneeling French shower again. One side of my body was always cold and there was no way to wash myself properly without completely flooding the bathroom. French people seemed to be inured to the ridiculousness of this arrangement and something in their DNA rendered them able to waltz out of the bathroom looking like they had emerged from the pages of French Vogue without getting a drop of water on to the floor. I, and all the other North Americans I knew, invariably left the bathroom looking like Niagara Falls.

I cursed as the hot water turned to frigid and then back again. As far as Franck and I could tell our hot water tank appeared to contain enough water for a three-minute shower for one person. Franck told me I needed to turn the water off every time I did not need it to rinse myself, but when I did that I shivered.

I got out of my "shower" just in time to see Franck hustling Charlotte and Camille into their coats and out the front door. I stepped forward to say one last good-bye but Franck shooed me back with repressed ferocity.

I got dressed, having a hard time shaking myself out of my melancholy mood. Were our girls going to be forever traumatized by this move and having to adapt to a million different new things like the guest with the Big Hair from Albuquerque prophesized? I thought of my own childhood. Besides a move down the street on my seventh birthday my formative years had been remarkably settled. My Dad worked, my Mom made us peanut butter and jam sandwiches and chaperoned our field trips. My sister and I played with the neighborhood kids and our parents all socialized together. It had felt safe and reassuring. What would my girls remember from this time in our lives?

I was pretty certain the food at the school cafeteria would be good – this was France after all – but it would be a long day for them, a full two hours longer than a school day in Canada. Still, if we didn't do this how could we possibly move forward with the renovations? I had somehow convinced myself that the work / life balance would be easier in France than in Canada but it was turning out that balancing family and work was not for the faint of heart in either country.

When Franck came back to pick me up and take me to meet Luc at the cottage I asked, "How did it go with the girls?" I wasn't sure I really wanted to know the answer.

"It was a good thing you weren't there."

"Were they crying?"

Franck motioned for me to get my coat on. "There were tears."

I bit my lip.

"The teachers assured me that they would take care of them," Franck said. "It will be fine."

It should be us taking care of them, my guilt shouted. Still, we did need to earn money for such trivial things as food and our mortgage. We also had to fulfill the promise that I had made to my family before we left and get this cottage up and running as a successful vacation rental. So far we didn't have much to show for ourselves.

CHAPTER 12

A few days later I woke up with dread clawing at my chest from the inside. It had little to do with our mortgage predicament or finding a roofer. The problem was direr; I was booked for my first foreign gynecologist appointment. I hadn't been able to schedule my annual physical before we moved. Things had just been too crazy, so shortly after arriving in France I booked an appointment with Monsieur Le Courbac, the gynecologist in Beaune my mother-in-law and Stéphanie had been seeing for years.

My yearly exam was not something I looked forward to more than any other woman. Still, having to go through all of *that* in French and when I was not sure of exactly how things worked with one's gynecologist in France…that added a whole new element of the terror. The unknown was not always a bad thing, but it was definitely not something I sought out at a gynecological appointment.

Franck's mother had informed me the night before gynecologists were not referred to as "*docteur*" in France, but as *Monsieur* or *Madame*. *Voilà!* There was one potential *faux pas* narrowly averted right there. How many more were lurking in the treacherous path between the receptionist and the stirrups?

Embarrassingly, I still hadn't overcome my phobia of doctors in general, particularly foreign doctors. Franck's family doctor (and now our family doctor) in Burgundy, *Le Père Durand*, had eventually gained my trust with his tatty espadrilles, prodigious smoking habit, and rotund stomach. Michèle and Stéphanie warned me that their gynecologist, Monsieur Le Courbac, was a completely different *genre* of doctor. He was technically competent, they assured me, but possessed all the warmth of hoar frost.

By the time I was ensconced in Monsieur Le Courbac's waiting room, thumbing through the vast selection of Paris Match and Madame Figaro magazines, my fight or flight response was in full bloom. Pounding heart, dizziness, burning face, nausea, a crushing sense of doom – the usual suspects of a full blown panic attack were present and accounted for. I plucked a magazine off the pile.

A tall gentleman with an impeccable white jacket over a suit materialized in the waiting room and announced a woman's name. A thin and elegant sixty-ish year old *madame* in capri pants and a Hermès scarf got up from a chair near mine and followed him. I plunged back into the magazine in an attempt to avoid thinking about the next hour of my life.

I was feverishly scanning a long article in Madame Figaro about Charlotte Gainsbourg and her alluring husband Yvan Attal when the doctor appeared once again and called for "Madame Germain." My heart made a strange thump and I shot out of my chair to follow him.

He didn't say so much as *bonjour* until he was seated behind his desk, a sleek structure of shining metal and glass. Even the chairs were a clear plastic and *très à la mode*. They were also uncomfortable for all but the smallest of skinny French *derrières*.

"What can I do for you Madame Germain?" he asked in a disinterested voice.

I noticed that he was wearing a silk neck scarf, or *foulard*. There was something deeply disconcerting about that urbane article of male clothing. It was an item that I associated with villains in old James Bond films and people who wintered on the Côte d'Azur. Whereas Le Père Durand's tatty espadrilles eliminated my fear, Monsieur Le Courbac's *foulard* ramped up my blood pressure. He watched me, waiting, with icy eyes.

"I just moved here from Canada a few months ago," I stumbled over my French. "I didn't have the chance to have my yearly physical before I left. My sister and mother-in-law are patients of yours, so I made an appointment."

I realized belatedly that I had used the informal *"tu"* form instead of the *"vous"* which I imagined was *de rigueur* in conversations with one's gynecologist. I always found myself slipping into *"tu"* without realizing it when I was under pressure, probably because it was easier to conjugate.

Monsieur Le Courbac narrowed his eyes at me for a few moments before opening what looked like an empty file on his desk with a plain piece of paper stuck inside. "Do you smoke Madame Germain?"

"No."

"How much do you weigh?"

Definitely more than his previous patient – I was certain of that - but I actually had no idea. "I'm not sure."

"Any major health problems?" He made no eye contact and did not so much as crack a smile. I began to shiver. The hoar frost effect.

"No."

"Children?"

"Two daughters. Two and four years old. They were both born by C-section."

His Mont Blanc pen paused for a moment. "Why was that?"

"My first one was…" I struggled to come up with the French words for 'coming out feet first' and mangled my explanation. "The second was just…kind of…." My hands flapped in bizarre movements as I tried to convey my answer. "She was positioned in a diagonal fashion…she wasn't coming out…she was…you know… stuck." I realized I had used *"tu"* again instead of *"vous."*

He raised a brow at me, and then scribbled a few more things on his piece of paper. "Very well Madame Germain, please go in the next room and remove your clothes."

My face was on fire. Time to cross the Rubicon.

I hoped the robe provided would be more stylish and self-explanatory than the Canadian version. Every year back home I would find myself in the exam room feverishly debating whether the ties went at the back or the front.

I somehow managed to get myself up from the chair and walk into the next room, which was large and bare except for an examination table.

"You can remove your clothes in the *cabine*," the doctor said, gesturing behind his head to a little room just off the main examination room. The *cabine*, I noticed immediately, appeared to be lacking a door or even a curtain. Luckily Monsieur Le Courbac was still sitting at his desk with his back turned.

"*Merci*," I said, trying to sound nonchalant, as though it was an everyday occurrence for me to disrobe a few feet away from a disapproving man who wore a *foulard* to work.

I put down my purse on the floor and removed my jacket. All I could see in the room was a wooden stool, a coat hook, and a digital scale. No gown. Now where would they hide the gowns in France? Was there some secret drawer or compartment that I was supposed to know about? Maybe I was supposed to bring my own, like the bags at the grocery store.

"*Pardon*," I called out. "I think you have forgotten to leave a gown in here for me."

Monsieur de Courbac swiveled around in his chair and eyed my still-fully-clothed self. "There is no gown." He turned back to his file.

No gown? How was I supposed to get from the changing *cabine* to the examination table? It looked like a long, lonely walk to take naked.

"Have you removed all of your clothes Madame Germain?" This question was infused with impatience. "Don't go to the examination table yet, I need to weigh you first."

I noticed a scale on the floor by my feet. So he was going to come in this tiny little room and weigh me once I was naked? "Ummmm...just a second," I stuttered, stripping off my clothes. A terrible thought occurred to me. What if I had understood him incorrectly and I wasn't *supposed* to be completely naked at this juncture? What if he came in and covered his eyes, horrified, "My God woman, put on some underwear for *l'amour de Dieu*!"

This was the awful part about conducting one's life in a second language - living in perpetual fear of misunderstanding some crucial tidbit of information.

When the doctor walked into the *cabine* where I was standing, naked, I was still debating whether to sit on the stool or remain standing. More importantly, where was I supposed to put my *hands*?

"Please stand on the scale Madame Germain," the doctor said, making no eye contact but at least not backing out, appalled. Part of me was very relieved at this, but the other part of me wished he would give me a more definitive clue as to whether I was doing this right or mortifyingly wrong.

I stood up on the scale. He peered down at the number after it beeped and scribbled something on his piece of paper.

"Please come to the exam table," he said, and went across the room to sit down on the little wheeled stool that was placed to one side of the table.

I took a tentative step into the exam room and then decided – just like that – that I was fed up with feeling cowed. People could only intimidate me if I let them, right? This rule applied with or, more to the point at this juncture, without clothes. I strode across the room and hopped up on the table.

"Please lie on your back."

I lay down.

I quickly noticed that there was a cluster of comics and quotes taped on to the ceiling just above my head. It was, I thought, strangely considerate of Monsieur Le Courbac to supply such strategically placed reading material for his patients.

"Everything has been figured out, except how to live," I read, a quote by Jean Paul Sartre and compared it to, "I may be no better, but at least I am different," attributed to Jean-Jacques Rousseau. Somehow being naked somehow made the quotes more touching and more profound. It was too bad I hadn't cottoned on to this fact during my Literature undergrad.

"Interesting quotes," I said. I hadn't expected to brush up on my French philosophy at the gynecologist's office.

"Yes," he said. "I choose them myself."

This, for him I was learning, constituted a remarkably expansive answer. All of the doctors in Canada were gifted at making innocuous chit-chat during a pelvic exam, talking about the weather, politics…anything expect what was actually going on down below. Monsieur Le Courbac clearly did not feel the onus of the conversation lay on his shoulders yet maybe I could divine something about him from his choice of quotes. I contemplated a Pierre Deproges quote, "Culture is like jam. The less we have the more we spread it around." Was this what Monsieur Le Courmac thought of New World countries such as the United States and Canada? Well, maybe North America did have less history and perhaps less culture than France, but at least the gynecologists supplied gowns.

"*C'est fini* Madame Germain," the doctor pushed his stool away from the exam table. "You may go and put your clothes back on again."

I walked tall back to the *cabine* but put my clothes back on with alacrity. I picked up my purse and went back to sit in one of the doctor's hard chairs. They definitely didn't encourage me to linger.

"Everything appears to be in order Madame Germain," he said, neither reassuring me nor alarming me. "Come back and see me if you have any problems, or if not in one year's time."

"All right," I said. "*Merci.*"

I watched as he wrote more things on my piece of paper, unsure of whether I had been dismissed or not.

He looked up at me after a few seconds. "You leave now."

I stood up. "I hope you have a good afternoon," I said in parting, trying to retain my dignity.

It was only after I sped down the stairs and out into the crisp pre-winter air that I realized I had committed the cardinal sin of "tu-toie-ing" my gynecologist yet again. I tried to remember whether I had used "tu" with him while I was prone on the table. That was something you did in France with people you were trying to seduce. I think I did. I wasn't sure what message he thought I was trying to send him with my naked informality but I knew it was the wrong one.

We told the girls they would be going to the cafeteria for lunch that day, but I checked my watch and realized that I had enough time to pick them up from school and take them home for a family meal. They had been to the *cantine* a few times now and still moaned about it every time. I was hoping they would start to get used to it sooner rather than later. Today though I would surprise them and pick them up when they thought they were going to the *cantine*. They would be thrilled! Maybe I wouldn't get much work done, but surviving my first gynecologist appointment in France put me in a celebratory mood. I had a few minutes to kill before going to pick up the girls, so I took my time walking to my car.

I'd parked it behind a very old stone building that stood in the middle of the parking lot under two *tilleuls* trees. I hadn't noticed the building or its age in my frantic pre-appointment state of mind, but now I walked towards it and put my hand out to touch the huge stones of its wall. Inscribed in the stone near the roofline was the four-pointed symbol of the Knights of the Templar. I knew this because I had always been a bit obsessed with the Middle Ages. There was also a well-worn carving of two knights on horseback wearing what looked like full body armor. What was this building? More importantly, what was in doing in the middle of the shared parking lot for the office of the Social Services and an elementary school?

I was halfway around when I saw a more modern sign that read "*Chappelle des Templiers*" XII siècle which meant I was standing in front of a chapel built for the Knights of the Templar in the twelfth century. I went around until I found the door. It was huge and wooden but unfortunately locked. Above it was a small nave window with what looked like some truly exquisite medieval stained glass set inside.

I walked all the way around and then got back into my car slowly. It was amazing for me to think about how around every street corner in Burgundy and even in the middle of a parking lot there were nuggets of the distant past strewn willy-nilly. I knew that most French people were quite blasé about living within the pages of a history book but I couldn't ever see that happening to me. As Rousseau and a certain *foulard* wearing gynecologist would say, "I may be no better, but at least I am different."

What did those medieval townpeople that came to this chapel to pray or hang out or maybe enjoy an illicit afternoon tryst in the nave, worry about? I didn't think they would be too preoccupied with how they addressed their gynecologist. Dying in childbirth surely trumped that particular concern for most women in the Twelfth Century.

Did they look for their *petit bonheur du jour*? Was it a freshly baked loaf of bread or a smile from a shopkeeper or a particularly delectable mug of mead? Something made me think that no matter how difficult things were at times there were nonetheless glimmers of joy for them too. I felt a lot less alone with my problems all of a sudden. Also, my problems seemed way less…problematic. They were just bumps in the tapestry of life that had begun way before me and would continue far beyond my lifespan. People centuries ago and centuries to come would experience similar rough spots, none of which meant much in the grand scheme of things.

How about their children? Did people back then worry about being good parents, or did they consider just the mere fact of keeping their offspring alive a resounding parental success? Survival was probably their primary concern but still, the people who had touched these stones before me probably worried about the well-being of their families, those people that they loved the most, just like me. They were also on this crazy journey of being a human, so I was sure that they struggled with the same paradox as me – their capacity to love made them much stronger yet infinitely more vulnerable.

I was still elated when I arrived in the parking lot of Saint Coeur. I panicked about finding a parking spot, as usual, but found my panic more amusing than alarming and was finally able to squeeze the car in a spot for service vehicles. Seeing as I didn't see any service vehicles in sight, I thought this slight bending of the rules was acceptable. I hopped out of the car, and for once it didn't bother me that none of the other *mamans* clustered in groups of two or threes outside the still closed wooden doors glanced in my direction.

I even smiled at *la dragonne* as I strode by. The girls would be thrilled to see me and we could all go back home to a nice lunch where I could bask in the relief of having survived my appointment and the knowledge that my problems were no match for hundreds of years of history. Besides, I knew Franck was cooking up a *roti de porc* with apples and that there would be plenty for everyone.

I went to Charlotte's class first, as her teacher was usually more than prompt at dismissing them at lunch and after school. Today, though, the teacher was still teaching them something to do with a clock she was holding up. Her back was turned to the glass door where I stood. Charlotte was facing me, but was still watching her teacher. I knocked gently on the glass and waved to her.

Charlotte saw me and her blue eyes flew wide open. Her lip start quivering and she promptly burst into tears so loud that I could hear them through the double plated glass window. The *maitresse* whipped around and sent me an accusatory stare. I grimaced. She opened the door and ushered me in. "Is anything wrong Madame Germain?"

"*Non, non, non.*" I gestured at Charlotte to calm down as I stumbled through my explanation. "My appointment this morning was over earlier than scheduled, so I decided to come back and pick up the girls for lunch instead of having them go to the *cantine.*" Charlotte heard this and began to cry even harder until her whole body was convulsed with sobs.

Charlotte's *maitresse* eyed me skeptically. "*C'est tout?*" she asked.

"Really. That's all," I pleaded. "I thought she would be happy."

"Well, please take her home now. She's clearly too emotional to learn properly."

I hustled Charlotte into her jacket and out the classroom door. Once I had grabbed Camille from her classroom I dragged my girls to the middle of the courtyard and stopped to bend down so that we were eye to eye. I gave Charlotte a big hug. "Charlotte, *ma chérie*. Can you explain to me why you're crying? Did you *want* to go to the *cantine?*"

It took her a few moments of gasping to be able to speak.

"I just saw you there and I was so worried about going to the *cantine*. I worry every time we have to go. I worried and worried about it all morning. It was almost going to be time to go and then I looked up and saw you there and I was so relieved…I don't know why I'm crying. I'm actually happy!" She let out a sob and tears began running down her cheeks again.

I squeezed her again. "I'm so sorry Charlotte. I knew you don't like going to the *cantine* but I didn't realize that you got so anxious about it every time."

Charlotte sniffed. "I'm sorry Mommy. I don't know why I'm crying."

I zipped up her jacket. "I think you were just *émue*. That can happen to everyone."

"What does *émue* mean?"

"It means you're so happy and relieved about something that it is like a big bubble in your chest that gets so big that it bursts and you cry. That's why sometimes we cry from happiness."

I watched her as she blinked and tried to collect herself. Now I was the one who was *émue*. I asked myself yet again reflexively, like a habit, was our dream of living over here in Burgundy selfish now that we were parents? Guilt washed over me as I thought of Charlotte's nerves. Yet I was sure that those twelfth century parents felt similar angst about shipping off their young ones to apprentice with the ironmonger. And I wasn't sending Charlotte off to forge metal all day long, but forcing her to endure a varied, fantastic four course French lunch at school. I could live with that.

CHAPTER 13

Back in Canada I would have told a friend about my visit to Docteur *Foulard* and we would have ended up in hysterics. I missed having girlfriends. Franck was, of course, my best friend as well as my husband, but there were some things that only another woman could truly understand. Friends made life seem so much lighter, I realized, and I craved that *légèreté* that I could tap into at any time.

I had noticed that every Thursday night at the village *Salle des Fêtes* just down the road from our house the lights were on and a bunch of women seemed to be doing some kind of aerobics. Later on that week when Michèle was over at our house I asked her about it and she said there had been a *cours de gymnastique* for the village women every Thursday night since time immemorial. Maybe not as long as the Knights of the Templar chapel had been standing in Beaune, but a long time all the same.

"Gymnastics?" I asked, traumatized by memories of chickening out in front of the vault and not being able to climb up a rope during the gymnastics unit at elementary school. "You mean I'd have to do somersaults and cartwheels?"

"Oh no!" she laughed. "Just exercises. You know, dancing to music, lifting weights, sit-ups...that sort of thing."

So it was aerobics then, even though it was called *la gymnastique* here in France. I could handle aerobics. "How do I sign up?"

"I don't think you need to sign up," Michèle said. "I think you just go. Tonight is Thursday. It starts at eight o'clock I think."

"You should go," Franck said, leaning against the kitchen counter eating a wedge of *Comté* and slices of a gala apple. "It would be good for you to get out of the house."

So he'd noticed I was experiencing a bit of cabin fever. Our house was a long way from being comfortable. We still had very little furniture besides the kitchen table and our mattresses on the floor. We brought over a buffet from the cellar in *La Maison des Deux Clochers* with the rest of the furniture from the house but that was it. Franck was over at the cottage most of the time and I was often stuck at the house, at a loss as to how to entertain the girls when they weren't at school.

Michèle had wandered into the girls' bedroom so they could show her how they had set up a Polly Pocket village in a cardboard box I'd given them.

"I'm busy all the time trying to find a roofer." Franck cut another slice of apple and held it out to me. "Not to mention dealing with plumbers and stonemasons, and the Architect of French Monuments and all that. You've been looking after the girls much more than me. Go have a break and do some somersaults with the other women from the village."

"I've always hated doing somersaults."

"Oh really?" Franck popped the last bit of *comté* in his mouth and reached out to pull me close. "I thought you quite liked *gallipettes*."

I'd forgotten that the French word for "somersaults" was a slang word for…well…doing gymnastics in bed…

I laughed against his chest, inhaling his lingering aroma of cassis and apple.

Michèle came in to say goodbye and I went into our bedroom and my "closet" (i.e. my suitcase that lay on the floor) and dug out a pair of yoga pants and a T-shirt. None of the bedrooms in our house had closets, which I didn't understand. Franck told me that most people just bought and used an *armoire* but we hadn't had time for that yet.

After we had dinner I looked at my watch and said, "I'm off!" relishing the fact that the timing of the class meant that I didn't have to do the dishes. The kitchen didn't have a dishwasher and the sink was a horrible little circular affair not even big enough to fit a plate in, let alone a pot. The tiles on the counter around the sink were in the process of rotting and caving in. Washing dishes by hand for a family of four was never fun at the best of times, but in our kitchen it very quickly became one of our most hated chores.

"What's this?" called Franck as I headed to the front door to put on my sneakers. "No leotard and tights?"

"Sorry to disappoint," I said.

I walked slowly down the road from our house past the old wine press and to the *salle des fêtes* –the building that hosted the village's celebrations –weddings, baptisms, birthdays and anniversaries, plus the ping pong club, the wine tasting club, meetings, and of course the gymnastics group. It was a long, squat building that had been designed and built by one of Villers-la-Faye's long line of Communist mayors and definitely would not look out of place as a bunker in a forgotten Soviet republic.

At that moment I felt in tune with my three-year-old self on my first day of preschool where I had insisted my mother stay with me the entire time. These women were from the villages around here and most of them had grown up together. I was in that no-man's land between an outsider (I was Canadian, after all) and belonging (I was married to Franck). I knew from experience that Burgundians often took quite a while to warm up to new faces.

I shivered in the cool air. Winter was nipping at our heels. We had to get the roofing situation sorted out fast at the cottage. Once the weather turned cold re-roofing would become a far more dicey business.

I pushed open the heavy door of the Village Hall and made my way from the foyer into the main room. All the women were all clustered together in the center of the room. They created a confusing tableau. They were all standing around talking loudly and holding champagne flutes even though they were dressed in exercise clothes. In fact, five of them were actually wearing leotards and tights suitable for a Jane Fonda exercise video from the 1980s.

They didn't notice me approach as they were all oohing and aaahhhing over the photos one of the leotard-clad women held.

I shucked my jacket on one of the chairs that lined the edge of the room and added my water bottle which, now amongst the champagne flutes, seemed oddly out of place.

Should I interrupt them? Was I in the wrong place? I fought against the impulse to sneak back out before they noticed me.

I walked over to them instead. *"Bonsoir,"* I said.

The din evaporated as they turned to look at me.

"I was wondering if I could try the *cours de gymnastique*, but perhaps I'm interrupting."

They must have picked up on my slight accent as they all stared at me as if trying to figure out what planet I had materialized from.

"I'm Laura Germain," I added. "Franck Germain's wife. We just bought the house on *la route des chaumes*."

Several of them began to talk at once. "Ah bon! *La Canadienne! Bien sûr!*"

"We were just looking at photos of my new grandchild." A heavyset woman in an ivy green colored leotard and white tights passed me over the photos. "Her name is Léonie. She was born two days ago in Beaune."

I studied the photos of the little bald newborn with her eyes shut firmly against the new world she had been thrust into. I could completely relate.

"She's beautiful," I said, passing the photos back. "You must be thrilled."

"Bien sûr! That is why we are celebrating. Jocelyne, go and get Madame Germain a glass. You will drink *un verre* with us to celebrate, *non?"*

How could I refuse? "Sure."

"Solange brought the *crémant*. She made it. It's as delicious as my new granddaughter."

In no time at all I held a chilled flute of Burgundy's delicious *crémant* in my hand that had been made in Villers-la-Faye itself. I took a sip. It maybe wasn't officially allowed to call itself champagne because the grapes were grown in Burgundy, not the Champagne region, but it was delicious. I savored this unexpected *bonheur*.

We sipped and chatted with Solange being, with typical Burgundian stealth, assiduous in refilling our champagne flutes when we weren't paying attention. Quickly I lost track of how much *crémant* I had actually consumed.

"How was the birth?" a woman in sports shorts, a T-shirt and an Adidas headband around her forehead in Olivia Newton-John style asked.

"Like it always is with the first," Jocelyne said. "Long and difficult.

They had to use suction in the end. My daughter was cut from stem to stern, poor girl. Anyway! That should make it easier next time."

"She should enroll in vaginal re-education as soon as she can," Solange said. Jocelyne nodded in fervent agreement.

Vaginal re-education? Why had I never heard of that before? I pictured a row of vaginas wearing little mortarboards but instead of providing more details the women veered off on the topic of the recent grape harvest and how their wines were aging in the barrels.

"Nice fruits and solid structure." Solange popped open another bottle. "But it's still too early to know for certain how things will evolve. "I've been tasting every day. The tannins are coming along nicely."

A wiry woman in a bright fuchsia leotard and electric blue tights downed her glass of *crémant*. "What do you think *mesdames*? The class is more than half over. Should we try to do some *gymnastique* while we are here?"

Opinions were split down the middle on this point, with Solange and Jocelyne's camp voting for opening yet another bottle of Solange's *crémant* and foregoing any pretense of being here for exercising anything other than our wrists by hoisting the champagne flutes to our mouths. The rest mumbled that maybe we should do a few minutes of exercise since we were here, although nothing too strenuous

The leader woman clapped her hands. "*Alors mesdames*. Let's collect the glasses and take our places."

She reached out and grabbed my hand. "Madame Germain, is that it?"

"Yes."

"Have you done exercise before?"

"Oh yes. I did it back in Canada."

"If you decide to continue next week you'll need to bring twenty euros and a note from your doctor saying you are fit to do the class."

Really? I felt like asking. I needed a note from my doctor to drink *crémant* and do some sit-ups? It seemed in France a doctor's note was required for pretty much every endeavor, from attending school to picking your nose.

"OK," I agreed, lulled into complacency by the *crémant*.

"My name is Aline. Just take a spot anywhere on the floor and follow along as best you can."

I found a spot right at the back, just in front of the big plate glass window looking on to Jacky's Bistro.

The teacher bent over an old school ghetto blaster that also looked, like the *salle des fêtes*, as though it had been ferreted out of communist era Russia. She inserted a cassette tape, not a CD, but an actual cassette tape. I didn't even know they existed any more. Memories of making mixed tapes for Franck at university while he was still in France flowed back, mixing with the *crémant* and bathing everything in a nostalgic glow. I remembered that I had put the Fine Young Cannibals on it, as well as some Tom Waits and Spirit of the West.

"Are you ready ladies?" Aline asked. Instead of the yays and cheers that usually were the result of this question in aerobic classes back home there were a few desultory "if we have to's" and several heavy sighs instead. I loved that the majority of the women here didn't seem to feel the compulsion to fake enthusiasm for exercise.

The music crackled to life through the static of the ancient speakers of Aline's ghetto blaster. I recognized the disco rhythms and high-pitched voice of the now-deceased French superstar of the 1970s and 1980s, Claude François.

"Clap your hands ladies!" Aline said and she side stepped from side to side and demonstrated what she meant. There were a lot of complaints and a few snickers from the women around me.

"Alexandri! Alexandra!" Aline sung along to the music. "Now ladies, leg lifts."

There was a chorus of groans. We did one side step and then one knee lift...one side step and then one knee lift...I almost fell over to the side. Maybe that *crémant* had made me a little light-headed after all.

"And now the arms!" Aline did some enthusiastic bicep curls as she side-stepped and did the occasional knee lift. The women in front of me were laughing and chatting with each other, most had already abandoned any pretense of following along. Aline did not appear surprised by this in the slightest.

We kept doing this for a few more songs, with Aline throwing in a slight variation in the exercises from time to time. "Do you think we should do floor exercises?" she said at the end of her tape.

"*Non!*" The opinions were unanimous.

Aline shrugged. "*D'accord.* That's enough for this week then."

Seriously? That was it?

The women gathered together chatting and laughing while Aline walked over to me. "What did you think?" she asked.

"Um…Super!" I said.

"We don't usually drink that much." She picked up her jacket over her leotard.

Jocelyne rushed over to us. "Don't listen to her," she said to me. "Of course we do! Why do you think we all come here every week?" She stopped Aline from putting on her jacket. "We still have fifteen minutes before we can go home to our husbands. Let's finish off the *crémant, hein?*"

Within seconds I had a full flute back in my hand again and I was regaling the ladies with my first visit with Monsieur Le Courbac.

"He's a cold fish," Solange nodded. "But he is actually an excellent doctor and a superb surgeon. When my daughter had her C-section I had never seen such exquisite stitching. She practically has no scar."

I realized that even though none of the women here actually felt warmly towards him the huge majority went to him due to his reputation. I realized then that I would probably keep going to him too, *foulard* or no *foulard*.

Why did I care about his surgical skills? I asked myself as I walked up the *route des chaumes* towards home and admired the bright stars. It would be crazy to even contemplate a third child. Our life was chaotic enough as it was and as great as Camille was now I honestly didn't know if I could survive another baby with her propensity for screaming. Still, if Franck and I ever *did* decide to have a third child it would be born via C-section, I had already had two so a third was automatic. Exquisite stitching could come in handy…wait! That was the crazy part of me talking.

When I got home Franck was lying on our mattress reading a book of poetry by Victor Hugo.

"Is that good?" I asked, collapsing down beside him.

He gestured over to a dusty cardboard box in the corner of our bedroom. "My parents brought this over just after you left. It's all my old books from when I was in high school and university. I forgot that Hugo was such a good poet."

"I've read all his novels," I said. "But I don't think I've ever read his poetry."

I went over and rifled through the box. Sartre. Rousseau, Voltaire,

Descartes…

"Wow. Did you actually read all these?"

"Yes. After…"

He bit off the word, but I remembered now. After he and his girlfriend before me, Juliette, had broken up he had locked himself in his bedroom and tried committing suicide by overdosing in philosophy.

"After Juliette?" I supplied.

"Juliette?" He smirked. "I don't know who that is. The first women I ever loved was you."

I picked up a volume of Pascal and tapped him on the head with it. "A bad memory is a fine thing."

"How was your *gymnastique?*"

I lay down on the bed again, intertwining my legs with his. "Most of the class was spent drinking *crémant* to celebrate one of the women's new granddaughter. I think I might be drunk, actually."

"Ah. Exercise the French way."

I laughed. "I guess." I flipped over on my back and the room began to spin slowly. "I AM drunk."

"It's the *crémant*," Franck said. "You know, bubbles."

"Hmmmmm," I closed my eyes.

"Did you make any friends?"

"All the women there are old enough to be my mother. Still, it was fun. I'll go back."

Franck rolled towards me. "For the exercise or the *crémant?*"

I thought about this for a moment. "The *crémant.*"

His lips began to work their way along my jaw-line. "You see? You're becoming Burgundian already. Alors, about those *gallipettes…*

CHAPTER 14

The leaves on the vineyards were thinning on the vines in earnest. Winter felt like it was breathing down our necks, and winter in Burgundy was not a good time to be roofing a house.

If we couldn't figure out this bank thing, something that I could never have even conceived would be a road-block three months ago, how could we possibly move forward with our renovations? We were stuck. Why were things going so slowly? Were we cursed? I shivered. I was having a hard time maintaining my newfound "problems are a mere bump in the grand tapestry of life" philosophy in the face of the multitude of "no's" we had been hearing from banker after banker as we tried in vain to find a mortgage for the cottage.

During our most recent visit to our bank in Beaune, an elderly teller who Franck *had* managed to charm beckoned him closer when he was filling out our withdrawal slip.

"A new banker has just arrived," she said. "I think maybe I should set up an appointment with him so that you can discuss your mortgage problem. Something tells me he may be able to help."

So the next week we found ourselves waiting in the reception area of the bank for twenty minutes for the mysterious new banker, Monsieur Pascal Dubois, to come and take us into his office. We were getting uncomfortable and impatient in our hard plastic chairs. The only available reading material featured overjoyed and stylish young couples being granted their first mortgages. I mean, *serieusement?*

Finally a lanky man with black but balding hair and long fingers emerged from an office, laughing at a colleague's joke while sipping on a paper cup of espresso.

He stopped when he saw us. "Are you waiting for me? Did we have an appointment?"

"Are you Pascal Dubois?" Franck asked, admirably keeping his temper in check.

"Most days I wish I wasn't, especially when my ex-wives are chasing me for alimony, but unfortunately *c'est moi*. I'm starting to think we did have an appointment."

Monsieur Dubois didn't even try to hide the fact that he had been drinking coffee and, judging from the tobacco scent emanating from his wrinkled jacket, smoking cigarettes while shooting the shit with a colleague and completely blowing off our appointment. Such disrespect for the anal-retentive ethos of the banking world earned my grudging respect.

"Yes," Franck stood up.

"*Bon!* Why don't you come with me then?" He sauntered down the hall to his office, not seeming to notice or care if we followed him or not.

There were two chairs wedged in front of a desk piled high with teetering stacks of files and loose papers. The path to the chairs was an obstacle course through stacks of tile samples and buckets of paint.

"Have you been doing renovations in your office?" Franck asked as we sat down.

Monsieur Dubois picked through the detritus of building materials to his desk then lowered his lanky form down onto his chair. "Not my office. I couldn't care less what my office looks like. I'm renovating a house with my new wife. We bought a ruin just near Nolay six months ago. That's why I asked for a transfer to Beaune. Well, that and the fact that people in Champagne are as cold as glaciers. We're planning on doing all the work ourselves."

I arched an eyebrow at this. Unless the new Madame Dubois was a very industrious woman, their renovation could take a long, long time indeed.

"We renovated our first house six years ago, in Magny-les-Villers," Franck jumped in and capitalized on our shared interest. "It was a complete dump. Rotting walls, snakes in the pipes, horrible wallpaper...*la totale*. We did it all ourselves with the help of friends in four months before our first vacation rental guest arrived. It was *folklorique*, to say the least."

Monsieur Dubois' eyes sparkled with interest. "Do you mind shutting the door?" he nodded at me. "I like to smoke when I discuss renovations and they have this ridiculous no smoking in the offices regulation now. God forbid, if they keep up with all these rules we're going to find ourselves living in Switzerland."

After I stumbled over the tiles to shut the door and got back to my chair he lit up and after taking a drag offered us each a cigarette.

"*Non merci,*" I said.

"I quit six years ago," Franck said, apologetic for refusing. "I know if I smoke so much as a puff I'll be back to a pack a day in no time."

"I should quit," Monsieur Dubois mused, savoring his cigarette. "But I don't want to, so that's that."

He propped his feet up on a stack of what looked like roofing brochures and began to pepper Franck with questions about the best stonemasons in the area. The two of them launched into an extremely long and detailed discussion about plastering old walls, the pitfalls of rewiring ancient light fixtures, and what were the best alternatives for replacing old windows. I actually found that I had a lot to contribute to the conversation and reliving the crazy four-month sprint to renovate our first vacation rental, *La Maison des Deux Clochers* was quite a bit more fun than being turned down yet again for another mortgage.

After a good three quarters of an hour had passed and Monsieur Dubois' ashtray had filled up considerably, Monsieur Dubois smiled at us and said, "*Au fait,* why did you make an appointment to see me today? Did you have a banking matter to discuss? I'd much rather discuss renovations, but banking is what I'm being paid for I suppose."

Franck briefly outlined our mortgage dilemma. We had to mortgage our cottage before we could begin the renovations, and we had to mortgage it through our company in Canada. Franck was short and succinct. We had told this tale so many times that it was honed down to spare language that even Hemingway would admire.

Monsieur Dubois's expression did not shut down immediately after the mention of a foreign company, as was the case with most of the bankers we had met with so far. My heart flipped. Dare I hope this was a good sign? If I wasn't mistaken, he looked intrigued.

Franck and I held our collective breath – not an easy thing in the smoke filled office.

"I like you two," he said, finally. "I'd like to discuss the renovation stuff some more. I tell you what…I have a friend who works in lending in Paris and between the two of us I think we may be able to push your loan through."

Franck and I looked at each other, wide eyed.

"That would be *fantastique*," I breathed. "*Merci.*"

He shrugged. "These bank regulations are so *énervantes* anyway. It gives me great satisfaction to get around them. You aren't planning on going bankrupt or defaulting on your mortgage, are you?" he added, as an afterthought.

Franck and I both shook our heads vehemently. "Oh no. We're good for the money," I said.

"That's good enough for me." He turned and rummaged around what looked like small bags of plaster, or perhaps grout, propped up against the wall behind his chair. He pulled out two bottles of wine and plonked them on the desk in front of Franck and me.

"*Voilà*. Take these."

Franck began to protest but I spotted the prestigious name of Vosne-Romanée on the bottles and kicked Franck under the table. Vosne was one of the most prestigious wine making villages in the *Côte* and their wines were amongst my favorites. I couldn't bring myself to refuse the bottles.

Monsieur Dubois waved away Franck's words. "Don't be ridiculous. Most of my clients are winemakers and they are giving bottles to me all the time, every time I do them a favor, which is often. Don't worry, there are many more where those came from. This will give you something to toast me with when I get your mortgage approved. We'll have to meet again soon for you to bring me the paperwork. Once I talk to my friend in Paris I'll call you and let you know what I need."

"Perfect. *Merci*," Franck extended his hand for a handshake. I did the same.

We walked out of the bank, each holding a bottle of wine, stunned.

"Do you think he can do it?" I asked, as we were clear of the bank's double doors.

"I think anybody could have," said Franck. "They just had to have the soul of an anarchist like Monsieur Dubois."

I gave out a little yelp of joy. "Won't it be wonderful not to have to worry about the banking anymore? The renovations will be a breeze."

Franck turned a skeptical eye on me, but broke out in a smile nonetheless.

Monsieur Dubois had us drop off a bunch of financial documents, most of which we had to translate from English, which took us a several days. Every visit involved much door shutting and smoking and discussing plaster versus drywall and the best way to scrub and polish old *tomettes*. He assured us time and time again that he would be able to push our file through the dense web of bank administration and that we could safely start lining up workers.

After months of searching for available roofers Franck found a roofer that was from our village of Villers-la-Faye and who actually agreed to come over and meet us. Who would have thought that roofers would suddenly become such a hot commodity in Burgundy?

He met Franck at the cottage where he took a brief walk about on the top of the cottage roof and then we retired back to our kitchen to discuss the quote and the job over an *apéritif.*

"How is your availability looking?" Franck asked.

The roofer stretched his legs under the table. *"Pas mal.* I'm actually not too busy right now." This was music to our ears. All the other roofers we had contacted were too busy to even meet with us. Maybe it wasn't a particularly good sign, I reflected, but we were hardly in the position to start getting picky.

"Can you start next week?" Franck asked.

The roofer began to laugh. "Next week? Are you joking?"

"No."

"C'est dommage. I'm booked up from now until the spring. That's what I meant when I said I wasn't busy. These past few years I have been booking a year or more ahead of time. The earliest I could begin is April. There is no way you are ever going to find a roofer who could start before then."

Franck raised a brow at me. April? Still, we had heard the word *impossible* too many times while renovating *La Maison des Deux Clochers* and we had still managed to pull it off. We could do it again, couldn't we? Still, a new roof was an essential piece of the puzzle and April was definitely too late.

"We need someone to start by mid next month," Franck said. "Our first guests are arriving on July 12th.

The roofer stopped drinking his *kir* mid-sip. "You are planning to renovate that house in eight months? *Bonne chance!*" he snorted. "The roof is just the beginning. You're going to have to redo everything - pierce holes in the stone walls for new windows, put up new drywall, install a new bathroom, new floor and plumbing and…"

"We know," Franck cut him off. "Our house in Magny wasn't quite as extensive, but we did it in four months by ourselves with just a few good friends."

The roofer appeared unmoved. "I still can't start before the spring."

Franck shrugged. "Send me your quote anyway. You never know."

The roofer began to protest, but Franck just poured him another drink and changed the topic of conversation.

CHAPTER 15

We had to wait two long weeks where Franck frantically searched for other available roofers in vain, and it wasn't until almost the end of November that the first roofer we had called – the man from our village who said he wasn't going to be free until April – called back and said he had a cancellation. He could begin our roof on December first.

"I had a hunch he would pull through," Franck said.

"You did?" I thought back to our *apéritif* with him, when he laughed at us for thinking we could get anyone before the late spring. "How?"

"It's more convenient for him to do a job in his village," Franck said. "He can go home for lunch, have some wine, maybe have a siesta with his wife…"

In any case, Franck swung into action and lined up all the trades that he had made contact with to begin work as soon as the roofer was done. Better yet, Monsieur Dubois had pulled through with his promise of a mortgage. I wasn't exactly sure by what means he and his accomplice in Paris accomplished the task, but he managed to bribe or cajole his fellow bankers in Dijon or Paris to accept our mortgage application for the family company. Every meeting Mr. Dubois shut the door and chainsmoked his way through multiple renovation horror stories. After an hour of this, we spent maybe five minutes on the paperwork for our mortgage. He always ended the meeting by handing us a bottle of wine from one of his numerous winemaker clients. It was, Franck and I decided, a highly satisfactory business relationship. I believed Monsieur Dubois felt exactly the same way.

Camille still wasn't talking at school, which worried me more each day. It had been three months now. If she hadn't talked yet, would she every talk again at school? That worry plagued me day and night and crushing guilt always followed quickly on its heels. One of the reasons I came to France was to create a joyous family dynamic and the idea that the move had instead traumatized Camille continued to haunt me.

Charlotte, on the other hand, had become quite a celebrity in the preschool schoolyard. In the end, the nonchalance and random violence of French preschoolers proved no match for her sunny smile. When Franck and I would come to pick her up we would often be pointed out by the children and hear murmurings of *"Ce sont les parents de Charlotte."* The girls were getting used to eating at the *cantine* and had admitted that the food was actually quite good, even though they were often wary about what was going to be ladled into their plates.

One day near the end of November I arrived at the girls' school early for once and actually had my pick of two perfect parking spaces.

La dragonne opened the door, a few minutes early for once. I walked through it, my head held high. I was not going to let things beat me. I was stronger than that.

I picked up Charlotte first and she skipped alongside me as we walked to Camille's room.

"Did you have a good day?" I asked her.

"Yes, we had a lady come in and talk to us about music."

"Music?"

"Yes, you know. Mozart, Beethoven, and all of that."

"Oh. Right."

"Bonjour Charlotte!" a group of girls passed by us and gave us a friendly wave.

"Bonjour," Charlotte waved back with a smile, clearly impervious to the innate charm she wielded.

Severine, Camille's *maitresse*, was searching the crowd of parents milling around the door with an urgent glint in her eyes. I hoped everything was OK.

She caught sight of me. "Ah! Madame Germain. I must speak with you."

"Is everything all right?" I demanded. "Has there been an accident?"

She laughed and pulled Camille around in front of where she was standing. "Not at all. *Au contraire!*"

Camille was sporting a self-satisfied look on her face that reminded me of the Cheshire cat.

"Did we have a good day today at school Camille?" Séverine leaned down and asked my daughter.

"*Oui. On a passé une très bonne journée,*" Camille said in absolutely flawless French. "I enjoyed the painting and learning how to write my name."

I stared at my youngest. She was speaking French in full sentences! Perfectly! Without the slightest shadow of an accent! "When did this happen? How...?"

laughed. "It started this morning as soon as your husband left. She just started speaking like that with absolutely no accent or mistakes. I almost fainted."

Camille smiled proudly. "Why did you wait so long to talk?" I asked Camille. "You must have known how to for a while."

Camille shrugged. "I wanted to be able to speak French like all of the other kids."

"You mean perfectly?" I asked.

She nodded.

"Mission accomplished," I gave her a hug.

There was at least one problem that was solved, and solved on its own without any intervention from me.

We filled Franck in on Camille's now fluent French as soon as we shut the door behind us in Villers-la-Faye.

Franck, for his part, was already excessively cheery that we were finally able to get going on the renovations of the cottage.

"*Enfin!*" he said. "I will be so relieved to get that roof replaced before the really bad weather sets in. Using his charm and countless bottles of wine and cassis he had managed to line up all the other tradesmen who had to descend on the cottage as soon as the roof was done and try to whip it into shape before July 12th.

I knew how worried Franck had been. While I fretted about being lonely and whether Camille would actually start talking in school one day, Franck had been up, often during the night, pacing around the still most empty living room calculating how we could possibly gut an entire house and rebuild it from the ground up in eight months.

I often felt him slide out of our bed at around two or three o'clock in the morning. Sometimes he came back to bed around five; sometimes he didn't come back to bed at all but poured instead over his spreadsheets and calculations. His eyes had dark circles and he seemed to get through most days only by drinking vast quantities of espresso.

For some reason the cottage renovations didn't stress me out the same way they did Franck. I knew the task was almost impossible. The thing was that I had complete confidence that Franck could pull off the impossible. I watched him do exactly that so many times before, when he managed to get a work Permanent Resident visa to come to Canada so that we could be together, when he carried my huge trunk on his shoulder ten blocks during a sub zero winter in Montreal when we moved to our first apartment, re-plastering the destroyed walls of *La Maison des Deux Clochers* in record time…I knew he could do it again.

He managed to sleep through the previous night, and in the morning, the first of December, he hopped quickly into the shower and put on his clothes. "I'm going to go over there first thing to meet the roofer," he said. "I don't want anything getting in the way of him starting fast."

He peeked out the window. "The weather his perfect." He rubbed his hands. "No snow. Clear skies. Just a little bit of frost but that should burn off quickly."

Despite her newfound fluency Camille was in her usual morning mood and didn't want to touch either her hot chocolate or her *tartine*, which she said I had buttered the wrong way. Charlotte, meanwhile, gobbled up hers and commented that the apricot jam that Franck's parents had given us was delicious. She was wearing little strawberry bobbles in her hair and her cheer was a welcome diversion from Camille's morning scowl.

"What is the weather perfect for?" Charlotte asked.

"For taking the old roof off the cottage we're renovating and putting a new one on," I said.

"I like the old roof," muttered Camille, kicking the table leg.

"That way the cottage will be all snug for the winter!" Charlotte exclaimed, impervious to Camille's black look.

"Exactly," I said. "That way the workers can get in and do what they need to do in the winter so when the weather turns nice the cottage will be all ready for our renters."

While Franck spent his days lining up trades I spent mine on the Internet trying to sell the idea of the cottage. Not as it was now, of course. That would cause any potential guests to run for the hills. I had to picture, then relay the finished product in my mind, a task which tested both my imagination and my writing skills. Potential guests would invariably ask for photos and I had to convince them that they were not necessary. Instead, I gave descriptions of images that for the moment only resided in my head; refinished stone walls, exposed centuries old oak beams, a sunny, enclosed courtyard where they could sip their morning *café au lait* in perfect privacy and tranquility... I thought it best not to mention that our next-door neighbor had chickens and had recently acquired a rooster. I just kept my fingers crossed that the bird in question would end up as *coq au vin* before July. I wove our prospective guests a fiction and the first step to converting it to a reality was the roofer showing up on the job.

The phone rang. Franck leapt across the living room in a single bound to pick it up.

"*Allô?*" he said. "Ah! *Salut* Patrice. I was just going to leave for the cottage in five minutes to meet you and your guy there."

"This is *dégueulasse!*" Camille pushed her *tartine* away from her and crossed her arms.

"Camille! You know how to swear in French?" I asked, secretly impressed.

"Mom," Charlotte reminded me. "*Dégueulasse* is a bad word."

"I know." I pushed Camille's plate back in front of her. "You shouldn't say that again Camille, but still, you used it perfectly! Did you learn that from the kids in school?"

"From Charlotte," Camille said, picking up her *tartine* again.

Charlotte's mouth dropped open. "That's not true! Don't believe her!"

I pulled Charlotte's ponytail. "Don't worry, I'm not mad even if you did teach it to her. It was one of the first French words I learned when I first came to Beaune for school too."

"Really?" Charlotte looked up at me, her blue eyes wide.

"Yes. I know it's rude and everything, but kids say it a lot, don't they?"

Charlotte nodded. "They say it all the time in the *recrée*."

I leaned down and gave her a kiss. "Well, if that's the case, thank you for explaining to Camille what it means. It's not a nice word to say, but I think it's important that you both understand what those words mean and how the other kids use them. I was teased when I first got to France because I didn't understand those words. I don't want that to happen to either of you."

"Hey Franck!" I yelled as I cleared away Charlotte's plate. "Camille just used the word *dégeuleasse* perfectly. Charlotte taught her."

This was met by silence. My stomach dropped. Were the roofers going to be delayed? If so, how long? One week? Two? It couldn't be that, could it? We had waited so long for them already.

Franck was clutching the phone with white knuckles and his olive skin had drained to an alarming shade of gray.

Two weeks delay would bring us to the Christmas season where we knew from our experience on *La Maison des Deux Clochers* that work ground to a halt completely until at least January 15th when everyone got back from their ski trips in the Alps and emerged from their holiday hangovers.

"You must be able to do something!" Franck said into the phone. "You can't just leave us like this..."

I heard *"desolée"* followed by a click on the other end of the line. Apparently Patrice the roofer could just leave us like that.

Franck hung up the phone.

"What happened?" I asked, clutching his arm for support, for him or for me I wasn't certain. "Is the roofer delayed?"

"Cancelled."

"Cancelled?" How can that be?

"The roofer who he was going to have do our job fell off a roof last night, just as he climbed down."

"Did he die?"

"No, but he broke his back and he'll be in the hospital for several weeks and won't be working for a long time, if ever."

"Surely he must have other roofers?" I realized that I was shockingly short on empathy for the injured roofer, but without a roofer the renovations would remain at a complete standstill for the foreseeable future. Were these renovations making me a heartless *pétasse?*

Franck cracked his knuckles. "They're all busy on other jobs. I tried everything. I pleaded. I really think there's nothing he can do."

"He can't just leave us in the lurch like this!"

"He just did."

"But..."

"He did say he would phone around to all the other roofers he knows and see if he can find someone who is available. I think he feels really bad but he didn't sound very hopeful." Franck gave our kitchen table an explosive kick which made me and the girls jump. "Who could have predicted this *merde!*"

My husband collapsed on a chair and dropped his head in his hands. "I don't know what to do," his voice came out muffled. "Should I call all the other trades I've lined up and cancel, knowing I'll lose most of them, or should I hope for a miracle and plan on us being able to find another roofer?"

I didn't have an easy answer. Once again, I found myself completely baffled by life. I was aware that I was probably suffering from a persecution complex, but still, we were trying so hard to make good on the trust my Dad had put in us and move forward with renovating the cottage. If he had at least started the job and fallen off our roof they would have felt obligated to finish one way or another, but because he fell before they began our cottage they could just abandon us, and there was absolutely nothing we could do about it.

Another possibility occurred to me. "Do you think that roofer really fell off the roof or do you think they just found a more lucrative job they wanted to do?" I never would have even contemplated this possibility four months ago. My lack of faith shocked me, but I felt like I couldn't trust anyone but Franck anymore.

Franck looked up at me with exhausted eyes. "Does it really make a difference?" I realized then how much work and energy he had been pouring in to getting the trades on board over the past few weeks. He didn't deserve this.

"I think the guy really did fall," Franck admitted. "Patrice sounded completely traumatized."

I put a hand on his shoulder and gave him a squeeze. "I'm sorry *cheri.* Don't call the trades yet. Let's hope for a miracle. I think we are due for one."

Camille appeared in the kitchen doorway, dressed for school in a denim jumper with a frilly pink tutu underneath.

She put her hands on her hips. "*C'est déguelasse!*" she declared.

Franck and I both looked at each other, stunned. It was another perfect use of the word. The roofer cancelling on us at the last minute…it was so unfair that, in other words, it was completely *déguelasse.*

"Yes it is *ma* Camille," Franck said. "It certainly is."

I took the girls to school and had to creep back home. The fog was so thick I could barely see the road in front of me.

I found Franck still sitting at the kitchen table, nursing the same bowl of coffee. The middle finger on his right hand twitched.

"Did he call back?" Before the question was even out of my mouth I already knew the answer. Frustration rose in my throat like bile. I hated not being able to *do* anything. More than anything I wanted to help Franck, but what could I do short of kidnapping a roofer and threatening them at knifepoint to reroof our cottage?

I looked for a spot to put my keys, but aside from our kitchen table and four chairs and the buffet we had extracted from the cellar of *La Maison des Deux Clochers*, we still had no furniture.

"Let's go to Dijon," I said, suddenly.

"*Quoi?*" he looked up at me. "What if Patrice calls back?"

"We have voicemail on our phone. He has your cell phone number. We'll go crazy if we wait around here all day for a phone call that might not come. We need to get some distance from the situation. Give the universe time to sort something out." I had no idea why I had become metaphysical all of a sudden, but right now surrendering seemed like the only sane option, at least until we both recovered a bit.

"What are we going to do in Dijon?"

"Go to the *brocantes.* You may not have noticed," I said, surveying the room, "But things are still a little sparse around here in the furniture department. "

Franck followed my gaze. "You know, the funny thing is that I hadn't really noticed. I guess that says something for my state of mind."

"Yes. It's one track. Always has been, always will be. That's how you get impossible tasks done time after time. Still, we could use some furniture."

Brocantes was the name for second hand stores in France. People used them to sell their things that were not valuable enough to go to a proper antique shop. The irony was that the items I usually stumbled upon at *brocantes* in Burgundy would be quite at home at the most upscale antique store back in Canada – huge oak armoires passed down through generations, ancient kitchen scales, vintage maps and paintings, not to mention gorgeous oak benches.

We learned the hard way after Charlotte was born that *brocantes* and children did not mix. I felt guilty that I was so gleeful about the prospect of visiting a *brocante* without my children, but Franck must have shared at least a spark of my enthusiasm as he stood up and drained his coffee.

"What did I do with my wallet?" he asked. "The girls are going to the *cantine* today, right?"

"Yes. It's beet salad then *blanquette of veal* with potatoes *risolée* and then a selection of Corsican cheeses with chesnut paste, so I'm not worried about them."

"We can eat lunch in Dijon," Franck said, his energy level coming back. "Le Gégé was telling me about a restaurant that he and Laurence just tried there."

"Perfect."

"Did Camille really say *"c'est déguelasse'* this morning or did I imagine that?"

"She said it." I wrapped my scarf around my neck. "Do you think she realized what she was saying?"

"I'm not sure," Franck said. "But in any case, she nailed it

149

Our favorite *brocante* in Dijon, called *Troc Vingt-et-Un* was my version of paradise and always packed to the rafters with stuff. We had a full two hours to trawl around the huge store before it closed for lunch at noon.

I started, like I always did, in the section near the front that housed what was known as *bric à brac*. I examined an espresso cup and saucer from a set that had clearly come from a café. There were also five yellow jugs of different shapes and sizes labeled with the "Ricard" brand to contain the water needed to mix with the *pastis*. These sat beside several old winetasting cups, some more tarnished than others, and a set of retro turquoise kitchen scales with the complete set of weights that went with them.

I moved on to the furniture section, and admired the accidental beauty of a *petrière* - an old wooden bench used by bakers for letting dough rise. An old mantle clock and a dusty stuffed fox with still bright beady eyes made up an unintentional tableau on its wooden top.

I walked through another aisle where the furniture was stacked up ten feet high. This was my kind of maze.

"Laura?" I couldn't see over the set of cane chairs that had been set upon a buffet to find out where Franck's voice was coming from.

"Where are you?" I called out.

"Armoires," Franck answered.

I pressed on past pine kitchen buffets and round oak tables with deeply scratched tops and old wooden school desks with ink wells.

I found myself in a space between two densely packed rows of enormous armoires. Franck was at the far end.

"Over here," he said. "I love this one."

I loved the fact that I was married to a man who enjoyed looking at old furniture as much as I did. Franck had once told me *brocantes* brought back memories of his grandparents' house and family parties with flowing wine and much dancing to Claude François records on Pépé Georges's scratchy record player.

My eyes wandered over Franck's choice. It was built of pale pine that had acquired a glowing patina from use over the years. It was simple in design with a large mirror on the front door flagged by inset pine panels with a worn, delicate carving in the wood.

I reached out and smoothed my palm over the panel nearest me. The wood felt as smooth as silk under my fingertips.

"How old do you think it is?" I asked. It certainly wasn't as old as the intricately carved armoires made out of dark wood such as walnut and oak that surrounded us, but I actually liked it better.

Franck shrugged. "Probably late 1800s. From a simple farm or country home. Nothing pretentious."

"It's gorgeous," I said. I opened up the pine knob and stuck my head inside. It smelt faintly of mothballs but more strongly of pine and beeswax. I inspected the back of the armoire and the feet for evidence of bugs but it was in perfect condition. It had to be out of our budget, however. Something like this is Canada would sell for a couple of thousand dollars.

"How much is it?" I asked Franck, not really wanting to know the answer.

"I couldn't find a price tag," Franck said. "Maybe it's already sold."

I tried to rally. "I doubt we could afford it anyway."

Just then a friendly woman in a bright yellow T-shirt with the "Troc 21" insignia over her left breast came down our alleyway with a clipboard in her hand.

"*Bonjour*," she said. "Can I help you?"

"We were just admiring this armoire," Franck said. "We recently moved back here from Canada but there aren't many of these over there."

"Canada?" she asked. "Québec?"

Franck launched into our life story as I continued to stroke and admire the armoire in front of me. There was something about certain pieces of old furniture – like this one – that possessed a soul. I felt that way about our old kitchen buffet at *La Maison des Deux Clochers* and even the towering and at times menacing pear buffet that stood in that small house's living room. New furniture never got the same reaction from me. With pieces like this armoire it was as if everything it had witnessed and experienced and been a silent part of had somehow seeped into the grain of wood, giving it a personality that was as individual as the wrinkles on a grandmother's face. Like the Templar chapel in the middle of the parking lot in Beaune, being surrounded by furniture far older than me had a way of putting the lumps and bumps of my life in perspective.

"We couldn't find a price," I heard Franck say and I snapped to attention. "Has it already been sold?"

The friendly woman began flipping through the sheaf of papers on her clipboard.

"No," she said finally. "There is no price because somebody just brought it in this morning. In fact, I have the price for it right here." She plucked a stack of bright red price tags from her back pocket and shuffled through them. "Ah! *Le Voilà.*"

"How much?" Franck asked. I could tell from his tone that, like me, he was not sure if he wanted to know the answer.

"Two hundred," she said, sticking the price tag on the side of the *armoire.*

"Two hundred euros?" I asked, my voice faint. Could that possibly be missing an extra zero? If so, when would she realize it?

"Well...yes," she said, apology in her voice. "I know it isn't one of the more expensive woods like oak or walnut, but it is in excellent condition. I find it quite *charmante* even though it's probably only two hundred years old so, *vous savez*, not really antique."

Franck nodded, solemn. Only I could detect the glee in his eyes.

"We'll take it," he said, plucking off the freshly affixed price tag and giving it back to the saleswoman. "But can we look around a little more first before we pay?"

"*Bien sûr!*" she exclaimed. "That was the quickest sale I've had so far this week. You'll have to tell your other Canadian friends to drop in!"

She continued on down the alley of armoires, sticking tags on as she went. As soon as she went around the corner, I grabbed Franck's hand.

"Two hundred euros! That's a steal." I almost felt inclined to thank the hapless roofer for falling off the roof. "We have to start importing furniture to Canada."

"Do you think we could?" Franck said, and then shook his head. "*Non.* One thing at a time. We need to finish the cottage and buy some furniture for ourselves, not to mention renovate our own place..."

"OK. Maybe not today," I said. "But the importing furniture thing...that should happen at some point. It's a good idea."

"Agreed," Franck said. "But first let's look for a dining room table."

We lingered at *brocante* until we were kicked out at noon by the employees who were eager to lock up the store and leave on their two-hour lunch break.

Besides the armoire, we also bought a beautiful oak dining room table that used to do service in a local monastery as well as eight bent wood chairs with wicker seats. I also bought a green and red manual coffee grinder for decorating the cottage and an enamel sign saying "*Toilettes*" for the door of the bathroom. Also, I had found a sky blue glass seltzer bottle from the turn of the century that I would keep for myself. I took the bag with the small items as Franck arranged to come up and pick up the big pieces in a truck the next day.

We walked out of the door into the crisp December air, bonded by our mutual satisfaction over our treasure hunting expedition.

"*Alors.*" Franck dug out the car keys from his jeans pocket. "Lunch! Let's go to the restaurant that *Le Gégé* suggested."

I had a knee jerk reaction of a North American that we should just find a place to eat quickly – that settling into a two hour lunch was a waste of time. I reminded myself that here in France the mid-day meal was invariably the main event of the day. All activities before merely were a prelude and everything afterwards an afterlude.

We hopped in the car, crossed the train tracks and penetrated the medieval heart of Dijon. We passed the Maille mustard shop and the old theatre where scenes from *Cyrano de Bérgerac* had been filmed and past shiny roofs of patterned black and yellow Burgundian tiles. Franck drove up a cobblestoned street that led to the large square where the ornate iron covered market building was located. Franck slid into a parking space and turned off the ignition.

"Good thing it's not a market day," he said. "We never would have found a parking spot."

It had begun to drizzle, but this just added a cozy edge to my already rumbling stomach. Once we were ensconced in a warm restaurant it could rain down all it wanted.

Franck took my hand and led me to the far corner of the market building and then down a narrow alley.

"Are you sure you know where you're going?" I asked.

"*Le Gégé* said it was right beside the anarchist café," Franck said. "God knows I spent enough time in there during my first two years of university."

"You were an anarchist when you were in university?" I knew Franck had been bulimic about his consumption of European philosophy, which more often than not had a distinctly nihilistic bent, but I didn't know that he had also been an anarchist.

"Isn't everyone?"

Not me. How had I missed out on being an anarchist?

Franck waved towards a chesnut colored café wedged in one side of the dark alley. A vibrant sign which read "*Café Chez Nous*" hung above the door. It was hard to see anything through the windows due to the cigarette smoke inside.

"What exactly do anarchists do?" I asked.

Franck smiled in fond remembrance. "Smoke a lot of cigarettes. Talk about how everything is terrible and how everything needs to be knocked down in order to be rebuilt. Read newspapers. Decry the corruption of the media. Plot to overthrow the Establishment." Franck shrugged. "The usual."

I nodded back at the café. "And you did a lot of that in there?"

"Oh yes. But not just there, we did it everywhere we went. That's what university students in France do, you know."

Not just university. I believed that most French people retained a slice of anarchy in their souls no matter where they went in life, or even, like Franck, if they eventually quit smoking.

Franck opened the door at the end of the alley. I peered up and saw a neon sign above the door that read "*La Ruelle*", or "the alleyway" which seemed apt.

"This is it?" I asked.

Before Franck could answer a friendly waiter in pressed jeans (where do French men learn to iron their jeans?) and a pink cotton button down shirt came over to offer us a cozy booth in the corner that looked on to Café Chez Nous. Out the window I saw that the rain had begun to fall in earnest making the setting even cozier.

"Perfect," I murmured.

Half an hour later Franck and I had both enjoyed two *kirs* each and had moved on to a bottle of white wine to go with my lamb tagine and

Franck's steak tartare.

I eyed his plate as he cracked a raw egg over the mound of raw ground beef and sprinkled some freshly cut herbs over top. He mixed it all together with his fork. "I can't believe you're really going to eat that."

He passed me a forkful. "It's one of the most delicious things on earth. You have to try it."

My insides contracted in revulsion but I reminded myself that I had moved to France to live a different life and to try new things. I closed my eyes and opened my mouth. Franck chuckled as he popped the forkful inside.

I chewed cautiously. The meat felt smooth and satiny against my tongue, and the bright flavors of the parsley and other herbs kept it from being too rich. Still, it was raw meat. I quickly swallowed my mouthful with a gulp of white wine.

"Well?" Franck ventured.

"Not bad."

"Do you want some more?"

"Baby steps *mon cheri*. Baby steps."

Franck snorted and then dug into his plate.

Our main courses were eventually replaced with a plateful of local cheeses served with fig compote and diced prunes. The bread had nuts in it – hazelnuts and walnuts that perfectly offset the creaminess of the cheese and the chew of the dried fruit.

I groaned with pleasure. "This is delicious. Is it wrong that we are enjoying ourselves this much without the girls?"

Franck frowned at me, perplexed "We're adults. Of course we enjoy doing adult things. Just because we're parents doesn't mean we have to stop being grown ups."

I leaned across the table. "But this wouldn't be nearly as pleasurable if Charlotte and Camille were with us. It makes me feel guilty to admit that."

"That is the most ridiculous thing I have ever heard. You know how in the airplane they have those safety announcements?"

"Yeah." I had taken countless flights and could probably recite one on demand if asked.

"You remember the part about the oxygen masks that drop out of the ceiling if the cabin loses air pressure?"

I nodded.

"They always instruct parents to put on their own masks before putting on their child's mask."

"Always."

"Why do you think that is?" Franck asked.

"Well…if the parents pass out before they can get their own mask on they're not going to be much help to their children."

"*Exactement.*" Franck popped a piece of nut bread topped with a creamy swipe of wonderfully smelly *Époisses* in his mouth. "That's how I see parenting. If we don't take care of ourselves and indulge in things we truly find pleasurable, we're no good to ourselves or our children."

I took a sip of my red wine. We each had ordered a glass of Gevrey-Chambertin as it would have been a sacrilege to enjoy all this Burgundian cheese without a good Burgundy pinot. Franck's oxygen mask theory was a revelation. As much as I loved my girls, self-care had completely fallen out of my life since they were born. I had no time. I had no energy. Worst of all, I was confused about what self-care actually meant anymore.

In my social circle back in Canada post-partum self-care meant throwing oneself into exercise and signing up for a marathon or a triathlon. It had nothing to do with the soul or one's mind.

I had spent so little time on things that *actually* nourished me instead of the things that I believed *should* nourish me that I had completely lost touch with what made me happy in the first place. I knew though that spending a morning trolling the *brocante* with Franck and enjoying a delectable lunch with him in this cozy restaurant definitely made me happy more than running a marathon ever would.

"I guess I feel guilty putting on my own oxygen mask," I admitted. "Somehow I feel that as a mother I don't have the right until everyone else's needs have been met."

"Laura." Franck reached across the table and squeezed my hand. "Children's needs are constant. It's like trying to fill a black hole. You don't need anyone else's permission to do things for yourself. You are the only one who can give that permission to yourself."

"That's true," I admitted.

"Once we get settled I think you'll have an easier time of it here than in Canada." Franck took a sip of wine. "The French don't believe in becoming slaves to their children at the price of their own happiness."

"Slave?" I withdrew my hand from his. "That's harsh."

"Maybe, but I think it's the truth in many cases. I saw parents in Canada whose mouths were telling me that having children was the best thing in the world, but their eyes told a different story. They looked exhausted, confused, disenchanted…"

"Do I look like that?"

Franck glanced at me, appraising. "Sometimes."

"I love our girls," I said.

"I know you do, but all I'm saying is that as a rule if the parents are happy, the kids will be happy."

I wasn't so sure about that. "Don't you think we should get our happiness from spending time with our children?"

"I think you'll find we enjoy the girls more if we are also able to steal adult moments like this on a regular basis. It's all about balance, you know…*equilibre*."

"What do you do about the guilt?"

"What guilt?"

"*What* guilt?" Since having Charlotte and Camille guilt had become a close companion in my life - guilt that I wasn't playing enough with them, guilt that I wasn't feeding them healthy enough food, guilt that I still yearned for adult pursuits like quiet meals out and writing and reading a book in an empty house when I had these marvelous daughters. "Are you seriously telling me that you feel no guilt about how you are doing as a parent?"

Franck cocked his head at me. "I just don't understand guilt. I mean, what's the point?"

The waiter came to clear away the cheese course and we ordered espressos.

I struggled to answer his question. What *was* the point of guilt? What did guilt do besides sap my energy and make me feel bad? Somehow part of me felt that guilt was the karmic price I had to pay for being gifted with a beautiful, healthy, intelligent child.

"There is no point to guilt, I guess," I conceded. "But for us WASPs it's a hard habit to break."

"Does your guilt improve Charlotte and Camille's lives?"

"No." On the contrary. It probably made me more crabby.

"Does it make you a better mother?"

"No."

"Does it make you a happier person?"

"Definitely not."

Franck nodded his thanks to the waiter who brought us two steaming cups of espresso with perfect little foil wrapped chocolates on the side. "Like I said, it serves no purpose. Just stop feeling guilty."

I unwrapped my chocolate and dipped it into my espresso so that it melted a bit before taking a bite. Motherhood without guilt? What would that even *feel* like? All the mothers I knew back home were similarly plagued.

"It would be hard for me," I said. "Maybe even impossible." I wondered if maybe guilt was simply in my genetic make-up. I sipped my espresso. Strong and bitter and perfect.

"It may be," Franck agreed. "But it might also be worth it, *n'est-ce pas?*"

Just as I was seriously considering how to best go about abandoning my guilt, Franck's cell phone rang. We both jumped in surprise. Could it be the roofer? Had he found somebody who could help us? Maybe things did have a way of working out. I had to let the universe just do its thing more often.

"*Allo.*" Franck answered. I watched him. "*Oui. C'est lui-même,*" he said. "Ah bon...Ah bon?" He nodded a few times, and bit his lip. "How is she now?"

It had to be one of the girls. What had happened? Panic coursed through my veins, quickly followed by a deluge of guilt. Bad things happened when I let go and started to enjoy myself, I *knew* it!

"We'll leave to come and get her right now," I heard Franck say. "We're in Dijon though, so it will take about half an hour."

Franck closed his phone and took his wallet out of his pocket.

"What?!" I demanded. "Tell me what's wrong."

"Camille threw up at the *cantine* at lunch. All over the table, apparently. We need to go pick her up."

First I felt relief, then of course more guilt. So that's why she had been so crabby over breakfast. We shouldn't have made her go to the *cantine* so we could drift through the *brocante* and indulge in a leisurely meal. I should have known she was coming down with something. My poor little girl. If she were in Canada she wouldn't even be in full day school. I pictured her at the school now, all alone, nauseous and embarrassed about throwing up all over her schoolmates.

"Let's go!"

Franck rolled his eyes and waved me to sit back down again. "I have to pay first. Taking a detour to jail is not exactly going to help us get to Camille faster."

I sat down, but began clicking my nails on the table top and tapping my foot. "Hurry," I muttered.

Franck paid but it galled me that he didn't seem to share my sense of urgency about getting to Camille.

Once we were in the car I found myself for once urging Franck to drive faster.

It seemed an eternity before we got to the school. When we passed the Virgin Mary statue in the preschool courtyard of Saint Coeur she looked down on us, inscrutable.

"Do you think she's in the nap room?" I asked.

"No. They said she would be in her classroom."

The classroom was dark inside, but I could make out Severine, Camille's teacher, kneeling beside a little cot on the floor. Géraldine, who Charlotte and Camille knew as the "nap lady" was on the other side of the cot holding a wet cloth to Camille's brow. My little girl lay on the cot, pale but with bright, wide eyes.

"*Maman! Papa!*" she said in perfect French when she saw us. "I threw up in the *cantine!* All over the table!" Was that a hint of pride I detected in her voice?

Geraldine nodded. "It was truly *spéctaculaire.*"

I knelt down by Sévérine and took Camille's hand which didn't feel clammy or too hot or too cold, but just right. "Poor you," I said to Camille, then looked at Geraldine. "Did you have to clean it up?"

Geraldine nodded. "It decimated the Corsican cheese platter. That went straight into the garbage pail."

I grimaced. "I'm so sorry. *Desolée…*"

"*C'était dégueulasse!*" Camille said with relish. "I just looked at the chesnut cream on the platter and the throw-up came up in my throat. It *covered* the cheese." It was traditional in Corsica to eat chesnut cream with all the crumbly local sheep cheeses but it wasn't traditional for it to trigger vomit.

Both Sévérine and Géraldine had to cover their mouths to stifle laughter.

"That's her new favorite word," I explained. "Unfortunately."

"That's a bad word," Sévérine told Camille, trying hard to resume her teacher's authority. "But in this situation it does maybe have some truth."

Camille twitched one very small shoulder. "I know."

Géraldine stood up. "She seems to be feeling quite a bit better now but I think you should take her home just to be on the safe side."

"Of course," I said. Franck bent down and gathered Camille up in his arms.

"I can walk!" she chastised him in his mother tongue. "I'm almost three, you know."

He set her down on her feet. I wrapped her up in her coat and zipped it up. After thanking Géraldine and Sévérine several times we hustled her out of the building.

We got Camille back up to Villers and settled her in front of a Barbie Princess DVD on Franck's computer with no further vomit incidents. I went into the kitchen where Franck was sitting at the table, chewing his thumbnail.

"Thinking about the roofer?" I surmised. "No messages while we were away?"

"*Non,*" he said. "How's Camille?"

"Vastly impressed by the splash she made at the *cantine.*"I bit my lip.

Franck looked up at me. "You're feeling guilty again, aren't you?"

"I feel as though I should have prevented Camille from getting sick, or at least had her home for lunch so it would have happened here."

"Do you regret this morning?"

I couldn't go that far. "No. I'm happy about the furniture and the lunch. Those had been big *bonheurs*, even though I felt guilty that they had been *bonheurs* that were distinctly child-free. "

"Don't you think you are dealing with Camille better now because you have some gas in your tank?"

"I guess." It was true. I was still enjoying the satisfaction of our morning excursion, so I probably was being extra patient and attentive to Camille.

Franck picked up the phone. "Oxygen. Us parents have to make sure we get some otherwise we'll keel over."

"Who are you going to call?"

"The roofer."

I cocked a questioning brow.

"I'm calling him. I'm not going to go over and strangle him, which I may have if we hadn't had a bit of a break in Dijon."

"Ah," I said. "Oxygen."

"*Exactement.*"

CHAPTER 16

That night we thoughtfully prepared an easily digestible dinner of *purée* and *jambon blanc* for Camille, but she ended up insisting on a large plateful of veal stuffed with a herb sausage mixture and tied together with a string so that they made little savory dumplings called *les paupillettes* cooked in a white wine sauce that Franck had made the night before along with a huge mound of rice.

"I'm starving!" she declared as she dug in. "This is delicious."

The phone rang and I looked at Franck questioningly. At seven o'clock – dinner time here in France - few people would think of calling. It was very poor manners.

Franck went into the living room and grabbed the phone. I heard a low murmur of conversation but thanks to Camille and Charlotte chirping to each other in French about the already legendary cafeteria Corsican cheese barf I couldn't make out what Franck was saying or even to whom he was talking.

"Who was it?" I asked when he returned.

"The roofer," he said. "He said maybe he's found someone who can help us. Another roofer who just started his own company."

"Is he any good?" I asked.

"Are we in a position to be picky? The new roofer has apparently invited you and me for dinner at his house tomorrow night. If he likes us we can talk quotes with him."

"What did you say?"

"I took the address and said that we would be there. What choice do we have?"

"Who is going to look after the girls?"

"I'll ask my parents."

I turned my attention back to my plate of veal *paupillettes*. They were delicious, the delicate herb and pork mixture inside the thin crust of crispy veal infusing the whole dish with deep, satisfying flavors. The sauce Franck had whipped up with cream and white wine complemented it perfectly and was soaked up by the basmati rice.

As I chewed, part of me appreciated my meal while part of me fretted about the dinner at the potential roofer's house. Deep down I am an introvert and I didn't like the idea of being parachuted into a dinner with a bunch of strangers. Burgundy meals were almost never short affairs. Would this be formal? Casual? More importantly, would they be serving innards? That was always a risk in France.

"If you go I can stay with the girls, then you won't have to bother your parents," I suggested.

"He wants to meet both of us. Laura, you know how badly we need a roof on the cottage."

I groaned. "We can't stay too long," I said. "Camille is sick."

"That will be our perfect excuse to leave early then," Franck said.

Hah. Famous last words in Burgundy.

The next night Franck and I were crawling along an icy road in *la plaine*, the flat part of land that stretched out beyond Beaune on the opposite side to the rolling hills of our *Hautes-Côtes*. We were lost.

Camille was feeling perfectly fine and had gone to school where she had become the source of pointed fingers and awestruck exclamations along the lines of "that is the girl who threw up all over the cheese platter at the *cantine!*" She glowed with her newfound fame. We had left her and Charlotte at our house with Franck's father playing a game of *petit chevaux*.

"Try not to come back too late," André reminded us. "I have to work tomorrow."

"I don't even want to go," I said, winding my scarf around my neck. "I just want to have him build our roof. Is that so complicated?"

"Ah," André raised a brow without looking up from the game, where he was allowing Charlotte to cheat shamelessly. "But that is not how things work in Burgundy."

I raged inwardly about this fact as we crawled past what seemed like endless fields. We left the vineyards behind us as we headed east. Why was it always so complicated to get things done here?

Franck never seemed perturbed by the Burgundian way of doing things. On the contrary, he was constantly shocked back in Canada when a tradesman didn't want to stop for a drink or didn't have time to chat. Also, Franck was a born extrovert and adored meeting new people.

Franck muttered. "Where the hell is this village?" We entered a patch of fog so thick that we could hardly see five feet in front of our headlights.

"Maybe we should call them and tell them one of us is sick," I said. "Then we can turn around and go back home and eat baguette sandwiches at our new dining room table."

Franck had rented the truck and gone up to Dijon and brought back, with the help of our next-door neighbor, our beautiful new monastery table and our honey colored *armoire*. They were set up in our living room and improved it immensely.

"*Alors Voilà*," Franck shouted and I glimpsed out into the fog to see our headlights briefly flare on a white sign that read Parigny-les-Eaux in black lettering.

My heart sunk. We had found the right village. There was no chance of fulfilling the seductive vision of eating sandwiches in the living room that night. Franck crawled along searching the address until he turned into the driveway, clogged with cars, of a rambling stone house.

"Here it is." He pulled up the parking break. "Ready?"

I made a non-committal noise in the back of my throat but opened my car door. The sooner we got in there the sooner we could head home. I had dressed in my best pair of jeans (which wasn't saying much) and a soft purple sweater with a huge cowl neck. I had no idea whether to expect a sit down dinner with linen napkins and fine crystal or a frozen pizza.

Franck knocked on the wooden door but there was a lot of shouting going on inside.

"I think you may need to knock louder," I said. "Or maybe just let yourself in."

I could tell Franck wasn't a fan of this idea. As much as spontaneous visits to friends and family were the norm in France, it wasn't considered polite to just waltz into a stranger's house. However, it quickly became clear that barging in was the only way we were going to get inside. Besides, it was a bitterly cold.

My Canadian pragmatism made me push open the door and step inside. I had a hard time pulling Franck along behind me. The rigidity of his body messaged me that he was still feeling sticklerish about this breech of etiquette.

The noise from the fifteen or so people drinking big tumblers of something stopped instantly.

"*Bonjour*," I said. "We're the Germains."

A tanned man broke through the crowd and planted *les bises* on my cheeks. "*Les Canadiens!*" he exclaimed. "I'm so glad you accepted my invitation. I've been told you have roofing troubles."

"Yes!" I pounced. "You see, we have this cottage that we need to…"

The roofer motioned me to stop talking. "We can discuss work later. First things first, what can I serve you for an *apéritif?* Pastis? Kir? Suze?"

"Kir," Franck said, taking off his jacket. "Please."

"Same." I regretted my warm sweater. Sweat was already beading on the back of my neck.

A rail thin woman with a cloud of frizzy black hair hurried over to take them from us and her husband, Alain, the erstwhile roofer, pulled us into the middle of the crowd, quickly pushed a drink in our hands, then introduced us to everyone. The crowd included Alain's parents, his wife's parents, an assortment of brothers and sisters, as well as several cousins and friends who all appeared to have identical sounding nicknames.

"Thank you for having us," Franck managed to make himself heard over the tumult of rapid French.

"*C'est rien*," Alain shrugged. "We do this every Friday night. Everyone just knows to come over to our house. Besides, I wanted to meet you. I don't get along with a lot of people you know. I have a *mauvais caractère*. Also, I would rather not work at all than work for assholes."

"We're not assholes," I assured him. "At least I don't think we are."

Alain hooted with laughter. "We'll see about that!" He slapped Franck on the back then began refilling everyone's drinks. I had been wise to wear jeans. The dress code was casual in the extreme. Pretty much everyone else was in jeans except one wizened specimen who was still wearing his faded indigo *"bleus de travail"* from his workweek – the uniform of the traditional French blue collar worker. Or maybe he wore them on the weekends too?

"You are *la canadienne*?" a woman with dyed blond hair and startling fuchsia earrings asked me.

"Yes. That's me."

"Do you have a dogsled back home?" she asked.

I started to laugh but then realized she was completely serious. "Ah no," I said. "Sorry."

"Do *you*?" she asked Franck.

"No," Franck answered, but I could hear the patent disappointment in his voice. Franck always wanted a dogsled. I blamed a youthful obsession with Jack London novels.

The woman searched our faces; perhaps suspicious that Franck and I were merely masquerading as Canadians. My head began to spin a bit. It had been so hot that I had sucked back Alain's potent kir. While the jeans had been a good idea, the hot cowl-necked sweater, not so much.

The woman frowned at us and I had an idea. We really needed a roofer. If all it took was a few little fibs about life in Canada, was that really such a big deal? I reminded myself of one of my favorite T.S. Eliot quotes "Only those who will risk going too far can possibly find out how far one can go."

"We don't need a dogsled because our next door neighbor has one," I said. "Along with twenty huskies to pull it. He takes us to work if the snow gets too high to drive."

Franck stared at me in stupefaction.

"What about igloos?" The ancient man in *les bleus* demanded.

I nodded as Alain sidled up to refill our glasses again. "Most of us Canadians don't choose to live in an igloo of course, but parachute me onto an ice field with a saw and I could build one in under an hour."

"*Vraiment?*" A heavyset man with a ruddy face asked, captivated.

"Yes Laura," Franck said, his voice unsteady. "*Vraiment?*"

"All Canadians can, of course. Igloo building is one of the first skills we learn."

"After crawling, you mean," Franck said.

"That's right." I arched a brow at him to stop his lip. Did he want this roof or not?

"*À table!*" Alain yelled, saving me, for the time being anyway.

He steered Franck and I by a strong hand on each of our shoulders to the table and sat us at opposite ends. The competition to sit beside us was lively and involved pushing and several heated arguments.

Finally a man built like an ox with florid face and bright blue eyes won the spot on my right and the old man with *les bleus* on my left. Alain introduced the younger man to me as his friend Hugo who was a brilliant stonemason and was considering going out on his own. "You may have lots to talk about." He winked at us.

"So you want to work for yourself?" I asked Hugo.

"Alain keeps insisting I start my own business," Hugo said with a roll of his eyes. "It's crazy. I'm basically doing it to get him off my back."

I was brought up in a family of entrepreneurs in a society of go-getters. There seemed nothing insane at all about wanting to be self-employed. In fact, in my mind it was the most natural and admirable of goals.

"I think working for yourself is amazing. What don't you like about the idea?"

"Besides the taxes?" Hugo answered.

"Taxes?"

"Have you not been in France long enough to know about the taxes?"

"Well, I guess we pay tax on our first vacation rental over here, but until we moved here we were more or less taxed in Canada for that. Franck is looking into the taxes now that we are officially French residents."

Hugo laughed and passed me the platter of raclette cheese to put on my little Tefal dish. Raclette, a traditional dish of the mountainous Jura and Alps regions of France, historically involved an entire half wedge of Racelette cheese which could measure up to two feet long, heated over a big toaster like contraption. The melty bits were scraped off with a huge wooden spatula. This melted cheese was then poured over a plateful of boiled potatoes and local *charcuterie*. This was accompanied, *bien sûr*, by small pickles called *cornichons* as the French believed that a little hit of vinegar made all of this eminently more *digeste*, or digestable.

However, because the French people in regions from Normandy to Marseilles had developed a love affair with raclette and it wasn't practical to haul around humungous half moons of cheese and massive wooden spatulas, Tefal had the smarts to develop a tabletop racelette machine that you plugged in the nearest wall socket. One would be hard pressed to find a French family who did not own one of these tabletop contraptions. The machine had eight little slots and each person had their own little Tefal tray.

Alain had three of these contraptions set up on his long table. One of them was placed right across from my chair. Not only did these little machines melt individual portions of cheese, but they generated some serious heat. Sweat trickled down my neck into my cleavage.

"You and your husband are in for a rude awakening!" Hugo said, still on the subject of taxes in France.

"Is it that bad?" I asked. "It can't be that bad…" I said, to Hugo or myself, I wasn't sure. I had always been mystified as to why the French lacked the entrepreneurial spirit that I had come to assume was the norm for most people. I had always assumed it was because the French were a bit lazy, not to mention the paradoxical combination of being secretly anarchist yet fond of being yelled at and told what to do like they are all the way through the French school system.

Hugo snorted. "For a tradesman like me or Alain, we basically have to plan on earning at least half of our revenue under the table just to break even. Guess how much it costs me for every Euro I pay to an employee?

"I have no idea," I said. "A Euro and twenty *centimes?*" That sounded pretty steep to me, but seemed like a reasonable guess. I plucked several *rondelles* of garlic studded *saucisson* off the plate being circulated and a roll of jambon blanc.

Hugo choked on his wine. "Try one euro and eighty centimes."

"That can't be right. It would make no sense for anyone in France to employ anyone else."

"Now you're getting the picture." Hugo refilled my glass. "Enough about work. Tell me more about Canada. Do you own a pair of snowshoes?"

The dinner grew increasingly raucous as pounds of *Racelette* cheese and platterfuls of delectable local *charcuterie,* pancetta, sausages both large and small, rounds of chorizo sausages, paper thin shavings of cured jambon de bayonne, were washed down with dry white wine and then a fruity red that Alain said was made by his cousin near Nuits-Saint-Georges. I also happened to love Cornichon pickles and had stationed a Maille brand bottle of them conveniently by my elbow.

"The wine cellar!" Alain hopped up from his chair and grabbed my arm. "You and Franck haven't seen my wine cellar yet. Come with us Hugo."

Hugo stood up – a little unsteadily, I noticed, and followed Alain.

"Hugo did the excavation for the cellar you know," Alain told us over his shoulder as he led us down a dark hallway.

"Excavation?" Franck said. In most homes in the winemaking area where we were, all houses came with a wine cellar, usually one that was several centuries old. The cellar was traditionally dug out in Burgundy before a house was even built on top. Clearly, the Burgundians have had their priorities straight for centuries.

"Yes, the cellar here was little more than a crawl space. We're kind of outside of the winemaking area here in *la plaine* you know," Alain explained, leading us down a narrow set of stairs.

We seemed to have ended up in the basement but I didn't see much besides a dilapidated washing machine pushed up against one corner and a five tiered drying rack festooned with underpants and socks. Apparently Alain had a taste for brightly colored *culottes.*

Alain turned to us. "Ah!" He put a finger against his nose. "I bet you think we have reached a dead end, *n'est-ce pas?* Are you wondering where we should go now?"

Alain walked a few steps past the washing machine and opened a trap door that I hadn't even seen in the floor. "*Voilà!*" he crowed.

I peered around the impressive bulk of Hugo to see a corkscrew staircase that lead downwards into dark and mysterious depths.

"*Ça alors...*" I murmured.

"Come! Come!" Alain disappeared down the stairs and called us to follow him. He must have got to the light switches, because all of a sudden the ground below us was bathed in muted golden light.

"How did you even get those stairs down here?" Franck asked.

Hugo gave a crooked smile. "Don't ask."

I was last going down the stairs, as I wasn't overly thrilled about going down this far underground. I knew from experience that wine cellars, like old houses that had been closed up for a while, often contained strange and unexpected things like albino rats, thick cobwebs, and strands of black mold.

When I reached the bottom of the spiral staircase I was pleasantly surprised. Amazed, actually. Hidden underneath this ramshackle house was a cellar fit for a small chateau. It boasted a vaulted stone ceiling, a pea gravel floor, track lights flickering an atmospheric light on the stucco walls, three barrels set up vertically for tastings, and row upon row of neatly stacked wine bottles lined the walls.

"None of this was here?" I asked, astounded.

"*Non.*" Hugo looped his fingers in the belt loops of his jeans and leaned proudly forward on the tips of his toes. We dug and we dug and we dug...we dug until that crack appeared." He pointed to a large fissure I hadn't noticed that wrapped around the expanse of the ceiling vault. "Then one of the exterior walls upstairs began to buckle. We decided that was a good time to stop digging."

"So...is your house unstable then?" I asked, claustrophobia clamping down on me

"That was a few weeks ago," said Alain. "We think it must be fine. It's still standing."

"But it could cave in at any time?"

Hugo shrugged. "Technically, any house could cave in at any time."

I caught Franck's eyes and widened mine. His hazel eyes danced with delight. He knew exactly how I was feeling but I could tell he was quite enjoying the absurdity of it all.

"It's beautiful," Franck said. "I've always dreamed of having a proper wine cellar like this."

We had quite a nice wine cellar at *La Maison des Deux Clochers*, but it kept getting filled up with renovation materials. It just wasn't the same conducting a tasting when surrounded by plaster buckets and wheelbarrows and old shutters. It was also not this far underground, so its temperature was not ideal. I had to admit the temperature in this cellar was perfect – cool without being cold. I was sure Alain would have no problem keeping it a constant temperature for his wines all year round.

"We can't come down here without having a tasting," Alain decreed, going over to the wall and selecting several bottles, studying the labels, clicking his tongue, and then putting them back again.

"Do you prefer *Côte de Beaune* or *Côte de Nuits*?" he asked, finally.

"Both," I said. It was the truth. Call me undiscerning, but I rarely encountered a wine in Burgundy that I didn't like.

"*Côte de Nuits*," Franck said. I remembered, Villers-la-Faye was in the *Côte de Nuits*, even though Magny-les-Villers straddled both appellations. I guess that meant Franck saw himself as a full-fledged *Villerois* again.

Alain pulled out a bottle that he handled lovingly. "Ahhhh…a Grand Échezeaux. That fits the bill. What do you think?"

Grand Échezeaux? That was a Grand Cru wine, ridiculously expensive but worth every penny.

"*Fantastique*," I said. Franck nodded.

"It's a "*Les Cruots*". It's made by Hector Guyot. There are eleven Grand Cru Échezeaux appellations and they can be middling to outstanding. Guyot makes one of the outstanding ones. I made sure of that before agreeing to a swap. I did his roof and he paid me in wine," explained Alain.

Not just wealthy people indulged in good wine in Burgundy. Wine lovers could be found in every layer of society and you were just as likely to find a true connoisseur at a tradesman's house then at a winemaker's dinner.

"How do you source your wine?" Franck asked.

Alain didn't answer right away. Instead, he eased the cork out of the bottle and we all joined in a collective "ahhhhh" of satisfaction at the soft pop.

"I work often for wine makers or people in the wine industry, *vous savez*, winemakers, *négotiants*, oenologues and the like. We always end up doing a tasting sooner rather than later and well…rather than pay taxes to the government we are almost always able to reach an agreement that fills my cellar and gets their roofs built. Here was a uniquely Burgundian twist on the thriving French black market.

"Do you think you'll do that too?" I asked Hugo as Alain passed us each a glass full of garnet colored nectar.

"I like wine as much as the next person but give me a glass of ordinary chilled white wine and I am a happy man. I don't need all this *frou-frou* like Alain." He gestured around the cellar.

Alain passed me a glass. "However, he would trade his own children for ancient tiles or floor *tommettes…*"

I sent a questioning look to Alain.

"Hugo is restoring a mini chateau," he explained. "It's a fourteenth century stronghold and it was an absolute ruin when he bought it, *hein* Hugo?"

"You could see the sky from the cellars." Hugo grinned. "My wife almost divorced me the day I signed the papers.

"Your wife is always threatening to divorce you and I don't blame her," Alain said. "Weren't you supposed to be at that play of hers tonight by the way?"

Hugo shrugged. "*Oui.*"

Alain raised his glass. "*Santé,*" he declared and we all took a sip of wine.

The wine perfectly balanced the flavors of tart red fruit that was almost sassy, but made serious with a caramel earthiness that quickly followed. I was amazed at how many wines in Burgundy had a soul as unique as a centuries old armoire from the *brocante* or a person like Mémé Germaine. They possessed that dichotomy of being timeless yet unique. We remained silent in admiration as we swashed the wine around our mouths and took further sips.

"Sublime," Franck concluded.

There was also an elusive something about Burgundy wines that I had never experienced anywhere else; purity, an art, a sublime mixture of nature and nurture…that made this bottle just as transcendent as the Savigny we had shared with Martial and Isabelle, yet at the same time utterly different.

"Thank you for sharing this with us," I said. "I love it."

Alain's harsh features softened considerably. "If the house caves in on top of us at least we will die happy."

The three of us made quick work of the bottle and by that point Franck and I had completely forgotten about roofing the cottage. The staircase up from the cellar seemed much longer and much windier than it had on the way down.

When we got back to the table everyone teased us about sneaking off and not including them in the tasting. Alain and Hugo then presented the bottles they had brought up from the cellar that they had been hiding behind their backs. Not Grand Échezeaux but a completely delicious Morey-Saint-Denis. We were treated to a rousing chorus of "Ban Bourgignons" and then plied with more food when we sat back down.

I decided that it would be prudent to get more food in my stomach. The room had begun to spin as though turning slowly around an invisible axis. I followed Hugo's lead and applied myself to devouring several platefuls of *charcuterie* and warm potatoes doused in melted *raclette* cheese. I chased this down with at least a dozen more vinegary Maille cornichons. Hugo and I got back on the topic of Canada, and my stories, involving seals, ice flows, and mukluks, became more absurd with every sip of wine.

"We have bears and cougars that come into town all the time too," I shrugged. "That's why everyone keeps their doors unlocked, so everyone has an escape route." Hugo's eyes widened, but with interest rather than disbelief.

I suspected Hugo kept refreshing my glass of wine every time I turned around to talk to my elderly neighbor, who kept making comments in such a thick Burgundian accent that all I could respond with was a smile and a nod.

Hugo then waxed poetic for a time about the different finishes of "*crépi*" or stucco that worked over stone. His favorite was the finish "*sablé*" which I could picture on the sides of our cottage.

"Could you redo a stone wall that has ugly gray cement joints?" I asked. One whole wall of the cottage was exposed stone, *beautiful* exposed stone except that the joints had been done in a horrific shade of gray. This travesty bothered me every time I went over there.

"I'll have to dig out all the old joints between the stones but, *oui*, of course. What color would you want? Ivory? Cream? White?"

"Cream," I mused. "I'm thinking of painting the walls yellow." Inspiration washed over me and I lapsed into a satisfying daydream where I could see the cottage come together in my mind's eye. I wondered idly if I would recall all of my inspiration when the effects of the wine were gone.

"Yellow is a good color," Hugo agreed. "When I'm finished laying the flagstones in our kitchen I want to paint it yellow but my wife wants blue."

"Or she'll divorce you?" I guessed, chortling at my own joke.

Hugo joined in. "Of course."

We launched into a discussion of Hugo's chateau renovation. I learned that this rustic sounding man beside me spent every minute of his spare time and all of his spare money into bringing the derelict property back to its former glory, with a strict adherence to the authenticity of materials. "You see," he explained. "I could never put rounded tiles on my house. They have to be the little flat tiles, the hand varnished ones, of course. Anything else would be a betrayal."

"Of course."

"I wish the Architect of French Monuments agreed." Hugo's face took on an expression that made me feel very grateful I had met him in a brightly lit kitchen and not a dark alley.

"I've heard of him," I said. "I think he has to approve our skylights or something like that. Come to think of it, has Franck completed the paperwork asking permission?" My brain was feeling quite fuzzy but I had to try to remember to ask him.

Hugo snorted. "*Bonne chance* with that."

"What problem does he have with your roof tiles?"

"He wants me to use modern tiles." Hugo's icy blue eyes glinted with menace. "He even threatened to come and make me change them all."

"How could he possibly object to using the more expensive, most authentic roof tiles?"

"Because he's a *conard*. Assholes don't need a reason to be assholes."

Just then Franck slipped into the chair on the opposite side of Hugo. "Laura, are you OK to drive?" he asked.

I leaned over and gave him a rather ill-aimed kiss. "I have to remember to ask you something, except that I forgot what it was..."

"I'm thinking you are not OK to drive," Franck said, studying me.

Franck was starting to periodically cleave in two as I talked to him then merge together again. "God no. Are you?"

Franck shook his head then clutched it as though it was at risk of toppling off his neck. "I don't think so."

That was a problem, to be sure, but first I remembered my question.

"How has that paperwork for the Architect of French Monuments been going?" I asked Franck. "We haven't talked about that in weeks."

"Oh that," he said. "I picked it up to fill out but then I forgot about it. What made you think about that?"

"He's been giving Hugo a hard time." I hiccupped.

"I hate the man," Hugo said, his countenance still dark. "If I ever encountered him on the road, I guarantee I would not be hitting my brakes."

"He's that bad?" Franck asked.

Hugo nodded. "He is a tyrant and there is no possible appeal. His immediate boss is the Minister of Culture in Paris, and if you think *he* is ever going to answer your calls you are sorely mistaken."

It dawned on me to check my watch. As usual Franck wasn't wearing one. "*La vache*! It's already one thirty in the morning. Your Dad is going to kill us."

"One thirty?" Hugo grabbed my wrist and checked my watch for himself. "I'm getting a divorce for sure."

"How are we going to get home?" I began to panic. It had been unbelievably stupid of us to be swept away in the ambiance of the evening without thinking of the fact that now neither of us could drive.

"I can drive you," Hugo offered. The French certainly had more liberal drinking and driving laws than North America and I was sure Hugo was a man who could hold his wine, but still...I was too Canadian to feel comfortable with that solution.

"Oh, I forgot! My wife has the car. I guess I'll be walking home," Hugo said, as if to confirm my instinct. "That might be a good way to clear my head."

"We'll just call a taxi," I said.

Franck went over to ask Alain to use the phone to call a taxi. I could see Alain waving his hands in protest but I was sure Franck would prevail.

About five minutes later, during which I was overtaken by a huge wave of fatigue and felt like laying my head beside my plate on the table for a little snooze, Franck tapped on my shoulder. "Alain says a taxi will never come out here at this time of night. He says he has another solution."

"He can't drive us!" I exclaimed. In fact, nobody around the table could. "What are we going to do?"

"He won't tell me what he's planning but he said he would be back over here in a minute or two. Let's just sit tight." Franck poked me in the ribs. "And don't fall asleep on me."

True to his word, Alain came trotting back into the dining room a few minutes later, accompanied by a wizened woman in a floral dressing gown who was giving him an earful.

"*Ouaaaiiiiss!*" cheered a man with an impressive anchor tattoo on his exposed bicep who I knew to be Alain's father. "*C'est la Mamy!*"

The entire table burst into a rowdy "*Ban Bourgignon*" to celebrate the apparition of Alain's grandmother in our midst.

"What have you been getting up to, the lot of you?" she shook her finger, including the whole table in her chastisement.

"You could have joined in!" Alain cried. "You know you are always invited Mamy. Here, have a glass of wine."

I had no idea what, or even if, Alain's Mamy had anything to do with our getting home, but I began to picture Franck's father pacing around our newly acquired monastery table, furious.

"I was brought over to do a job, so I'll only have one glass. *Rapidement.*" She narrowed her eye at her grandson. "It had better be good wine seeing as you got me out of my bed."

Alain poured her a glass and she tasted it, swishing it around in her mouth and smacking her lips. "Not bad. Now where are these drunk Canadians I have to drive home?"

I gasped but everyone else burst into laughter.

"You dragged your grandmother out of her bed to drive us home?" I said to Alain.

"Yes," he said, unrepentant.

La honte. I covered my eyes. The shame.

"That's us." I looked up in time to see Franck point at us cheerfully.

"Your son and his friends ambushed us with kir and wine," Franck explained to Alain's Mamy. "We were powerless."

"It wouldn't be the first time." Mamy tipped back the rest of her glass into her mouth. "Now. Where do you two live?"

"Villers-la-Faye," Franck said. "I'm sorry but it is a good twenty minute drive."

"I know it," she said. "I used to pick blackcurrants up around there. There used to be a good bakery in Villers-la-Faye near the church, but I suppose that was well before your time."

"My grandmother used to own and run that bakery," Franck said.

"Tall woman with an efficient air?" Alain's grandmother asked.

"That sounds like her," Franck said.

"Is she still alive?" she demanded.

"Oh yes, she has a studio in *Les Primevères* in Beaune."

"Then payment for me driving you home safely is her recipe for *les feuilletés au fromage*."

"I'll see what I can do."

"She was quite a cook."

"She still is," Franck said.

With that Franck arranged with Alain to come and pick up the car the next day, and La Mamy led us outside in the driveway. Our feet crunched on the pea gravel and the bite of the air made me shiver. I was surprised all the alcohol in my blood didn't keep me warmer. Alain's Mamy motioned us to follow her with a crooked arm. "My car is in the barn," she said. "I don't drive it very often." That didn't bode well, but beggars couldn't be choosers.

She extracted a mammoth iron key out of her dressing gown pocket and opened the wooden door of the stone outbuilding.

Franck helped her push it open. The light from Alain's kitchen reached us here, and I noticed that a bit of what appeared to be moldy hay had fallen on my shoulder. A shirring sound came from the corners of the cavernous barn. Mice or rats?

It took my eyes a few seconds to adjust to the darkness but there in the barn was a Citroën Deux Chevaux, that mythic French car. In the dim light I could make out a reddish hue.

"Do you like her?" Mamy asked, patting the domed hood. "She's my baby. You'll have to squeeze in the back. If I hear any comments on my driving I'll toss you to the roadside."

Franck and I crawled in the back, no easy task given the lack of light and the amount of wine we had both consumed.

"Do you think Alain will roof the cottage for us?" I whispered to Franck, nestling my head in the crook of his arm.

"I think so, although I'm not sure if it was your prodigious wine consumption or that story about our neighbor's dogsled back in Canada that clinched it."

"I just gave the crowd what they wanted." Franck leaned down and gave me a kiss.

Just then a horrible grating noise emerged from the Deux Chevaux.

"She's got a bit of a temperamental clutch," Alain's Mamy explained. She must have pushed her ancient foot down on the accelerator. The car shot out the back of the barn so fast that I had to stifle a shriek of terror.

La Mamy managed to turn on to the road and in no time we were rumbling along in the direction of Villers-la-Faye. This involved a lot of grinding of the clutch and under-her-breath curses.

"Your Dad is going to be furious with us for staying so late," I said.

"Did you have fun?" Franck asked.

I thought about that. The evening had begun feeling like a wretched obligation, but somewhere between the tall tales about Canada and the Grand Cru Échezeaux I had begun to enjoy myself. Franck possessed the gift for dragging me, kicking and screaming, on crazy adventures that afterwards I wouldn't trade for the world. These kinds of evenings were what life in Burgundy was all about. Even if there had been no question of the roof, I would have agreed to come anyway if I knew how the evening was going to play out.

"I did have fun," I said. "But I still feel bad about your Dad. He has to work tomorrow."

Franck considered this as the headlights illuminated the fields that whipped past us, then vineyards. Mamy had the *Deux Chevaux* rattling fast along the narrow country road. "What could we have done?" he said finally. "You must have realized early on that there was no way we were going to get out of there quickly."

"True."

Franck dropped a kiss on my temple. "It has always been my opinion that it is better to ask for forgiveness than permission."

The next morning Charlotte and Camille jumped on us at six thirty. Young children were the universe's built-in punishment for overindulgence.

"We're starving!" announced Charlotte. "You need to get up and make us breakfast."

"*Oui*. We're starving!" Camille chimed in.

I cracked open an eye. The room spun above my head. "Oh my god," I murmured to Franck. "I think I'm dead."

Franck made a groaning sound.

"How mad was your Dad last night, do you think?"

"He wasn't mad so much as groggy," Franck said. "Didn't you see that he had fallen asleep on the couch and we had woken him up?"

"Somehow I didn't notice that." I was probably still trying to get myself out of the back of the car and thank Alain's Mamy in hopelessly disjointed French.

Camille began pulling my hair. "*On a faim! On a faim!*"

"Can you go and get them breakfast?" I ventured.

"*Impossible*," Franck said. "I'm sure I feel worse than you."

"I beg to differ."

"Just give me half an hour," Franck said. "I'll give you a back massage."

I was powerless against a good massage. "A long one?"

"Whatever you want."

"Half an hour long?"

Camille began kicking Franck with her little but surprisingly pointy feet.

"*Oui, oui, oui!* Just take the girls and let me sleep for a bit longer." Franck dropped his head to the pillow again.

I rolled out of bed and staggered around trying to find some clothes while Charlotte and Camille trailed after me claiming they needed a *pain au chocolat* right away or they would expire on the spot.

I slipped on a pair of sneakers without socks and shoved my arms in a fleece. I instructed the girls to put on boots over their pyjama bottoms and bundled them in their warmest coats. This was one of those times I gave thanks for living in a sleepy winemaking village instead of Paris or Lyon, where leaving the house with the children still in their pajamas and everyone looking like they'd just been dragged through a knothole backwards didn't cause anyone to blink an eye.

We trundled down our road and past the ancient wine press on the corner, then past the *Salle des Fêtes* and through the door of Jacky's store and bistro. I couldn't stop yawning. Jacky's store was redolent of fresh baguette and aging cheese, pleasant most of the time, although in my present state any reminder of eating wasn't welcome.

Jacky was holding court amongst the hodge podge of his store filled with cheeses and meat and postcards of the rock quarry outside of Villers-la-Faye that were black and white and dated back to 1952. He wiped his hands on his apron. I appreciated the fact that he did not seem to notice our strange attire.

"*Bonjour les Canadiens!*" He picked the Chup-a-Chup lollipop display from a high shelf and plopped it down on the counter in front of the girls.

"You can each pick one," he said to them, winking at them. "But *surtout* don't tell your mother!"

While the girls were choosing their lollipops I asked for two baguettes, three croissants and three *pains au chocolat*.

"You must come to lunch in the bistro one of these days!" Jacky said, patting the girls on the head. "We haven't seen you and Franck in there yet."

"Soon," I said.

I reminded the girls to say *merci* for their lollipops and thanked Jacky, eager to get back home to my massage.

We pulled into Alain's driveway in Stéphanie's orange Kangoo van around three o'clock that afternoon to reclaim our car. The scent of strong coffee brewing had drawn Franck out of bed, although he did do a lot of kvetching just to inject a bit of drama into the morning, as well as try to convince me that he was incapable of doing the dishes.

We agreed he would give me my massage that evening when he was feeling a little more energetic.

"Where are we Mom?" Charlotte asked from the backseat.

"This is the house of the man who is going to build us a new roof at the cottage," I answered. "Fingers crossed."

"*C'est vous!*" The voice came from Alain's grandmother who was standing at the far side of the driveway carrying what looked like a basket full of eggs. She was still wearing her housecoat from the night before. "Did you bring me my recipe?"

We did indeed. We had stopped by Mémé's on the way and after chuckling heartily over our exploits of the night before, she had penned out her recipe for her famous *feuilletés au fromage*.

"I'm only doing this because it's you," Mémé squeezed her favorite grandson's chin. "You know I usually don't share my recipes."

"Did you leave out any important ingredients or steps this time?" Franck asked. Mémé had a reputation for doing this, then protesting that clearly the reason her recipe didn't work is because the person trying to replicate it didn't know how to cook.

Franck passed the recipe card over to Alain's Mamy. She scanned it, then smiled up at Franck. Several of her teeth were missing.

I pushed Camille, who shyly offered a boquet of orange roses and Franck nudged Charlotte who held out a bottle of Franck's cousin's wine from Ladoix-Serrigny.

After Alain's grandmother accepted the gifts I introduced her to Charlotte and Camille while Franck went into the house to get the car keys and thank Alain for the dinner.

"Beautiful girls," she said patting them on the head. "Still, girls are nothing but trouble when they get older. You'll have to give your husband a few boys as well."

Before I could think of a response to this startling statement, she added, "Do you know what I did last night when I got back here?"

"What?"

"I went into the house to say that you and your husband had been delivered safely to Villers-la-Faye and that naughty son of mine sat me down and started filling up a wine glass for me. "I didn't get into my bed until about five o'clock in the morning!"

"Really?"

"Oh yes." She cracked another toothless grin. "Do you know how old I am?" She looked roughly one hundred and twenty so I wasn't about to start guessing.

"Eighty-seven!" she declared. "Five o'clock in the morning drinking *les canons* at eighty-seven."

"Wow," I said and meant it.

Franck came out just then, brandishing our car keys with a smile.

"Here we go!" he said. "You drive our car and I'll drive Steph's. Thank you again," he smiled at La Mamy."

"My pleasure." She trundled off towards the house

We transferred the car seats into my car, and while we were doing it, Franck whispered in my ear. "Alain will be meeting us at the cottage tomorrow morning with his team to build our roof."

I didn't say anything, but my smile stretched from ear to ear. We listened to the French top forty on the radio on the way home, and Charlotte and Camille and I sang at the top of our lungs.

CHAPTER 17

True to his word, Alain was at the cottage at seven in the morning. I got the girls off to school while Franck met our roofing crew. When I arrived at the cottage I could already make out men tearing shingles off the roof through the swirling fog in the air.

The door was open a crack and I let myself in.

Franck and Alain were both munching on croissants and without a word Franck passed the bag to me. I was happy to see all the *pain au chocolat* hadn't been taken and plucked one out for myself.

Alain kissed me on each cheek absent-mindedly like we were old friends. After that evening spent together, maybe we were.

"You have to do it," Alain was saying to Franck. "You have to do it today or it will be too late for us to put in those skylights"

"The mayor's office is closed today. But I'll think of something." Despite Alain and his roofers being here, Franck's features were strained.

"What are you talking about?" I brushed building detritus off the stone hearth in front of the fireplace and perched on it.

"The Architect of French monuments," Franck said, his voice ominous. "I need to get that paperwork completed by him and get his approval for the skylights right away."

"I'm getting really sick of hearing that guy's name." I took a bite of my *patisserie*. Mmmmm. It was still so warm that the chocolate was all gooey and melted between the buttery layers of pastry.

"We can't put in the skylights until you get the signed approval,"

Alain said.

Just then Luc came in the front door. Franck introduced him and Alain. Alain studied Luc for a moment and then seemed to decide that he was somebody he could work with i.e. not an asshole.

"I was just telling Franck that he has to ask for permission for the skylights from the Architect of French Monuments," said Alain.

Luc stared at my Franck. "You mean you haven't done that yet? We talked about it ages ago."

"It's not like we've been lazing around." Franck rubbed his face. "Remember I had that small thing to take care of? Find a mortgage so we could pay for the renovations in the first place? I'll go and see this architect fellow today, but don't let your guys stop on the roof," he said to Alain. "Also, tell them I expect them back at my house after work for an *apéro*. You two as well." He nodded to Alain and Luc.

"We need to start discussing where we're going to put the French doors out to the courtyard," Luc said after Alain had left.

"I have an idea," I said. Luc and Franck shared a knowing look. "Don't be like that." I tapped on the stone wall that lay between the main living room and the patch of yard outside that was attached to the house. "How about putting the French doors right here?"

"Just wait a sec," Luc measured something on one side of the wall and then disappeared out the front door with his measuring tape.

When he came back in he was looking pleased with himself. "I think you'll have to reconsider that idea."

"Why?" Was this another incident like wanting to paint instead of wallpaper the walls at *La Maison des Deux Clochers* when everyone had insisted it was crazy? I had dug my heels in and won that battle, and admired the freshly painted walls every time I went over there.

"I just measured that wall," Luc said. "It's about a meter thick and it is crooked as they come. If you try to cut a hole in there, even with the best stonemason in the world, the entire house is going to crumble around your ears.

Hm. The argument was persuasive.

"I guess we'll figure out something else," I said.

"We're going to leave you," Franck patted Luc on the back. He took a deep breath. "I'm going to see about the skylights. "

"Don't resort to violence," Luc said. "Trust me, you'll be tempted."

While Franck was in Beaune I made us lunch. Swayed by the allure of a *roti de porc* with apples and *fromage blanc* for dessert the girls had opted for the *cantine*. It still took some getting used to, this stopping at around eleven to eleven thirty every day to make a hot lunch and sitting down to enjoy it at a leisurely pace. Still, rushing through lunch just in order to find yourself unable to talk to anyone on the phone (because they were having lunch) or have anyone answer your emails (because they were having lunch) was a waste of time. Besides, as much as I found it difficult to start cooking at eleven thirty in the morning, by the time Franck and I were slicing ourselves off paper thin slices of *Comté* cheese at the end of our meal and enjoying our little espresso cups of coffee with a perfect little square of dark chocolate this whole two hour lunch thing began to seem like a very fine idea indeed.

Today I braised some chicory in butter and a splash of Père Magloire calvados. I stirred up a béchamel sauce and then wrapped the chicory in slices of freshly cut ham, securing each one with a toothpick. I lined them up snugly in my favorite Emile Henry casserole that I had found at the Louhans market when we were renovating *La Maison des Deux Clochers* over five years ago. I poured the béchamel over the top. Last but not least I sprinkled the dish with freshly grated Emmenthal. I slid the heavy casserole in the oven to bubble and crisp.

I took the stinky Soumatrin cheese out of the fridge as well as a pure white, ash covered Selles-sur-Chère, my favorite goat's cheese. I set the coffee up to drip and made a big green salad with *frisée* lettuce and a mustardy vinaigrette studded with minced shallots. I plopped a half-finished bottle of Médoc in the middle of the table. Maybe it was a travesty to enjoy a Bordeaux wine in a Burgundian kitchen but I had always enjoyed a solid Bordeaux. By the time I was slicing the fresh baguette Franck had bought from Jacky's that morning I was feeling rather pleased with myself. Franck was a bit late, but the *gratin* was keeping warm in the oven and my husband had surely charmed the Architect of French Monuments. Perhaps they were enjoying a nice chat about building techniques in Canada.

The door slammed open so hard it hit the wall.

Franck stormed into the kitchen and his eyes feverishly scanned all the hard surfaces. "I need to hit something!" he announced through clenched teeth.

"Pillow," I pointed to the direction of the bedrooms. "Go hit a pillow." My heart sank.

But Franck just kept punching his fist into his other palm and pacing around the kitchen. *Distraction.* He needed distraction.

"I made *endives* wrapped in *jambon blanc* for lunch," I said, taking them out of the oven. The cheese bubbled perfectly and a heavenly aroma enveloped the kitchen. "Eat first and then you can tell me about it."

"I'm too angry to eat." Palm punch. "I cannot believe that such a *conard* exists." Palm punch. "It boggles the mind." Palm punch. "You wouldn't believe what he said to me…"

"I'm hungry," I said. "I've spent the last hour making this nice lunch so I'm going to eat it before it gets cold." It may have seemed heartless, but I suspected that the inevitable conversation would go better on satisfied stomachs.

"Here, have some wine," I motioned to the table and poured him a very large glass. He took it and swigged it down. He licked his lips. Palm punch.

"I'll be right back," he said. A few seconds later a primal scream of frustration echoed in the WC.

I was ladling out the chicory on our plates when he came back in. "Better?"

"Marginally," he said. "Enough to eat."

We ate our lunch in silence, as Franck was completely preoccupied with his meeting. I decided not to be offended and instead concentrated on my meal. My béchamel hadn't separated at all and was perfectly spiced with the freshly grated nutmeg I had added.

Despite his silence Franck ate heartily. He served himself two more *endives* as well as several servings of my salad. It took a lot to disturb a Burgundian's appetite.

I cleared off the plates and put out smaller plates for the cheese. I refreshed the basket with more slices of baguette.

I took a piece of each and served myself a little bit more wine. The tastes were sublime together. I sighed. No matter how the meeting had gone, the Architect of French Monuments couldn't take this moment away from me.

Franck and I had a theory about moments of pleasure or joy. We likened them to a French game-show where you had to "bank" your money frequently so as not to lose it. Often, after enjoying a particularly good meal or a lovely evening walk or a cuddle with the girls one of us would quip "Banked!" Nobody could take away those "banked" moments. This meal that I had prepared and enjoyed – it was my *petit bonheur du jour* and I was banking it, dammit, no matter what Franck was about to tell me next.

I let Franck finish his meal wordlessly and then cleared his cheese plate away and replaced it with an espresso and a square of chocolate.

"Can you talk about it now?" I ventured.

Franck took a sip of espresso. "I'm not sure," he said. He took a deep breath. "I can try."

"I take it he didn't approve of our skylights?"

Franck snorted. "No. He wants us to put in dormer windows instead. They would not only look terrible and bring in only a tiny fraction of the light that skylights would, but they also cost about ten times the price."

"*Merde.*"

"That's not all," Franck warned. "He wants us to roof with ancient polished flat tiles that are impossible to find and cost a fortune. He also doesn't want us to make any opening out to the court yard."

"No French doors?"

"No French doors."

"That's ridiculous," I said. "Does he just want us to leave the property a total hideous ruin?"

"I don't think he functions according to any logic whatsoever. I think he's just a bitter, power drunk pseudo-Napoleon whose only joy in life is exerting power over lesser mortals in insane ways."

"I thought Hugo was joking about wanting to run over him," I said. "Now I'm not so sure."

"He wasn't joking." Franck bit off a corner of his chocolate. "You know what else?"

"What?"

"He also wants all of the shutters in Burgundy to be gray."

I had already planned on the cottage's shutters being a vivid shade of turquoise. "But that would be so depressing!"

"He's demented."

"So what do we do now?" God help us. So soon after getting the roof and the mortgage crises solved here was another possible dead end.

Franck shook his head. "I have no idea. The only thing I know is that his secretary, who I chatted with for a long time before going in to meet with him, whispered at me as I left that she was going to call me this afternoon after lunch to follow up. She said it in a way that I could tell she didn't want him to overhear her."

I thanked the heavens for Franck's ability to charm secretaries. "What do you think she's going to say?"

"I have no idea but it's our only hope with this guy. Do you know those three men from the village that are always walking around the streets?"

"The old guys who always have their hands in their pockets.

"Those are the ones. They are all retired and have nothing better to do than to spy on anyone doing any renovation or work on their homes and report back to the mayor and perhaps even the French Monument Architect himself."

"Villers has its very own spy network?"

"Of course."

Unbelievable. Villers-la-Faye looked so sleepy from the outside, but inside it was as full of machinations and feuds as The White House.

There wasn't much more to do but wait for the secretary's call and hope that Franck had done a very good job of charming her. "Did you like my *endives?*" I asked.

Franck reached over and caressed the palm of my hand with his thumb. "I always love your *endives.*"

I blushed, but just then the phone rang.

Franck leapt up to take it. I checked my watch. Ten minutes after two o'clock. Everyone in France had officially finished their lunch.

I began to clear away the dishes while trying to listen to Franck's conversation in the next room.

"*Ah bon?*" he kept saying, and then followed that with several heartfelt "*mercis*".

When Franck came into the kitchen I handed him a dishtowel so he could dry. "So was it the secretary?" I asked. "What did she say?"

Franck began drying the washed dishes I piled up on the concave of the counter.

"Good news," Franck said. "She told me that many people didn't know this, but her boss has different levels of influence depending on the exact status of the national monuments in that area."

"I imagine he does nothing to enlighten the public on that point."

"Exactly."

"It turns out that in Villers he can make recommendations but that ultimately the mayor has the final say

"That's good then?" I didn't know much about the mayor except that he was young and his name was Yves.

"I think so," Franck said. "Yves family was from Villers, but I think he was in Lyon or somewhere for a few years but now he's moved back."

"Do you know him?"

"Not very well but he's young which I hope may help. Keep your fingers crossed that he likes skylights." Franck checked my watch and put his dishtowel down on the counter. "I wish I could thank you properly for that delicious lunch, but I should go now. The mayor's office is only open for the next two hours."

I eyed the massive pile of dishes that still needed to be washed and dried. Eating a home cooked French meal was wonderful, but cleaning up after it without a dishwasher, not so much.

"Go," I said. "You can thank me by going to Dijon with me this weekend to pick out a dishwasher."

"They don't work here." Franck's family didn't believe in dishwashers because the calcium rich soil in Burgundy, while perfect for the vines, wreaked havoc with appliances and left a white film on even clean dishes.

"Dishwasher or divorce," I said. "Your choice, just like Hugo's wife. First go and try to charm the mayor though."

"Wish me luck," he said. He took his coat out of the armoire.

About forty minutes later, just when I had sat down with a second cup of coffee after finally finishing the dishes, Franck came back in.

"How was it?"

"I'm not sure," Franck was antsy and couldn't seem to settle. "I think it may be OK, but I'm not completely certain."

"Did he say he would override the architect's recommendations?"

"He didn't make any promises but he did say he would look at it…"

"That has to be good."

Franck grimaced, too shaken by the day's events to get caught up in my wave of optimism.

"Think about something else," I recommended. "Like a new dishwasher."

The next few weeks took on a certain pattern. Franck would be gone pretty much all day while I was responsible for getting the girls to and from school and pretty much everything domestic. The young mayor of Villers had pulled through and issued Franck the permission to install the three skylights in the cottage roof. That was an enormous victory. Every evening we welcomed anywhere from two to seven tradesmen at our house for the *apéro* that usually lasted until well after eight o'clock.

However, as Franck often reminded me when I complained that it would be nice to have one evening when we sat down to dinner before nine o'clock, our strategy was working. The roofers kept returning to the job every morning (Franck also provided three bottles of chilled white wine in the morning to cement the temptation). My husband was in his element. After living in Canada for the past four years where work was a comparatively matter-of-fact, serious affair, here it involved a lot of drinking, laughing, and joking around. As for me - not so much.

I had never been particularly domestic. In fact, housework filled me with existensial rage. Not only were cleaning the toilets and doing the dishes fist-gnawingly boring, but these jobs, like pretty much every domestic activity, were circular in nature. They were finished only to be undone again in a short period of time. The fact that there was no lasting result of any of this work irked me in the deepest part of my soul. I did the best I could, but felt myself sliding down that slippery slope of despair as December wore on, to the point where on some days I couldn't even remember to find a *petit bonheur du jour*.

I also worried about the effect the new rhythm of our life was having on Charlotte and Camille. Surely it was not healthy for an almost three and an almost five years old to be sitting down at the dinner table every night at nine o'clock and to have their house invaded every evening by a bunch of thirsty, boisterous tradesmen. Granted, the men were unfailingly chivalrous and always asked the girls what they had learned at school that day, but still…this was anything but a normal life.

I thought back somewhat obsessively to what that client with the big hair from Albuquerque had said to me about moving my children around as being the ultimate disservice a parent could do for their child. Were we asking too much of them? Franck was consumed with getting the cottage well on its way before Christmas, I was turning into a disgruntled housemarm, and their bedroom still didn't have any proper furniture. Two mattresses on the floor and a set of drawers from IKEA didn't really count.

When the girls were at school and I wasn't at home either preparing a new meal or cleaning up from the last one, I spent my time at the cottage. I learned to wear my warmest gloves and hat and scarf as it got downright frigid waiting around there talking to tradesmen about what axis to align the roof tiles or where we should place the new heater now that we had removed the old one from its place of pride in the middle of the hallway.

One afternoon, just a few days before everything ground to a halt for Christmas, Luc beckoned me into the open space that used to be the back bedroom.

In the past weeks, he and Franck had taken great joy in knocking down every freestanding non-supporting wall in the cottage. Now we had to figure out what the new configuration of the rooms would be, and how on earth we were going to squeeze in a toilet, shower, and washer and dryer and still leave room for at least a queen sized bed in the bedroom. The old bathroom was in an awkward space off the hallway between the main living area that no longer existed. This meant that you walked right out of the bathroom door smack into the ugly oil furnace that we removed.

Now we had an open space that would have been perfect for a bedroom with an area for a desk below the window and French doors that led on to what would eventually be a flagstone courtyard. We spent hours over the past several days tossing back and forth ideas of how to make the bathroom fit but nothing seemed to work.

Franck kept coming back to the idea of having the toilet and shower and sink integrated into the bedroom itself, but I informed him and Luc that North Americans definitely wouldn't go for that.

"Why do you think us North Americans say we're going to the bathroom and not the toilet?" I asked.

Luc and Franck shrugged.

"Because nobody wants to admit what they're actually doing in there," I explained. That's why so many North Americans are unnerved by the whole idea of a room where there is just a toilet, like the WCs in France."

"What do they think everyone believes they are doing?" Luc asked, confused.

"Washing their hands…well, no. Actually, everyone knows what is really going on but it's a conspiracy of silence, like the emperor's new clothes."

"Then having a toilet in the bedroom should make them really happy," Franck said. "They can say they need to go have a nap when in fact they are actually…"

I held up my hand. "You don't need to say it."

Luc had stopped lighting his cigarette, as he was laughing too hard. "You North Americans are so weird." He wiped his eyes. "How can you possibly be embarrassed about going to the toilet?"

Explaining that would take hours, and I wasn't even certain that I knew how to explain the cultural inheritance of centuries of Puritan prudishness. "Let's not get off topic," I said. "The important thing is that North Americans don't want to be able to see the toilet from their bed."

"Why not?" Franck asked. "I think it's romantic."

Franck and Luc began to snicker like a pair of schoolboys.

"Come on you two. We have to figure this out. If we can't make up our mind today we'll delay things."

"You're right," Luc said. "All right. Serious now."

Franck walked over to the far wall of the bedroom and knocked on it. "I don't think this is stone," he said. "The little lean-too room on the other side of this wall is where the chickens used to sleep at night. During the day they ran free all over the house though. That fascinated me when I was little."

"I peeked in a few days ago," Luc said. "It's still full of chicken shit. Probably fossilized. It's not a place that inspires you to linger. I guess we'll have to clean it out at some point though. Do you want to go have a look?"

Luc and I followed Franck out the front door of the house, through the main room where a hole was being cut in the new roof for the first of the three skylights. I crossed my fingers briefly and sent a prayer to Franck's guardian angels that it wouldn't snow or rain until the skylights arrived.

We walked around the side of the house, past the massive trunk of the vine that wrapped around the cottage, dormant now for the winter.

Franck led us to a little wooden door underneath the shallow slope of the roof that abutted the neighbor's property.

"Plug your noses," Luc instructed.

I did and made a concerted effort to breathe out of my mouth.

The door stuck – probably due to centuries of chicken poo congealed against its hinges. Franck had to apply all his body weight against it before it finally creaked open.

Luc had come armed with a flashlight. He pointed the beam into the fetid darkness. The floor was speckled white and black but Luc didn't tarry on that. He pointed the beam, instead, at the ceiling.

"Decent ceiling height," he mused. "I'm surprised." He turned to Franck. "I think I understand now what you have in mind. Clever."

Franck nodded. "There's no floor, but that's probably an advantage as if you put a bathroom in here we'd have to rip up a floor so we could put in the plumbing anyway."

"Do you really think we could put the bathroom in here?" I asked, trying to not breathe out of my nose as I spoke. "Do you really think it would fit?" My interest was definitely snagged.

Franck ventured inside. "Are you sure you want to do that?" I asked, but he had always enjoyed venturing places where others feared to tread.

"Somebody has to." Luc followed him and aimed his flashlight at Franck. Franck knocked against the crooked wall. "It's stone, but not as thick as that other stone wall I don't think. Maybe we could open it up."

"That would mean we could use the whole other room for a

gorgeous bedroom and have the bathroom off here – it would give us so much extra space!" I started rearranging the bedroom in my mind."

"Don't get too excited," Luc warned. "We have to check with a stonemason first that we could open up a doorway between the bedroom and this room without having the cottage collapse.

"We know one," I said. "His name is Hugo. He's a friend of Alain."

Franck was still inside the chicken poo lean-too, apparently deep in thought. "We could actually split this space in half and have two thirds be the bathroom off the bedroom and this front part hold the furnace and the hot water tank and to store the patio furniture and the garbage bins."

Luc nodded slowly. "*Possible*." He pointed the arc of the flashlight at me. I was still lingering at the opening of the door. "Do you want to come in Laura?"

"No," I said. "I'll stay outside so I can call for help if you two suddenly pass out from fumes or erupt in boils."

Luc and Franck stayed inside the space for far longer than I could have ever endured and emerged reeking of chicken excrement but also full of ideas and possibilities that might all of a sudden increase the cottage's square footage by about a third.

"I'll call Hugo right now." Franck pulled out his phone from his jacket pocket.

"I'd better go and get the girls from school and get the apéro ready," I said.

"One last thing before you go," Luc said. "I don't think we have room to have both a separate WC and a separate bathroom in there…it will all have to be in the same room, *une salle de bain à l'amercaine* .

"So our guests can say they are going to wash their hands when they are actually going to take a poo?" Franck asked.

"Exactly."

"It couldn't be more perfect!" I declared.

That day, despite the heady possibilities provided by converting the former chicken coop to a bathroom at the cottage, after picking up the girls from school I fell into what was becoming my usual early evening emotional slump. Charlotte and Camille were crabby from school, I had to prepare yet another *apéro* and then a dinner to shovel in to everyone after the tradesmen left and here I was again, doing it on my own.

I knew of course that Franck needed to be spending most of his waking hours at the cottage – it was the only way that things would get done by July. Still, I felt terribly alone and weirdly dissatisfied. Leaving me in charge of the bulk of domestic work was a recipe for not only a messy home but for me, a messy mind. I never regretted my decision to abandon my career as a high-powered lawyer but at least that job had structure and clear outcomes. Looking after the children, the laundry, the house and the food was such a vague and infinite undertaking. The renovations at the cottage were maybe finally coming together with the mortgage, the roof, and the newfound bathroom space but the renovations I had planned in our family life were not panning out the same way. Despite still trying to look for my *petit bonheur du jour* being stuck at home 100% of the time, even a home in France, was never going to make me happy.

The whole renovation of *La Maison des Deux Clochers* had been messy. It had been wonderful, in the end, but during those four months I had often felt like I had no idea where I was headed and was just doing everything all wrong. I thought somehow this time would be different. I was a parent now, after all. Wasn't I supposed to gain some sort of universal ability to glide through life like a real adult with the birth of my first child? Instead, my life seemed more disorganized and I seemed to be falling short on even more fronts.

I should make better dinners every night, but then how could I with often up to ten tradesmen in my kitchen until nine o'clock? I should iron my girls' pretty dresses, but that would mean either hauling the ironing board up from the basement or doing it down there and I just didn't want to. I should be taking more photos of them, doing more crafts – hell, doing *any* crafts - with them. I should also, I reminded myself, be reading them more bedtime stories in English so they didn't lose their mother tongue.

By the time I was finished hand washing the glasses I was in a foul mood. I had always had the bad habit of blaming my bad moods on others but as nobody was around except me and the girls I blamed it on the house. I stalked around our French abode, taking note of every shortcoming. There were a lot. It felt oppressive to be surrounded with such ugliness. The stupid round sink and the rotting counter in the kitchen were just a starting point. Next was the ugly tile in the floor in the living room and the hallway, and the hideous textured wallpaper that was partially ripped by the fireplace. The WC and bathroom boasted a host of complaint fodder. The WC was a tiny room for the toilet that meant my knees banged up against the closed door (and at 5'4 I was hardly blessed with gangly limbs). The strange "L" shaped bathroom housed a tub that never produced enough hot water and a sink that wasn't secure against the wall. All the bedrooms came with filthy carpets and a sole light-bulb that hung from the ceiling. We still hadn't bought light shades and I felt vaguely like I was entering into a Mexican prison cell every time I went into one of the bedrooms.

We needed new paint, we needed new floors, we needed to rip down the wall between the WC and the bathtub and start from scratch there-

My thoughts were interrupted by a knock on the front door.

Charlotte got there before I did. "Bonjour," she said to Luc, who stood on the doorstep.

"*Bonjour Charlotte*," he said and bent down to give her *les bises*. "How was school today?"

"We learned how to write a capital "S", she said.

"Very good. My son Alain probably did the same thing," he said. "He's in *moyenne section* like you. Did you know that?"

Charlotte nodded, her hands clasped behind her back. "I don't hold my scissors properly," she confessed.

"What?" I came to the door.

"The teacher told me today that I don't hold my scissors properly and that she wanted to talk to you about it again next time you pick me up."

I rolled my eyes. When were they going to stop about the scissor-holding technique? "It doesn't really matter how you hold your scissors," I said to Charlotte and gave her a hug.

She skipped off back to the bedroom to play horses with Camille.

"So she doesn't hold her scissors right?" I ushered Luc into the kitchen. "Who cares?"

"Actually, it is important," Luc said, washing his hands at the sink. "It means they may have difficulties with their penmanship later on."

"Not you too," I muttered, in English.

"*Quoi?*" asked Luc.

"Nothing. Are you by yourself?" I asked, surprised.

"I was finished before them. Franck sent me over to warn you that they'll be on their way soon."

"Can you look at a few things with me while we're waiting?"

"All right," he said, wary.

I took him and aired all my woes about the bathroom and the bedrooms and finished the tour at the impossible sink.

"The kitchen is too big a job," he said. "But we could maybe do something about the bedrooms and the bathrooms…"

"Great. When can you start?"

"Not until after Christmas."

Patience had never been my strong suit. I was disappointed of course that we couldn't start changing things yesterday, but still, at least I could start planning.

"I'm not a tiler you know," he added. "Tiling takes a very particular *coup de main*. I mean, I've done some at my own house, but…"

"I'm sure you'll do it just fine," I said. "Can you prepare us a quote?"

"*Mais…*"

Just then Franck breezed in the door. "The other guys will be here in five minutes."

Luc looked at me and then at Franck, a bit nervous.

"Perfect," I said. "Luc and I were discussing some jobs he could do around here during the slower parts of the cottage renovation."

"After Christmas," Luc clarified.

Franck went to the sink and rinsed his hands. "Such as?"

"Ripping out the bathroom."

Franck looked accusingly at Luc.

He threw up his hands. "Your wife ambushed me. I just came over here for my *apéro*."

"She does that." Franck searched in vain for a dry dishtowel to wipe his hands. "I guess we have to do it sooner or later," my Franck said. "But the money…"

"We're not going to have more money six months from now," I

said. "But six months from now that bathroom *will* have driven me crazy. That's a guarantee."

Franck gave up and dried his palms on his jeans. "All right. Can you give us a quote?"

"Sure," Luc said. "You'll have to go and choose some tile first though."

"Done!" I said, feeling like at last I was taking control of my destiny. Enough of sitting around and waiting for things to happen; I had to *make* them happen.

The clatter of men at the door interrupted us. I heard many familiar voices, one in particular that I remembered vividly.

I peeked into the hallway. "Hugo!" There he was, Hugo the stonemason, in our front hall. "How did you know we needed you?"

He tapped a finger to his broad forehead. "Psychic," he said. "It's the white wine. Has magical properties, you know…"

"Also, I called him." Franck said.

Franck and Hugo shook hands and Franck introduced him to Luc.

"What can I serve you?" Franck asked. Hugo requested a *kir* and they all sat down while Franck and I served them and then we joined the table.

Luc, with the help of many hand gestures, was describing to Hugo the idea of piercing a hole in the wall and making the chicken lean-to into a bathroom.

Hugo's ice blue eyes began to sparkle. "I love taking down those stone walls," he said. "You just never know what is going to happen."

I thought back to Alain's cellar and the fissure in the foundation of his house. Franck and I exchanged glances and Franck raised an eyebrow. I could tell he was thinking the same thing.

"I'll come back and look at it first thing tomorrow morning," Hugo promised. "Then we can see what we're dealing with, *n'est-ce pas?*"

"Have you decided to go out on your own yet?" I asked.

"I'm almost there," Hugo answered. "In fact, you two would be my first customers. You don't mind if I don't have all the accounting and stuff completely figured out do you?"

"He threw his last two computers out the window," Alain added.

"Shut up," Hugo said easily to his friend. "My invoices will be hand written for the first little while."

"As long as they're official," Franck said.

Hugo waved his hand. "Oh don't worry. They will be. My wife is doing that side of things."

Alain piped up. "She hasn't divorced you yet?"

Hugo smiled. "Maybe tomorrow."

CHAPTER 18

Before we knew it, it was the week before Christmas. This would be our first Christmas in our very own home in France. It still wasn't much of a house and all of our energies were being poured into the cottage renos. Still. We at least needed to get a tree and some decorations.

I noticed Christmas trees for sale in the parking lot beside the *ABC Auto-École* where Cyrile had inducted me into the mysteries of the stick shift and Beaune's lingerie stores.

During the girls' last week at school we stopped there after picking them up.

As we passed the ABC *Auto-École* Cyrile was just pulling out of the driveway with a terrified looking teenager in the driver's seat beside him.

"Madame Germain!" he greeted me. "Killed anyone yet?"

"*Non,*" I said proudly and went over to shake his hand.

"Then I have done my job," he said, taking a satisfied drag of his *gitane.* "*Joyeux Noël a toute la petite famille.*"

"Still using the same driving routes?" I asked.

"But of course."

"I'm sure I'll see you soon then," I said. "I know where to find you."

Once in the Christmas tree lot we surveyed the selection. A man in a heavy wool jacket came over to enquire if we needed assistance.

"Why are they all so small?" I asked. "Don't you have any larger trees?"

"These *are* the large trees," the man answered, pointing at the biggest one, which stood about five feet tall, several inches shorter than me. Back home in Canada we generally went for the seven or eight footers.

"My wife is from Canada," Franck explained.

The man shed his disgruntled attitude in an instant. "Ah! *Le Canada*! Do you snowmobile?"

"Yes." Since the drunken evening at Alain's this had become my standard answer to that question.

"The trees are bigger in Canada," Franck added. "Much, much bigger." Franck held his arms up to the already dark winter sky to indicate just how big. "Including Christmas trees."

"Of course," the man said, very *sympathique* now. "Everything must be bigger in Canada. I'm sorry, but ours all come from tree farms you see, we don't really have any real forests left in France. It is a tragedy. My wife and I have been dreaming of a trip to Canada to see the *grandes éspaces* – the big spaces." He held up the bushy five footer in a pot. "This is the biggest one I have, I'm afraid."

"Why is it in a pot?" I asked.

"We sell all our trees like that. That way you can replant them afterwards."

Our garden was a jungle. Right now in the middle of winter it was a mercifully dormant jungle but it was a jungle nevertheless. We needed to clear away trees instead of replanting more.

"Stéph might want it," Franck said. It's true Stéph and Thierry had a huge yard in Magny-les-Villers and had been talking about planting trees and creating a little forested area.

"OK," I said. "I guess at least we don't have to buy a stand."

Franck transacted with the man who now, even though he had several customers waiting, seemed reluctant to let us leave and seemed to want to talk more about Canada. Franck and I gave him a little exegesis on our prowess in snowshoeing to leave the salesman happy.

We then went to Bricorama where we loaded up on Christmas tree lights and decorations.

We finished off by going to the Place Carnot in Beaune for a glass of *kir* for Franck and me and a hot chocolate for the girls. We were all feeling quite merry, and appreciated the beautiful display of twinkling white lights in all the bare trees and canopies of swooping lights that branched off the *rue d'alsace* and the *rue pietonne*.

On our way back home Franck had the idea of inviting Martial and Isabelle and the boys over for waffles and cider to celebrate decorating our first ever French Christmas tree, small as it was. He phoned Martial on his cell phone and they accepted with alacrity.

It was cold and crisp, perfect weather for waffles. We stopped by Franck's parents on the way home to borrow their ancient waffle maker. Despite its frayed wires it possessed an indisputable ability to turn out the perfect waffles.

As soon as we got back to our house I began setting our monastery table in the living room while Franck moved the tree in and phoned Mémé to get her famous *recette* for waffles.

Charlotte and Camille were bouncing off the walls with excitement and had begun to open the boxes full of Christmas tree decorations. Most of them I had picked up at a Christmas market in Vienna the year Franck and I lived in Paris.

"Can we start?" they demanded. "Let's start decorating the Christmas tree now!"

"Hold on!" I said, and wrested the boxes of decorations from them. "We have to put on the lights first."

Franck materialized just then and slid a glass of *kir* in my hand. "For sustenance," he said. "I'm going mix up the waffle batter."

I took a deep sip and then told the girls they had to be patient for two seconds while I got the lights out of the box and sorted them out. They sat down at my feet and looked up at me, their eyes sparkling. They didn't seem to be at all bothered by the ugliness of our house. For them, Christmas was still every bit as magical.

I removed the lights from the box and unwound them, looking for the end of the string. I wondered for a moment if my second kir of the evening hadn't already gone to my head more than I had realized but no, I wasn't just imagining it, the strands of lights had no ends. They were large circles, like huge multi-colored hoops.

Franck came in to refresh my drink. I held up the lights. "What am I supposed to do with these? Lasso the tree like a calf?"

He came and inspected the lights. "Huh," he said finally. "I've never noticed that before."

The doorbell rang and Martial, Isabelle, Gabin, and Arthur came tumbling in, laden with bottles and a box from Bouché, one of the best pastry shops in Beaune.

Isabelle came over to give me a kiss. "It was a challenge to figure out what we should buy for desert after waffles. I voted for fruit but the boys wanted a *gateau*. I was outvoted."

I peeked at the cake and saw it was a *boucheron*, made out of whipped chocolate ganache and meringue and topped with curled black chocolate. "Yum," I said. I slid it in the fridge and beckoned Isabelle to follow me into the living room where I picked a hoop of lights off the floor.

"Why are the lights like this?" I asked.

"Like what?"

"In a circle. Why don't they have ends?"

"They never have ends," Isabelle said. "That's how Christmas lights always are."

"Bizarre," I muttered. "How are you supposed to wind them around the tree?"

Isabelle took one of the strands and dropped it over the top of the tree. "You don't wind it really. You sort of loop it around."

"They really work better when the strand is not in a circle."

Isabelle nodded, ever diplomatic, but did not look convinced.

Franck came and put Isabelle's glass of *kir* on the table. Isabelle and I continued to lasso the tree and quickly dissolved into hysterics as the kir went to our heads and we knocked it over several times in the process. We sat back on the couch afterwards and let the kids ransack the boxes of decorations and decorate the tree. Thank goodness Arthur was older and taller, as his job mainly consisted of moving up the decorations that were all clustered on the bottom third of the tree.

I found myself amazed at how sometimes the most unexpected things were different in France than in Canada. Toothpaste tasted, for example, completely different – more paste-like than minty. Also, toilet paper tended to be pink instead of white, not to mention rather scratchy. Milk was bought in tetra pack boxes I kept in the cupboard instead of jugs I kept in the fridge. It also tasted sweeter and more syrupy. Now I could add circular Christmas tree lights to that list.

Martial and Franck eventually called us into the kitchen, where they both looked adorable dressed in identical white aprons. They had begun a waffle production line.

"Call the kids in," Martial said.

I took out the sugar, various jams, and Nutella out of the fridge.

We fed the ravenous children and then sat around the kitchen table and enjoyed waffles ourselves along with cider from Normandy and the continuation of *kir* for my part.

Even if lasso-ing a dwarf Christmas tree was part of our new traditions in France, Christmas was beginning to feel magical for me too.

On the last day of school before Christmas break the entire student and parent population of Saint-Coeur school was invited to the Cathedral in Beaune for a family Christmas service. The girls were eager to go as all their friends had chattered about it at school. I don't think they really knew what it was all about, but they had learned in class how to say the Lord's Prayer in French and they were also learning their Hail Mary during recess on rainy days in the chapel. This meant they were already far better Catholics than their mother.

We were all supposed to bring something to add to the shared "*goûter*" after the service. I whipped up some sugar cookies that Charlotte and Camille and their cousin Lola helped me decorate. I wasn't sure how this would go over with the French crowd as everything produced in France, even craft projects made at school by the children, looked as though they had been executed by Martha Stewart or one of her minions (I suspected the teacher). Just before the service all the children in each class came out holding identically made and perfect Christmas gifts for their parents - a candle holder from Charlotte and a bookmark from Camille.

Our sugar cookies, on the other hand, definitely looked like small children had decorated them. On some the sprinkles had mixed together (with spit, most likely) so much that they transformed into a muddy gray color. Others had a surfeit of icing but hardly any sprinkles at all. I was determined to be my Canadian self and not get self-conscious about our cookies. We had had a blast decorating them (though I could not say the same for cleaning up the kitchen afterwards) and that was what mattered.

The church service was in the Notre-Dame cathedral in the heart of Beaune, which dates back to the 13th century. It was a beautiful church that had recently been cleaned of the accumulated grime and pollution of centuries, so that it's huge blocks of stone glowed pale ivory. Charlotte held my hand and Camille held Franck's as we walked up the wide stone steps. Inside, the pews were already filled with families from the school. I recognized a lot of people; although of course there was nobody there I could call a friend yet. We found a spot and sat down. Families definitely seemed to be larger here in Burgundy than back home, I mused as I looked around. A minimum of three children appeared to be the norm and families of four or five or even six children were not unusual. This made for a lot of babies and toddlers.

We didn't have to wait long after finding a spot for the service to begin. When the priest came out and began speaking at first I thought he was an altar boy. He wore round glasses and looked exceedingly young - maybe twenty years old, if that. Like most Catholic services I fell into a half-asleep state where I stood up and sat down with the congregation and mumbled the responses because I wasn't, like everyone else in the congregation, sure what I was supposed to be saying. I never could figure out why church services weren't designed around just staying seated. These contemplative trains of thought were always interrupted by another directive to stand.

The children, even though they were exceedingly well behaved, started to get as restless as I began to feel. Wooden pews were hard on the *derrière*. Some children were allowed to wander up so they could listen to the service from the base of the half-moon staircase which led to the altar.

The priest said a word that caught my attention. "*Avortement.*" Abortion? Why was the priest talking about abortion at a family Christmas service? I snapped to attention.

"Even from the moment of his arrival in Mary's womb, Jesus was a holy being, as are all children. How can abortion be allowed in any civilized country?" the priest asked.

I couldn't believe what I was hearing.

The young priest was displaying a lot of fire and brimstone and I noticed many of the French people around me also looked rather shocked by the turn this family service had taken. They exchanged glances with widened eyes and eloquent shoulder shrugs.

A couple of the smaller children, all of that age range around eighteen months when toddlers were blessed with mobility but had zero comprehension of danger, had begun to creep up the stairs towards the priest. One particularly bold specimen in an adorable outfit of sky blue overalls, a red cardigan, and red patent shoes actually managed to summit the stairs and began crawling around the priest's feet and tugged at his robes.

The priest, hardly pausing from his anti-abortion rant, began to nudge the child away from him with his foot. These "nudges" grew so firm that one would be hard-pressed not to call them kicks. He did this without so much as smiling or acting with any kindness towards the toddler. Suddenly the mother, perhaps realizing that despite the fact that the priest was banging on about how every child was precious he would have no compunction about giving her son a solid kick in the ribs so that he didn't disrupt his sermon, ran up to the front and rescued her child. She cast a dirty look at the priest as the child began to wail. She promptly carried him outside.

"Did I just see that?" I hissed to Franck.

"Yes," said Franck. "This is exactly why, even though I believe in God, I don't feel obliged to spend every Sunday in Church."

As we made our way to the room behind the main area of the cathedral to share the snack, I pondered this off-putting priest. I had always wanted to believe in something, but often the actual humans representing religions made this difficult, if not impossible.

I was unaccountably hurt, although not surprised, to discover that our cookies weren't overly popular. Even the French children seemed to avoid anything that didn't look esthetically appealing, no matter what the sugar content.

I watched as the priest plucked one off the plate absent-mindedly while he was talking to a very grandly dressed parent.

He nibbled at one, made a face of disgust and then put it back down on the plate. "Too sweet for me," he said.

And not enough for me, I thought.

The next night it was time for my last "gymnastics" class before our group broke up until mid-January. The older women, mostly winemakers or wives of winemakers themselves, had not become friends exactly but they now considered me a part of the group and were unfailingly friendly.

They had been sure to tell me at the end of our last class the week before that this week we were going to indulge in a "Christmas *apéritif*". I assumed the class would be cut short fifteen to twenty minutes early so we could all enjoy a holiday drink together. I dressed in my yoga pants and sweatshirt and made my way down the road, looking forward to a few stretches and halfhearted sit-ups before enjoying a glass or two of *crémant*.

I was a bit late, as Camille had insisted that I had to stay and watch her put on her pajamas before leaving. This turned out to be a very protracted exercise during which she put both legs through the same hole and tried to put her head through the arm-hole and then fell onto the floor in hysterics.

I pushed open the heavy door into *la salle des fêtes* and welcomed the rush of warm air. A babble of French came from the room where we normally had our class. I opened that door to find myself in a room with a bunch of *grandes dames* that were unrecognizable. Gone were the bizarre sports togs, replaced by elegant dresses or pantsuits, and artfully arrayed chunky necklaces or gorgeous scarves. A long fold out table in the middle of the room was covered with beautiful linen tablecloths and red candles as well as several sprays of flowers. Overflowing baskets of *gougères* and *feuilletes au fromage* and little slices of *saucisson sec* and baguette topped with *paté* were crowded out by the sheer number of bottles and glasses on the table. There were champagne flutes and white wine glasses and red wine glasses. Lesson: Do not forget that Burgundians take their festivities seriously.

The women all stopped talking and gave me a strange look.

"I didn't realize we weren't doing any *gymnastique* today!" I explained.

"Ah but we are Madame Germain!" Solange slid the stem of a

champagne flute in my hand. "We are exercising our wrists and elbows."

"And our mouths!" added Dominique. "Would you like some Dom Perignon?"

I wasn't sure if I'd heard properly. "Dom Perignon?"

"Yes. Dominique and her husband went up to Champagne to visit friends and they brought several bottles back. Would you like a glass?"

"Who in their right mind would say no to Dom Perignon?"

Solange laughed. "Nobody!"

She handed me a flute and I took a sip. I had only had Dom Perignon on a few other occasions but it was exquisite, not the slightest bit acidic and perfectly balanced.

"Have one of my *gougères* with it." Dominique held out a miniature version of the double-barreled winemaker's harvest basket filled to the brim with golden cheese puffs. I took one and took a bite. It was delicate and crispy on the outside and soft and unctuous and studded with Emmenthal in the inside – the perfect match to the Dom Perignon.

I took another sip of my glass of stars. That's what the monk Dom Perignon who accidentally discovered the technique to make champagne called to his fellow monks when he took his first sip, "Come quickly! I'm tasting stars!"

"When you said a Christmas *apéritif* I wasn't expecting this." I looked down at my ratty yoga pants and sneakers.

"In Burgundy, you should always expect a celebration," Dominique said.

I took another sip and another bite, quickly forgetting what I was wearing in the sublime perfection of the food and the drink.

"I will from now on."

Over the next few days the tradesmen started to come for shorter and shorter periods of time until they evaporated entirely by Christmas Eve day. Enquiries always ground to a halt during the last half of

December so Franck and I had used the time we weren't at the cottage to go out and buy our girls presents for Christmas.

Our budget was pretty meager, but I was determined not to let their first Christmas in France slide by without adequate celebration. We found them each a stuffy dog as well as a Polly Pocket magic fashion change disco bus to share. We picked up a bag of *"papillottes"*, brightly foil wrapped chocolates to put into their slippers that they would leave out for the Père Noël. There were no stockings in France, which was a good thing as the girls' tiny slippers, or *pantoufles* (one of my favorite sounding French words along with *poubelle* for 'garbage') were much easier to fill. Franck and I decided not to buy presents for each other but instead to concentrate on the girls. We strung lights up outside on the roof and wound them around the trees. Our house still looked like the dog's breakfast, but at least it looked like a festive dog's breakfast.

Waves of homesickness crashed and receded. My family had always done Christmas on a grand scale, so much so that when Franck came to our house for his first Christmas he ran out of steam before he ran out of presents to unwrap. He just sat on the couch, rendered catatonic by the sheer quantity of gifts and the massive, glittering tree. Christmases in France were far simpler. This Christmas would be much more modest but I hoped that my girls were too young to notice the difference.

"What should we do for dinner tonight?" I asked Franck when we were all down in Beaune standing by the *manège* after buying a few last minute gifts for Franck's family. We indulged the girls in one ride on the merry-go-round in the center of the Place Carnot. Charlotte chose the big black horse and Camille the elephant.

I knew that the next day Stéphanie was having us over for a proper French Christmas lunch. Some years Franck's family did a huge meal on Christmas Eve as well as, or instead of, the Christmas Day extravaganza. But this year it was decided due to the proliferation of young children to stick to the meal on Christmas Day when they would all be wide awake and excited to play with their presents. We would all be left to our own devices for Christmas Eve dinner.

"Given what we're going to eat tomorrow, we don't need to eat much tonight," Franck said.

"Still, we have to do something," I mused. "Something festive."

Just then the music ended and Camille and Charlotte came over to beg tickets for another ride.

I dug in my purse – I knew I had a few more. "What would you like to eat at dinner tonight?" I asked them.

"*Les escargots!*" Charlotte declared. "*J'adore les escargots.*"

"Me too!" chimed in Camille.

Snails? When had my daughters tasted snails?

"Where did you try snails?" I asked.

"*La cantine!*" Charlotte answered. "We love them."

Franck and I looked at each other once the girls had hopped back on to different animals, the donkey for Camille and the white horse for Charlotte.

"This is a proud moment for me as a father," Franck said, reaching for my mitten-clad hand. Indeed, the past few months since we had arrived in the summer had been at times lonely, exhausting, and acutely discouraging. Still, one of the main reasons we had decided to move to France was so that our girls appropriated their father's country for themselves. The fact that our daughters chose snails - Burgundy's classic dish - for their Christmas Eve dinner made it seem all worth it.

CHAPTER 19

Later that evening, we sat around the monastery table in the living room as Franck brought in the sheet of bubbling, fragrant *escargots* straight from the oven.

Once we had had the idea we were inspired to invite Franck's parents and Mémé as well. After all, what is the point of cooking sixty snails when you could just as easily cook one hundred? André brought a mystery bottle of wine that he unearthed in his cellar. After much conjecture, it was decided that it had been put there many years before by Franck's grandfather, Pépé Georges. The bottle had been found in a stash in a far corner, covered with an impressive layer of dust. The cork had definitely seen better days too, but when uncorked and poured we found it contained a delectable *aligoté* that had probably been the production of Franck's grandfather's vineyards just outside of the village from sometime in the 1970s. It felt almost like Le Pépé was here with us, sharing our Christmas Eve *escargot* scoff.

"Who wants snails?" Franck asked.

"*Moi! Moi! Moi!*" Charlotte leapt up from her chair and waved her arm as high up as she could get it in the air.

"*Moi aussi!*" echoed Camille.

Franck started them each with six on their plate, even though they both insisted they wanted more. Michèle took the escargot tongs and tiny fork and showed them how to extract the delicious beast from the shell.

"I know how to do it!" Camille declared as Franck filled each of our plates with a solid dozen, plus one for good luck. She grabbed hold of the tongs and picked up the escargot shell from her plate. She stuck her fork in and tried to extract the snail, but the shells were slippery affairs, as they were covered with the melted garlic parsley butter. Her escargot shell shot across the table, narrowly missing Mémé's eye. A splat of parsley butter dribbled down the wall.

I walked over and picked up the escargot shell, which still had the escargot inside and deposited it on Camille's plate. "No harm done," I said. "I was planning on ripping off that wallpaper anyway."

Mémé began to sing the *Ban Bourguignon* which, like loving snails, the girls had somehow learned in the past few months through some sort of magical cultural osmosis.

An hour later we adults were all sitting back in our chairs rubbing our stomachs while Charlotte and Camille, each fortified by over two dozen *escargots*, were tearing open the wrapping paper on their traditional Christmas Eve gifts, a pair of warm flannel pajamas for each of them, purchased in a wonderful little clothing shop in the pedestrian-only streets of Dijon.

"Can we put them on right now?" Camille asked.

"We're going to midnight mass," I said. "Remember? We can put out the things for the Père Noël before we leave though, so everything is ready for when we get back."

Charlotte and Camille each ran to get her slippers.

André and Michèle convinced Charlotte and Camille that, in France, the Père Noël liked *papillottes* and a glass of *ratafia* instead of milk and cookies. It sounded to me like the *Père Noël* had excellent taste.

I went down to the cellar and fetched a bottle of *ratafia*, sweet, fortified wine, made by my friend Sandrine's family just up the road from our house here in Villers. We poured it into a plain kitchen glass and the girls selected a bunch of shiny wrapped *papillottes* from the bag in the kitchen to put in a *café au lait* bowl.

We bundled up and headed over to the village church, our stomachs full of snails and white wine.

The church bells rang clear in the frigid air, just as they had done six years before. Back then, we were in the midst of renovating *La Maison des Deux Clochers* and as Père Bard went on about the Virgin Mary of Fatima I pondered faith, renovations and panic attacks. I wondered what my girls would think of the service.

Many villagers were also on the way to the church and we wished each other *"Joyeuses Fêtes"* and kissed and caught up on village gossip as we walked towards the sound of the bells.

I shucked my heavy wool coat at the door, remembering the balmy temperature of the church at my last midnight mass.

I began shivering almost immediately.

"Look, I can see my breath!" Camille announced. She and Charlotte pretended they were smoking cigarettes as we slid between the pews. I supposed this was a natural consequence of going to a school that was populated by hundreds of older students who smoked at every opportunity before and after school, not to mention the people smoking on café terraces and all the tradesmen who lit up as soon as they were outside our door after their evening *apéritif.*

"I guess they haven't repaired the heat," André said. "I heard it was broken."

Mémé grimaced. She was happiest during the dog days of August in Burgundy when the thermometer went well above forty degrees.

"I think I'm going to take Mémé back home," André whispered to Michèle, who nodded. "She could catch her death in here."

We found some space in a pew about half way to the front. It was crowded, which was actually fortuitous given that without body heat coming in from all sides the chances of developing hypothermia were high.

"Why is it so cold in here?" Charlotte asked between puffs of her imaginary cigarette.

"The heater is broken," I said.

"Are churches always this cold?"

"Last time I was here it was boiling hot."

"Is this going to be boring?" she asked me.

"Probably," I admitted. "The Père Bard is very old and he doesn't always speak very loudly. It's sometimes hard to understand what he is talking about." If he was going to go heavily into a discourse about the prophesies of Our Lady of Fatima like he did at my last Midnight Mass in Villers-la-Faye I would have to refer the girls over to Franck if they wanted an interpretation of the sermon. "Look at the decorations." I fell back on distraction.

There were no teetering arches this year, but instead a multitude of cut out children's drawings of stars and what looked like a woman in a hijab (perhaps a Muslim Mary?) as well as the occasional indeterminate animal hanging down from poles that were set up at the end of every third pew.

The Père Bard came out and sat down gingerly on a very old and wonky chair placed in front of the altar.

He clapped his hands. "Can all the children come near me?"

Franck gave Charlotte and Camille a nudge and they gratefully slid out of our pew and joined the other village children at the front of the church, surrounding Père Bard.

"Jump!" the Père Bard said. The children stood around, fingers in their mouths, looking at each other. Had they heard this ancient, wizened old priest correctly?

"I can't jump anymore so I can't show you how, but pretend you are a bunch of frogs and people are hunting you to cut off your legs and eat them. Have you eaten frogs' legs before?"

Most of the children nodded.

"Then you know. Frogs' legs are delicious. Jump as high as you can and show the hunters that you *need* your legs!"

The children didn't need any further encouragement. They began leaping around Père Bard like kernels of corn in a hot pan. They did this for several minutes, colliding into each other as Père Bard laughed and egged them on, telling them that if they wanted to save their legs from the hunters they needed to jump even higher.

"How this makes me wish I could still jump!" he cried. Finally, a little boy was bumped by a bigger child and went crashing down on the flagstones. His nose gushed blood and he began to wail.

"I think we need a mother up here!" The Père Bard raised his voice to be heard over the commotion. "We have an injured frog!"

The mother scooped up her child and took him to the back of the church.

The injury did not make the priest curtail this activity right away. He let the frogs jump for several more minutes before telling them that they had escaped those nasty hunters and jumped very finely indeed.

"Now that you are all toasty warm, you can go sit by your parents or here by me or really wherever you want. This church is your home too, you know. It always will be. Never forget that. Make yourselves comfortable."

Charlotte and Camille opted to stay up front with most of the other children, playing and rolling around at the foot of the Père Bard's chair.

The service went on, carols were sung, we heard a bit of a ramble about our Lady of Fatima, but not as involved as last time, and then before I knew it the church bells were ringing again and it was midnight. The service was over and it was Christmas.

"*Joyeux Noël.*" We all kissed and shook hands with the people around us. The bells thundered overhead. I couldn't see Charlotte and Camille anymore over the tumult of people and running children and taller heads.

After a few seconds I felt a familiar small pair of arms wrap around my leg. "*Joyeux Noël Maman,*" said Camille, looking up at me smiling with shining hazel eyes. "That was fun. Has the Père Noël come to our house already?"

"Not yet," I said. "We have to get you and Charlotte back home and asleep in bed for him to come."

"Charlotte! Charlotte!" Camille called her sister. "We have to go home now so that the Père Noël will come!"

We made our way slowly out of the church, despite the girls tugging at our hands to go faster, kissing and greeting and saying good-bye to fellow villagers on the way out.

The presents were quickly disposed of on Christmas morning. Charlotte and Camille ripped off the paper and squealed over their stuffy puppies and Polly Pockets. They ate a prodigious amount of *papillottes* and their enjoyment of the day didn't seem to be at all affected by the torn wallpaper on the walls or the ugly floor tiles. The tree and the decorations and the fact that the Père Noël came during the night, drank all the *ratafia*, and ate the *papillottes* made it a perfect Christmas in their eyes. A big Christmas was fun, but a modest Christmas had its rewards too. Fewer gifts made us aware of what was important, and increased our appreciation of what we did have.

Stéphanie told us to be at her house by 11:30 for the *apéritif.* She would not hear of me bringing anything to contribute to the Christmas meal. When I asked Franck why she was turning down repeated offers of help he said that it was her pride as a hostess to do everything herself. I wondered briefly why I had never seemed to possess that particular brand of domestic pride.

Tom and Lola greeted us at the door, jumping up and down and telling us about the presents Père Noël had brought them. The most popular was Lola's stand up microphone. The four cousins rushed upstairs to her bedroom to try it out. By the time Thierry had poured us each a flute of *mousseux* the strains of very loud but out-of-tune voices floated down the stairs. We were the last ones to arrive. There was Steph and Thierry, Thierry's parents, his aunt from Dijon, Franck's parents and of course La Mémé, equipped with several exquisite shawls to stave off drafts despite the roaring fire. We caught up with Thierry's parents and his aunt and Stéphanie passed around homemade *gougères* – crunchy on the outside and rich and airy on the inside - made with Mémé's recipe.

Eventually Steph went back in the kitchen and André went to help her. I was shooed away. We were told to sit down at the table, stunningly decorated with tones of red and gold, and an abundance of freshly picked holly.

Steph handed out the plates, beginning with Thierry's aunt and Mémé and then moved on down the line in order of age. On each plate were two artfully arranged slices of *foie gras*, two slices of toasted *brioche*, and a scoop of fig jam.

Thierry busied himself with filling our glasses with a dark yellow Sauternes, perfectly chilled.

We waited until Steph and André were seated at the table and then Stephanie said *"Bon alors, Joyeux Noël et bon appetite!"* I scraped some *foie gras* on a piece of toasted, buttery brioche, topped it with fig jam, then washed it down with the beautifully paired Sauternes. The foie gras was silky smooth on my tongue, enhanced by the sweet pops of the fig jam and the honeyed richness of the Sauternes. They mingled together to form a holy trinity of yum. The table fell silent for several minutes as everyone relished this first sublime bite of the holiday meal.

We talked about preparing the *foie gras* which Stephanie had done from scratch this year - well not completely from scratch - she hadn't force fed a goose but she did buy a freshly fattened goose liver and prepared, deveined, marinated and cooked it herself.

"Do you like it Laura?" she asked. I knew I should feel guilty about the force-fed goose, but all I could think of was how it was so incredibly delicious.

"*C'est délicieux*," I answered. Why did nothing in Canada taste this satisfying? Why were flavors never quite so carefully and artfully matched? Here on my plate and in my glass was the perfect harmony of sweet and savory. The crunchy butteryness of the *brioche* and the syrupy fig jam highlighted the savory unctuousness of the *foie gras*. Individually all these things were delicious, but married together they were sublime. There wasn't a lot of the food on the plate but because it was so perfect it was all that was needed.

We took a good hour nibbling away at the first course. The children came down and they all ate a full plate just like the adults, all except Lola who was turning out, much to the despair of Franck's family of *gourmets*, to be a picky eater. I wasn't sure if my kids realized if they were eating fattened goose liver or, if they did, whether they would even care.

Without me realizing exactly when or how, their eating habits had improved drastically since we moved here. They sat down to eat three proper meals a day and a snack when they got home from school around five o'clock. There were still a few things they didn't like, spinach for Charlotte and brussel sprouts for Camille, but they would try more or less anything else, mainly because the kids around them had to try everything too. Also, I believe the fact that most things they tried actually tasted *good* inspired them to be adventurous.

Charlotte and Camille proclaimed that the *foie gras* was delicious and declared it one of their new favorite foods, then asked if they could go upstairs to play. The cousins disappeared again and Steph and Thierry and André took their time doing the dishes from the first course while Steph periodically checked the oven.

Finally she removed what had been in there and the house was filled with an irresistible smell. It was a *chapon* - a rooster castrated at a young age – filled with a chestnut and pork stuffing.

Stephanie served this with a side of chestnuts for anyone who wanted them. I had grown up in Canada seeing chestnuts cover the sidewalk every autumn but I had never tasted them before or, indeed, ever seen anybody eat them. It was in France that I first discovered them and realized how much I loved their earthy taste and texture.

Stéphanie also served her bird with a reduced *jus* from the cooking. Thierry, meanwhile, had taken out several bottles of *Hospices de Beaune* wine and served one that was a Pommard *premier cru*.

He gave it to Franck to taste. Franck swirled it around in his glass, sniffed, and swashed it around his mouth and proclaimed it perfect. No one rushed on to anything else, and each plateful was just the perfect amount of flavors to savor without overwhelming the palate.

I thought back to our Christmas dinners in Canada. They were joyous affairs, but it was always such a race to get everything on the table at the same time; the turkey, the stuffing, the brussel sprouts, the scalloped potatoes, and the green beans. Everybody filled their plates and rushed to the table to eat before it got cold (which it inevitably did). The flavors were good, but there were too many of them at once, and the whole thing was over far too fast. Afterwards, everyone sat back with prodigious gut aches and a kitchen full of dishes to clean.

The protracted nature and the small portions of meals in Burgundy meant that everything was properly savored. It forced everyone to slow down. Slowing down while eating, I realized now, was key to true appreciation and enjoyment of food. There were no distractions apart from the flowing conversation.

After the *chapon* came a *trou normande* in the form of a lime sorbet with strong alcohol poured over it. This was, according to French belief, the secret to digesting well and making more room in our stomachs for the cheese and dessert courses.

The *fromage* platter was massive, and included a truly pungent and perfectly oozing *"Ami de Chambertin,* a half round of *Cîteaux,* and a crumbly and salty *Cantal* sheep's cheese amongst other offerings. Here too, the different textures and tastes of the cheeses riffed off each other creating an amazing taste experience. For the wine, Thierry served another Pommard from *les Hospices* that was groaning with ripe fruit flavours and structured tannins – absolutely the perfect foil to the cheeses.

Dessert came sometime after, along with a *vin de paille* from the Jura, a sweet intensely yellow wine that used half rotten grapes that had been aged on hay. Its richness complimented Mémé's two *"buches de Noël"*, one mocha, one chocolate. Next came a praline *kouglouf* made by Franck's father, served with the tiny china cups of strong espresso and bowls of *papillottes* and *clémentine* oranges.

As I was unpeeling my second orange the conversation ranged from wine to the best markets in the region. Thierry's father, nicknamed "Le Cadou" so insistently that I had never learned his actual name, was a loyal attendee of the Friday morning market in Nuits-Saint-Georges where he went without fail to visit with friends and his favorite merchants and to buy whatever struck his fancy. Franck's favorite market remained the Monday morning market in Louhans that featured veal's brains and chilled white wine for the traditional pre-market breakfast. Mémé had always liked the market in the nearby town of Chagny. I argued for Beaune even though Franck's family didn't like the fact that it had seen an influx in tourists over the past decade during the summer months.

I glanced at my watch for the first time that day. "It's ten o'clock at night!"

Indeed, darkness had fallen over the vineyards behind Steph and Thierry's house a long time before, but somehow I didn't have the impression of time passing. We had been at the table for almost twelve hours.

"A perfect Christmas Day," Franck said, rubbing his stomach and reaching across the table to caress my palm.

CHAPTER 20

Six and a half months...we had six and a half months before our first guests arrived at *La Maison de la Vieille Vigne* I thought, as I surveyed the destruction of the cottage. If things didn't start coming together fast I would have to include a different packing list for our guests from the usual shorts, sweater, and slippers. Instead I would have to ask them to equip themselves with a bucket, spade, hammer, clothing that has already been destroyed, tent, sleeping bags... The tradesmen began to dribble back during the second week of January and now that the roof was finished, with the exception of installing the eaves, the work inside could begin.

Luc convinced Franck and me that ripping up the floor in the entire cottage and starting afresh was the best possible solution. That way some of the plumbing and heating pipes could run through the new concrete and make everyone's job easier.

Hugo attacked the destruction of the floor with enthusiasm. Demolition fit *parfaitement* with his aptitudes and enthusiasms. Why did men love demolition so much? He had brought along helpers including a huge man who never uttered a word but always wore a red beret. We dubbed him "*Beret Rouge.*" Beret Rouge wielded a sledgehammer with a ferocity that made Luc, Franck and I give him wide berth.

Hugo also brought along a hefty friend named Auguste who was easily pushing sixty and who broke out into an alarming sweat every time he picked up anything weighing more than five pounds.

"I bring him along and pay him a bit because I feel sorry for him,"

Hugo explained. "He used to work in a mustard factory in Dijon before he got laid off. Then he had the heart attacks."

"Heart attacks?" I asked. "As in plural?"

"Should he be working at all?" Franck added.

"Probably not," Hugo admitted. "I'm really careful with him though. I yell at him if he tries to do anything too strenuous. If he stays home he gets completely depressed and watches soap operas all day long, particularly *Les Feux de L'Amour*. I can't in all good conscience leave a friend to such a fate."

I eyed Auguste, not particularly reassured. He was leaning on a wedge that the Beret Rouge had used to pry up stubborn pieces of concrete on the floor. His face was an alarming shade of garnet.

"Do you know CPR?" I whispered to Franck in English so only he could understand.

"Sort of, but rusty," Franck admitted.

"I'm worried he may have a heart attack at any moment," Franck said to Hugo.

"He might." Hugo shrugged. "But if he does drop dead, isn't it a better way to go doing a man's work than sitting at home crying over *Les Feux de L'Amour* like a woman?"

Franck apparently saw the logic in this because he went into the bedroom with Luc to discuss some fascinating matter concerning pipes.

"By the way," I said to Hugo when they'd left. "I'm a woman and I have never watched a soap opera in my life."

"Yes, but you're Canadian," Hugo said obliquely. "The only thing that worries me is all the wine."

"The wine?" I asked.

"You know we go to Jacky's before we start work to begin the day with *un petit blanc*, then we go there for lunch, and then we come to your place after work?"

"I didn't know that you went to Jacky's in the morning," I said. "That is a lot of wine when you add it all up."

"Nothing a working man can't handle," answered Hugo. "But Auguste is taking about a hundred different medications and I'm not sure if he is supposed to be drinking quite as much as the rest of us."

"Probably not." I was no doctor but the answer to that question seemed pretty self-evident to me.

Hugo looked troubled for a moment, then waved this concern away. "Oh well, *un petit blanc* has never hurt anyone."

Franck came back in the room. "Haven't found any Roman ruins?" he asked Hugo.

I laughed at this question, but Hugo took it seriously. "Not so far. What should we do if we do find something though?"

"You can give any coins to me but for anything else just cover it up and keep going."

Hugo took these instructions with a nod.

The *Beret Rouge* was digging closer and closer to the meter thick and ridiculously crooked stone wall that, according to Luc, supported the entire cottage.

"He maybe shouldn't go too close to that and dig too deep," Franck said, nodding towards the wall.

Hugo screwed up his mouth, considering. "It'll probably be fine."

"I'm trusting you to ensure it is *definitely* fine," Franck said.

Hugo grimaced but finally conceded *"D'accord, d'accord"* and went over to talk to *Beret Rouge*

I shivered. The thermometer was hovering around zero and a freezing fog swirled outside. "I'd better go get the girls," I said. "I have to start planning Camille's birthday party."

Franck groaned. "I told you. We don't have to do a birthday party. Lots of years I didn't have one." Franck walked me out to our car. "People don't do them automatically here in France like they do in Canada."

It was tempting to just let things slide this year, especially as I didn't know the parents of Camille's little friends very well, but not hosting a birthday party for my children seemed sacrilegious. I remembered all the incredible birthday parties my Mom had thrown for me.

Franck and I hadn't been too clever when conceiving our girls. Camille was born on January 15th and Charlotte on February 21st. Both of these dates fell in the dead of winter in both Burgundy and Canada. This meant house parties rather than garden parties. Why hadn't we planned for a spring baby? Truth be told, in our typical fashion we hadn't planned much at all.

Franck opened the car door. "Are you sure you don't want me to go and pick up the girls? I'm worried that all this fog is going to turn to ice if the temperature drops."

"I think your presence is needed here to make sure Hugo and *Beret Rouge* don't end up being overzealous and make the whole cottage fall down. I'll be fine." Cyril the driving instructor wouldn't believe how far I had come. I wasn't completely reassured about the road conditions but it was all a matter of degrees; I was even less reassured about Hugo overseeing the demolition.

Franck looked back at the dust and dirt billowing out the cottage windows. He gave me a kiss. "Drive slow and be careful."

"*Bien sûr.*"

Part of the daily life in the villages of Magny-les-Villers or Villers-la-Faye was "*La Chaine*" the local nickname for the winding road that serpented through the vineyards down to the village of Ladoix-Serrigny and the main road. *La Chaine* was steep and, because that wasn't exciting enough, villagers made a game of just how fast they could make it up and down.

The fog was denser by the time I started down on *La Chaine*. I was luckily driving slowly when my wheels started slipping. I slowed down even further and put the car into second gear. Despite my shaking hands, Cyril would be proud.

I was almost at a crawl when I saw the headlights of another car in my lane. Would they see me in time? I tried to pull over even farther to my right, off the road where thankfully there was a guardrail preventing the car from plummeting into the *Premier Cru* vineyards below.

The other driver finally saw me because the car squealed into its own lane just as I heard the sickening scrape of metal against metal as my side view mirror scraped his. I must have slammed on my brakes without thinking about my clutch, because my car stalled and rolled to a stop.

"*Merde! Merde! Merde!*" I hissed. My heart pounded and despite the frigid temperature inside the car I broke out in a sweat. I wanted to call someone for help, but I had forgotten to take Franck's cell phone. How was I going to get down the rest of *La Chaine*? My tires no longer gripped the road and it felt as though it was now covered with a solid sheet of ice.

I couldn't sit here though. The next person who came whipping down *La Chaine* would slam into me in this fog.

My heart pounding, I turned the key in the ignition and pointed the car downhill. I never took my foot off the break completely, and shifted myself into second gear and stayed there. It must have taken me four times as long to drive the usual distance to the bottom of the hill. The main road didn't look very pretty either, but at least the fog had dissipated slightly here at a lower altitude and the visibility was better. I cursed the early winter nights though. It was dark already but the road ahead of me sparkled with ice in the light of my headlights.

I crawled along in the slow lane. Even then I had cars honking and then zooming around me. How could they all be driving so fast on this skating rink,

As I drove by the village of Aloxe Corton my headlights illuminated three cars that had skidded into the vineyards alongside the road. I wondered if I should stop, but then caught a glimpse of one guy lounging against the hood of his overturned car chatting on his cell phone.

Why hadn't I let Franck drive? I hadn't realized how fast the roads here could turn treacherous.

I breathed a sigh of relief when I saw the salting machine in front of me at the roundabout leading into Beaune. I followed obediently behind it, grateful to feel my tires grip the road.

I circled the parking lot at the school once, but I was of course running late and there were absolutely no available spots left. Usually I kept circling until people began to leave, but today I just did not have it in me to be the polite Canadian.

I double-parked in front of two cars by the school door, leapt out and went to go and get my daughters without so much as looking back to see if I was inconveniencing anyone.

By the time I had fetched the girls and we were making our way back to the car I was already panicking about the best route to take back up to Villers-la-Faye.

The lights in the parking lot illuminated the woman I blocked, and who was now stalking around her Peugeot in sky-high heels as she yelled into her cell phone. As soon as she caught sight of me unlocking my car's door she began berating me.

"*Vous!*" She pointed an accusing finger. "I have been waiting here for fifteen minutes thanks to you!"

"That's *impossible*," I answered. "I only parked in front of your car five minutes ago. Come on Charlotte and Camille," I added, hustling them into the car. "Do up your seatbelts."

The woman launched into a spiteful French diatribe. I stared at her for a second, wondering if I should even try to respond but really couldn't think of anything but getting the girls safely back up to Villers. Finally, I just shrugged and drove off to leave her screaming to herself

I drove up a different way, via the village of Corgoloin. Even then, it must have taken me almost an hour to do the drive that I usually accomplished in ten minutes. Halfway up, fat white snowflakes began to fall and within seconds obliterated the lines of the road. I decided to go straight to the cottage as it was closer than our house and I couldn't wait one second longer to turn the wheel of our car over to Franck or someone who was far more qualified than me to drive in these conditions.

Before I could even get out of the car Franck ran out of the cottage. "There you are!" he said. "I've been going crazy and have been back and forth to our house about ten times to see if you got home. How was it?"

"Awful," I buried my face in his warm wool sweater.

"I was just about to borrow my Dad's car and go looking for you. I'm not letting you go again without the cell phone. I should have gone. I didn't think the roads would ice up so fast…"

"Can you drive me and the girls home? I don't want them to get cold sitting there in the backseat."

"Of course." He popped his head back in the cottage then was back in the car before I had even done up my seatbelt in the passenger seat.

"I double parked behind someone at the school," I said. "She yelled at me."

"What did you do?" Franck asked.

"I was so preoccupied with getting the girls back up here safely that I just shrugged and took off."

"Maybe it took a death defying drive," Franck said. "But you're finally learning to park like a French person."

The next day we woke up to find the village covered in snow under a sparkling blue sky. The snowplow, which was shared by ten villages, hadn't made it up to Villers-la-Faye yet and Franck said he doubted it would anytime soon. Franck walked over to the cottage to meet any tradesmen who were foolhardy enough to try and drive up their *camionettes*. He came back a half an hour later as I was toasting yesterday's leftover baguette for breakfast.

"Nobody showed." He banged the snow off his boots on the porch. "We're all going to take a snow day."

"Snow day! Snow day!" Charlotte and Camille danced around the kitchen table, shrieking.

"I wish we had a sled," I said.

Franck grabbed a piece of toasted baguette from the plate and began to butter it with the salted butter from Brittany that caught my fancy on our last trip to the grocery store. "Maybe we do." He dolloped on some blackcurrant jam his parents made in the early fall.

"Do we?"

"I had a great sled when I was little. My parents never throw anything out. It has to be somewhere in the barn. After we're done breakfast let's go over there."

Camille took a sip of her hot chocolate. "I'm done!" she said. "I'm going to get ready."

"Go ahead and get dressed," I said. "But we're not leaving until *Papa* and I have had our coffee." When did I start calling Franck "papa" - the French word for father? I wondered.

Despite my warning, our morning *café au laits* ended up being a lot less leisurely than we had planned. The girls dressed in lightning speed and began tugging at us and asking where they could find their gloves.

"Bottom drawer of the *armoire*," I said, getting up and washing out our *café au lait* bowls in the sink then going to help them.

Franck had already put on his jacket by the time the girls were dressed. He was almost as excited as the girls. "I hope we can find it. It was the fastest sled in the village."

We tramped over to Franck's parents' house. The village took on a magical quality without the sound of a single car or tractor. The church bell rang over in Magny and we could hear the crystalline sound travel across the snowy hills and vineyards. Just then the church bell of Villers began clanging as well, drowning out the crunch of our boots in the snow.

The girls ran ahead, then tripped and fell in the white snow and insisted on making several snow angels before letting us help them up again. We heard cries of joy coming from beyond the mayor's office and a little boy in a bright red jacket and hat flew out, sledding on a humble plastic garbage bag from behind a stone house at the base of the Mont Saint Victor.

"*Chouette!*" he called up to his friends who must all have been primed to go after him.

"Let's go get our sled!" Camille began to run again as fast as her little legs would carry her through the thick snow.

There was a cluster of people outside the *boulangerie* across from *chez* Germain, most with baguettes under their arms.

"*Bonjour!*" Franck and I greeted them as we walked by. Franck would have stayed and talked, but Charlotte and Camille had him each by one arm and were pulling him down to the gate to his parent's house.

We rang the doorbell and a few seconds later we heard André's voice. "*Oui?*"

"*C'est nous Papy!*" Charlotte and Camille jumped up and down. "We've come for Daddy's sled."

"Your sled?" André opened the door wide, looking understandably daunted.

"Don't worry," Franck said. "I'll climb up on the ladder in the barn and look for it myself."

"I don't even know if it's up there," André said.

"It has to be up there!" Charlotte insisted. "We need to go sledding today. Have you seen all the snow?"

"I have," André said. "Do you want to come in the house and I'll make you a hot chocolate while you wait?"

The offer sounded enticing, but for once even Charlotte and Camille turned it down.

"No," Charlotte answered for both of them. "We'll go and help

Daddy."

"You're not climbing up on that ladder." I brushed the crust of snow off Charlotte's jacket.

"We'll just wait at the bottom."

We all went and waited in the barn across the courtyard from the house and stood below Franck as he climbed up the ladder and ventured into the attic of the barn.

Charlotte began to try to climb up the ladder several times but I managed to detach her each time before she got too high.

"Any luck?" I called out after a few minutes. The natives were getting restless.

"I can't believe it," Franck called down. "Here is Papy George's old *mobilette!*"

"Bring it down! Bring it down!" Charlotte and Camille jumped up and down, the sled momentarily forgotten in the thrill of a mysterious discovery. I was pretty certain they had no idea that a *mobilette* was a type of motorbike and not the easiest thing to get down a ladder.

"I found it!" Franck shouted. "I found the sled!"

Camille and Charlotte erupted into cheers.

Shortly after Franck climbed down bearing a solid old-fashioned wooden slat sled that curled up at the front. Within a few seconds Franck was leading us to his secret hill.

"What about the Mont Saint Victor?" I asked. "Isn't that where you used to go sledding when you were little?"

"Sometimes," Franck said. "But it looked crowded. We're going to try somewhere different." He led us past the church and up the hill towards the rectory where Le Père Bard and his sister lived.

At the top of the hill, the high vineyards were almost unrecognizable under their blanket of white crystals that sparkled in the sunshine. Franck veered to the right.

"There is a hidden field down here." Franck beckoned us. We arrived at a rusty but firmly locked gate.

"Private property?" I surmised.

"I guess." Franck shrugged, as though he had never considered this before.

I looked beyond the gate where a pristine hill covered in white beckoned. "Who owns this field anyway?"

"I think it was sold in the past few years. I heard that the people who bought it are going to build a house here eventually but for the moment-"

"Perfect sledding hill," I finished for him.

"*Exactement.*"

"Yay! Yay! Yay!" Charlotte and Camille, not slowed by any compunction about trespassing, had already begun scrabbling over the fence.

"Olivier and I used to sneak over here all the time when the others were sledding down the Mont Saint Victor. Chumps," added Franck with no small amount of satisfaction.

Franck and I stood at the top of the hill for a second, breathing in the pristine air. The hill sloped down a huge wide expanse before leveling out and ending at a snow topped and extremely ancient looking rock wall. Beyond the fields the vineyards flowed down from *Les Chaumes* into the carpet of *Les Hautes-Côtes*. On the horizon I could make out a distant row of snowy peaks.

Franck kneeled down and put an arm around each girl. "Do you see over there?" He pointed at the mountains. Those are the Alps and the one in the middle is the Mont Blanc. It is over three hundred kilometers away. You only see the Mont Blanc from here a few days a year."

During this speech Charlotte had somehow managed to sit down on the sled that was tethered to Franck's wrist with a decaying piece of twine and was now rocking it back and forth in the snow.

"Can you believe that?" Franck stood up. "It's been years since I've seen the Mont Blanc from here."

"Weeeeeeeeeeee!" I heard. I looked down just in time to see Charlotte flying away on the sled, her feet up in the air. Franck was left with the frayed piece of twine around his wrist. Her laughter rang back up the hill.

Camille plopped down in the snow and began to wail. "Charlotte didn't wait for me!"

An hour later we were soaking wet and our muscles were screaming from our tramps back up the hill, frequently dragging a recalcitrant toddler on the sled.

"Someone's here!" Charlotte hissed as I dragged her up the last hump of the hill. I looked up, ready to have a strip torn off me for trespassing.

I spied a familiar wiry figure scale the fence, followed by a smaller figure in a full snowsuit.

Franck burst into laughter. It was Olivier and his son Dominique.

"I should have known I would find you here!" Olivier called down to him.

"Best sledding spot in the village!"

CHAPTER 21

Camille's third birthday was fast approaching and I had to get my act together and plan what was known here in France as a *"goûter d'anniversaire,"* or "birthday snack."

"Who do you want to invite?" I asked Camille as she played with her Polly Pockets on the kitchen table while I hand washed the dishes for the umpteenth time.

"All my friends from school. The whole class, except for Paul."

"Why not Paul?" I realized that I was chatting with Camille in French instead of our usual English and that somehow it felt more natural.

"He tries to kiss me every day." Camille rolled her eyes. "He wants me to be *son amoureuse* but I'm not interested." I certainly hoped not. *Amoureuse* translated directly meant "sweetheart" or, for adults, "lover."

I paused drying an Emile Henri casserole dish, fascinated. "What do you do when you are someone's *amoureuse*? You are both in preschool, for heaven's sake."

Camille shrugged. "You love each other."

"That's it?"

"You smile at each other. You lend each other crayons or paints sometimes."

"And you don't love Paul?"

Camille stuck her tongue out and made a gagging sound. "He gets in trouble at school all the time. I don't like that sort of boy."

That was good news, I supposed. "How about we invite six friends

besides Lola?" Inviting the whole class seemed a bit beyond my skill
level as a hostess.

Camille chewed her lip. "OK. *D'accord.*"

"What kind of cake do you want?"

"*Chocolat.*"

It was pretty intimidating to be throwing my first party in France,
even if it was just for three-year-olds. In Canada we usually rented out
the gymnastics hall or the kindergym space and everything was
orchestrated down to the minute. People didn't seem to do that here.
Like Franck had said, it was not a given that every child had a birthday
celebration every year in France and when they did it tended to be a
small party at home. Camille's friends would all be coming to our
house. What exactly would I do with them? Eating cake and opening
presents wouldn't take up that much time and as our boxes still hadn't
arrived from Canada Charlotte and Camille didn't have many toys
besides some dolls and their Polly Pockets.

We found invitations and Camille, with considerable difficulty,
narrowed the list of her invitees down to seven. I was amazed that for a
little girl who only recently started to speak in school, she had already
acquired so many "best" friends.

The day rolled around too quickly. I had been busy with the
demolition of the hole between the bedroom and the chicken coop – a
space we now optimistically referred to as the "bathroom". It had been
a touch and go affair, with Hugo continually wanting to take a
sledgehammer to it and Franck and Luc trying to curb his enthusiasm
so that he didn't bring the whole house down. Of course, the ancient
stonewall ended up being thick and unbelievably crooked.

One day Auguste plucked a huge rusty key from the refuse pile.
Hugo had found it wedged between the stones and tossed it on the pile
of detritus to go to the dump. Auguste beckoned me over.

"Come see this Madame Germain. Your husband told me how
much you love old keys."

"Call me Laura," I said. "And I do love old keys."

He held it out to me, reverently. "Look at its size," he said. "It was hand forged, one of a kind. I can't even guess how old it must be."

The key was indeed heavy in my hand and at least six inches long. It was coated with rust but its elegant shape could still be discerned.

"I wonder what it was used for?"

"Probably something in the cottage…but who knows where it came from, really? It could have come from the chateau for all we know."

I tried to imagine the lock that went with the key and also the door, and the house and the village that surrounded it back then.

"Wow," I said. "A mystery. I love mysteries."

"Would you like me to take it home and polish it up for you?" Auguste asked.

I handed it back to him. "Do you know how to do that?"

Auguste nodded. "I like doing things like that."

"Why don't you keep it?" I said. I loved it but I knew from what Hugo said that Auguste's life hadn't been very cheerful since his heart attack. If the key gave him any joy then…

He tucked it in the back pocket of his light blue work trousers. "We'll see," he said. "I love working on old things. I don't know why, but it makes me happy."

I looked around me at the cottage that was currently in complete shambles. "I'm the same," I said. "Though at times like this I sometimes forget."

I had found balloons and almost exploded my lungs trying to blow them up. We tied them outside on the fence and on the back of Camille's chair at the monastery table.

The chocolate cake was baked and iced in shocking pink icing. I had entrusted Charlotte with decorating the top with M&M's and she had encrusted the cake with the candies like a fancy watch encrusted with diamonds.

Camille was decked out in a black velvet dress, white stockings, black patent shoes and a purple princess dress she received for her birthday pulled over the whole ensemble. She held a wand in her hand; to welcome or hex her guests, I couldn't be sure.

It was a Wednesday. There was never any school for the smaller children on Wednesdays, this was the daywhen things like extra-curricular activities and birthday parties were planned.

Unfortunately Franck couldn't be present for the occasion as the positioning of the metal bar to support the now pierced wall to the bathroom was being installed at the cottage. This was a delicate maneuver that required much supervision from Franck and Luc. Franck tried to hide his relief that he had a "get out of jail free" pass for Camille's birthday party but he wasn't doing a very good job.

"*Bonne chance!*" he waved a cheery good-bye and hustled out the door after lunch.

As for me, I was starting to have serious doubts about my wisdom of inviting the children for a full three hours. My logic had been that most of the parents were coming from the other side of Beaune. I didn't feel it was fair to have them drive a quarter of an hour just to go home and head back here an hour and a half later. Still, that meant I was going to have to fill three hours. I planned some crafts and printed out a stack of coloring pages, but it was raining outside and I was suddenly aware that our house was very small.

Somebody rang on the doorbell. It had never worked and made an odd metallic scraping sound, but Camille heard it even from her bedroom.

"They're here! They're here!" she shouted. She raced to the door, followed by Charlotte who I noticed had changed into a full pink princess ensemble that she insisted on bringing from Canada.

The mother at the door looked harassed and was frantically pushing buttons on her cell phone. "I had such a hard time finding you," she said. "Why do you live all the way up here? I can't even get a signal for my cell phone!"

"We're less than ten minutes from Beaune," I reminded her. Villers-la-Faye was hardly the wilds of the Yukon.

She blew air out of her lips in exasperation. "Anyway, I could never live in one of these villages. They're so depressing."

I knew that this woman and her daughter lived across the very busy street from the school in Beaune. I would find *that* depressing instead of the rolling vineyards, but I was too Canadian to say it out loud.

She gave a cursory glance inside the house which, granted, did not look particularly appealing, especially not in its pre-renovation state. I could pretty much tell it confirmed her conclusions about the kinds of people who lived in "these villages".

Somebody else was coming up behind her, a chic man in a royal blue sweater, dark jeans and Italian loafers. He all but jettisoned his daughter in the house. "I'll be off Céline," he said, although she had already run off with Camille. "Some of my favorite winemakers are in Villers and I think I'm overdue for paying them a visit," he said to me. "What time did you say pick-up was again?"

"Five o'clock," I said, doubting that he would retain that tidbit of information by the time he got to his Mercedes parked outside.

The first women's attention was caught. "There are the winemakers here?" she asked. "Where?"

Céline's father laughed. "Everywhere! There are at least seven in this village alone."

"Are they any good?" I heard her asking as they walked back down the path together.

An hour later the children had run around the house countless times, screaming at the top of their lungs. They had tried on all of Charlotte and Camille's dress-up clothes, including the boys and fought over the three fairy wands in the dress-up box. I was asked repeatedly where all my furniture was and if there was the second floor of the house. They also told me my wallpaper was ugly. I knew it but still, the truth hurt.

My forehead started to break out in a sweat. "Time for cake!" I cried.

Charlotte and I ushered all the three year olds to the table and then scurried into the kitchen to light the candles in secret.

"Do you think she'll like it?" Charlotte asked, nervously proud of her decorating job.

"Of course," I assured her. Truth be told, the cake did look a bit odd but what three year old could resist an M&M encrusted cake?

Charlotte carried the cake and I helped as we all sang "*Joyeux Anniversaire*" to Camille. We proudly sat the cake down in front of Camille. She grinned and blew out the candles.

"Now. Who would like a piece?" I asked, picking up my knife.

"*Moi!*" Camille said, but then there was silence.

"*Ce n'est pas très joli,*" observed a blond girl dressed in Camille's gypsy outfit. Not pretty? Sure, the M&Ms were a little disorganized and maybe the color had run on a few of them from Charlotte licking her fingers but, come on, they were *M&Ms!* Besides, since when had three year olds become so picky? Sugar was sugar.

"I helped make the cake," Camille informed her friends. "It's delicious. You'll see."

At least half of the children around the table gave a Gallic shrug, doubtful of this assertion.

"You don't have to eat the M&Ms," I assured them. "Come on…who wants a piece?"

"*D'accord,*" conceded a little boy with a scattering of freckles over his nose. "I guess I'll try it."

I rolled my eyes and muttered in English. "How exceedingly *kind* of you."

I dished him up a large piece and set it in front of him, realizing I felt nervous, as though I was about to be judged by the food critics who awarded (and took away) the coveted Michelin stars from French restaurants.

He stared down at the cake, drawing his eyebrows together. We all watched as he poked at the crust of pink icing and M&Ms with his fork. "The icing is too thick. What were the M&Ms supposed to be?"

"What do you mean?"

"Weren't they were supposed to be a picture of something?"

"A rainbow!" Charlotte answered, affronted. "Can't you tell?"

The boy seemed momentarily cowed. Charlotte was two years older than him, after all, and fetching with her blond hair and blue eyes.

He screwed up his mouth, his French honesty battling with intimidation, but finally the truth burst out. "It doesn't look like any rainbow I've ever seen."

The blond headed girl beside him added, "Proper cakes aren't supposed to have rainbows on them."

Camille dug into her cake and ignored her friends.

"It's a special Canadian cake," I said, then asked my eldest pointedly, "Charlotte, do you want a piece?"

"Of course!" She declared. I was filled with incredible love for my girls. "I know Canadian cakes are delicious."

Charlotte took her plate with a big smile and sat down and, after casting a meaningful glance at all the three year olds around the table, dug in. "It's perfect. Soooooooooo delicious." She smacked her lips.

Thanks to Charlotte all of the children allowed me, some more willingly than others, to serve them a piece of cake and set it in front of them on their paper party plate.

Little spoons were picked up and the children began to delicately, eat wouldn't be the accurate word, but rather *"déguster"*, or "taste," my cake.

Nobody except for Charlotte and Camille seemed at all enthusiastic. Most only picked at their piece and almost all left the icing and M&M layer.

A young girl named Amélie pushed back her plate. "It's too sweet."

"Yes," said the freckle-faced boy. "It doesn't need to be so sweet. The chocolate flavor is overpowered."

I found myself blinking back tears as I took my rejected cake back into the kitchen.

When I came back, eager for the party to be over with, Charlotte had organized a game of spin the bottle for opening the presents. After that I bundled everyone up and took them to the *pétanque* court at the top of our street to play tag in the cold. When we returned home I checked my watch. Parents should start arriving soon to collect their miniature culinary critics.

I listened for a car or the grating of our broken doorbell for the next twenty minutes, but nothing. I had put the right pick-up time on the invitation, hadn't I?

The children were getting fractious and a few skirmishes broke out. Camille came into the living room sobbing that the freckle-faced boy had poked her Polly Pocket jackets down the grate in the bedroom floor.

"They'll all be leaving any minute," I said. "Maybe we should give everyone their treaty bags."

Camille agreed, her tears drying in an instant. She ran into the kitchen where we had put all the treat bags in a big metal bowl. She took it into the bedroom and began handing them out.

I could hear the yelps of enthusiasm crescendo.

Two little girls ran into the kitchen. "Are these presents for us?" they demanded, shaking the treat bags, which contained some Haribo candies, some stickers, and a bouncy ball, each.

"Yes. Don't you get treat bags at birthday parties in France?"

They shook their heads, and poked through their bags reverently.

"I guess it's a Canadian thing," I said.

"Like the cake?" the smaller girl asked.

"Like the cake."

She drew her eyebrows in, inspected the contents of her treat bag more closely, then said, "I guess all Canadian things aren't bad then."

The first parent arrived a full forty minutes late. She didn't even excuse herself, she just took her daughter's hand, made her daughter thank both Camille and me for the party, then left.

After that the parents dribbled in one by one, some with lame excuses of bad traffic and so many errands to do fresh on their lips, others blithely ignoring the fact that they were almost an hour late in picking their child up.

Finally there was only one small girl left, Céline, the one whose father had planned to visit some of his favorite local winemakers in the village.

I sat the three girls in front of the TV and slid in a DVD of Barbapapa. Franck and I called the animated TV show from his youth "children's Valium."

"Don't worry about your papa." I put a reassuring hand on the shoulder of the abandoned child.

"Oh, I'm not." she assured me, not even bothering to tear her eyes away from the screen. "He's always late."

Franck came home just then, dirty from the day at the cottage but triumphant that the metal beam had been placed above the opening between the new bathroom and the bedroom without the entire cottage falling down around our ears.

"How did the party go?" he asked.

"They insulted my cake."

Franck washed his hands and dried them on a dishtowel. "Ah.

Maybe I should have warned you about that.

"They are three! Who would have guessed they would be so discerning?"

"Laura. They are French."

"What they are is rude."

"Or honest. Depends on your perspective, Franck said. "Maybe we should just have bought a *galette*." Franck said, far too late to save me the humiliation I had suffered at the hands of Camille's friends. *Galettes* were the wonderful marzipan filled puffed pastry that appeared every year at the beginning of January to celebrate Epiphany and which were so delicious that they almost made one want to convert to Catholicism.

"Ya think!?" I filled that second word with every ounce of my exasperation at being abandoned with a cabal of three-year-old gastro-snobs.

There was a knock at the door. "That must be Celine's father," I said, parking my disgruntlement momentarily. "He's over an hour and a half late."

Before I could get to the door, however, it opened and in came the tradesmen for their evening *apéritif*. There was no sign of Céline's father.

I went back into the living room and looked at the girls, trying to figure out what best to do. It was a school day the next day.

"Do you know your phone number?" I asked Céline. "Maybe I could call your Daddy and Mommy in case they forgot to come and pick you up."

Céline examined my face as though looking for signs that I was mentally deficient. "I can't remember big numbers. I'm only three."

There was nothing else I could do except return to the kitchen where I helped Franck serve up kirs and baguette and little squares of Comté for the tradesmen, as well as chopped up slices of *jambon perseillé*. Just then there was another knock on the door.

"*Enfin!*" I couldn't help saying and went to open the door to find Céline's father leaning against the doorframe for support, looking considerably more disheveled than when he had dropped off his daughter.

"*Tiens!*" he said. "I had some wonderful tastings. It's hard to get me out of the cellar once I get down there. I knew Céline would be happy to play a little longer at your house."

Franck came beside me at the door. He stuck out his hand. "*Bonjour.* I'm Camille's father. Franck."

Céline's father shook his hand and nodded. "Jacques," he said, and then came in without being invited and peeked around the corner into the kitchen. "Is it the hour of *l'apéritif?*"

Franck raised a brow. "Would you like to join us?"

Surely good manners would dictate that Jacques refuse and hurry on home. He had been over two hours late to pick up his daughter, after all.

"*Bien sûr!*" he answered, instead.

I watched, stunned, as he sat down at an empty chair at the table and nodded in thanks as Franck poured him a *kir.*

Franck made the introductions and it was discovered that Luc had done work on the house of a friend of Jacques' in Aloxe Corton.

Jacques regaled the table with highlights of the wines he tasted when he was down in Villers-la-Faye's cellars.

"A Ladoix Premier Cru...*comme ça!*" He kissed his fingers with a loud smacking sound to indicate just how delectable was the wine. "As fine as any *Grand Cru*, let me tell you. Finer than many, in fact, but at a fraction of the price."

"Did you buy any?" Franck asked.

"Sixty bottles. The trunk of my car is scraping the road."

The conversation then veered to the *négotiants* in Beaune, many of the tradesmen were familiar with their wine and had worked on their various properties and didn't have much good to say about the wine they sold at highly inflated prices.

"Rich as Croeusus!" declared Hugo. "I cannot believe people are so stupid as to buy their *merde*."

"There are a few that know what they are doing," Jacques countered.

"*Ah bon?*" Hugo demanded. "Such as who?"

Thus began a rollicking argument to the mutual satisfaction of all the men.

I went back in the living room to check on the children. "Your father is just staying for a drink," I told Céline.

"I knew he would," she shrugged, sanguine.

It was not before nine o'clock at night that the kitchen party broke up. Jacques was not in any state to drive his shiny Mercedes home, so his new pal Hugo offered him a ride.

As I finally waved a long overdue *au revoir* to him and Céline, Jacques smiled up at me.

"What a wonderful afternoon in Villers!" he said. "I really need to get up here more often. One would think it was an hour away from Beaune instead of ten minutes."

"Seven minutes," Franck said. "When I'm driving, at least."

"We named her after your favorite singer," Jacques called back to me as his daughter took his hand and began to lead him down the path towards Hugo's van.

"What?" I said, confused.

"My daughter. Céline. My wife and I named her after Céline Dion."

"*My* favorite singer?"

"All Canadians love Céline Dion, *n'est-ce pas?*"

"Not exactly."

He guffawed. "Of course they do! *Bonne nuit et merci!*"

CHAPTER 22

The third weekend in January was marked on everyone's calendar in Burgundy. While the vineyards lay quietly slumbering under the winter snow, the winemakers actually had some spare time to celebrate. Luckily, January 22nd was also the day in the Catholic Calendar when Saint Vincent, the patron Saint of winemakers, was feted. The Saint Vincent Festival happened on the third weekend of January every year in Burgundy and was one of the most important fixtures of the winemaking year. It was a weekend of partying, to celebrate wine and winemakers, to give thanks to Saint Vincent for the year's harvest, and to pray for delectable grapes in the year to come.

Every year in Burgundy, a different town or village was chosen to host the Saint Vincent celebration. This year it was in Beaune itself, which was a big deal. The town was the epicenter of winemaking in Burgundy. It was bound to put on an amazing party. Franck and I had been looking forward to going to the Saint Vincent festival since we had contemplated moving back to Burgundy.

All of the Saint Vincents I had attended in my life had been joyous, but frigid affairs. In Burgundy, the third weekend in January invariably coincided with the coldest snap of the year.

On Saturday morning we roused the girls before six o'clock so we could watch the procession of the Saint Vincent statues from each winemaking village be carried through Beaune's vineyards before finishing at Notre Dame.

"Why are we going so early?" Charlotte asked when I roused her out of a deep sleep. "I'm tired."

"It's to see all the saints."

Her eyes widened. "Real saints?"

"No. Wooden statues of saints actually, but they are beautiful and most of them are hundreds of years old."

Charlotte didn't bother hiding her disappointment.

I knew from past experience that the procession was one of the most picturesque French experiences imaginable and it was the type of photo opportunity that didn't come along very often. We were in desperate need to redo our website and add new photos, but we needed to *take* actual photos in order to do so. At the moment the cottage wasn't exactly the stuff of inspiring images.

"This sounds boring," declared Charlotte. "A bunch of saint statues? What's the point?"

"The point is Mommy and Daddy want to go," I said, zipping up her jacket. "Don't get all existential on me."

"I'll buy us all *pain au chocolats* on the way there," Franck added as we hustled the girls out to the car. There was a sudden upswing in enthusiasm.

We pulled up to a spot in the vineyards outside Beaune where we knew the procession would be arriving. As promised, we stopped in Ladoix -Serrigny to pick up the *pain aux chocolats*. They were hot out of the oven and the chocolate was still melted inside. Franck had also bought a *pain aux raisins* for each of us as, in his opinion, cold weather was best counter-acted by lots of warm pastries.

I passed the girls the bottles of Evian I had in the front seat and had them take a sip. "I should have brought a thermos of hot chocolate instead," I whispered to Franck.

"Now what do we do?" Camille asked, passing the bottle back to me.

"We wait," Franck said. "Do you want to get out of the car?"

"Yes!" Both girls leapt out into the frozen vineyards.

"I guess we're getting out of the car," I said to Franck, even though I would have voted for staying put as long as the remnant heating felt warmer than the outside.

By the time I got out, Camille and Charlotte had broken branches off the vines closest to the car, faced off and began to fence.

"Wait," said Charlotte. "Mine isn't long enough." She went to snap off another, longer section of vine. A few of the spectators clustered around watched her, aghast. Children were generally adored in France, but not when they were breaking off grape vines.

I grabbed her arm just in time. "Charlotte, you cannot break the vines," I hissed in English.

"They're just branches." Her blue eyes peered up at me. "Why not?"

"There not just branches," I continued in English. "They're precious. These are the vines that the grapes will grow on when it gets warmer." I looked up at where we were standing. This area was *prémier cru* for sure. "If you take them off, the grapes won't grow."

"Oh," she said, studying the bare branches. "I didn't realize." Her eyes filled with tears of regret.

Camille jumped closer to us. "I can't feel my toes."

The sharp, penetrating cold had made my toes go numb as well. I started to hop around a little bit to keep myself warm. I looked down at the girls.

"Maybe this wasn't such a good idea," I said to Franck, who was preparing his camera for the arrival of the saints.

We waited for what seemed like a very long time until both girls had begun fighting, because what else do you do when you are cold and bored and under six? Why couldn't this thing run on time? I wondered.

Charlotte was almost five yet I still found myself forgetting how often something fun for adults is absolute misery for children. Franck and I had celebrated several Saint Vincent Festivals pre-children and although it had always been bitterly cold that had never somehow gotten in the way of our enjoyment. We had even covered the story one year as journalists for "France Magazine" when the celebration was held in Chablis on an absolutely frigid morning. We spent hours taking photographs as the sun was coming up. It was nothing a few glasses of red wine and a few hot espressos couldn't fix. Things were more complicated with children. Why did I always forget that?

Franck glanced down. "If they don't come soon we'll go find a warm café in Beaune."

Just then the sound of trumpets and music faintly flowed over to us from further down the vineyards. I leaned forward and caught a glimpse of two men holding the first saint in the procession on their shoulders. Each winemaking village had a carved saint, which was carried on a wooden platform supported on the shoulders of two winemakers from each village.

"Look for Villers-la-Faye!" I said to the girls.

"And Magny-les-Villers!" Camille added. "We have two villages, don't we?"

"There's a problem though," Charlotte said.

"What's that?"

"Neither Camille nor I know how to read yet."

"Well, *Papa* and I will pay attention and we'll show you."

The girls agreed, but only lasted about ten saints before they started complaining about the cold again.

"I'm freezing!" Camille said.

"This is boring," Charlotte concluded. "I want to go home."

"Don't you see how beautiful this is?" I demanded. "How special…"

I shut up, taking a moment to think about how I would have liked this when I was three or five. Not much. The austere beauty and solemnity of the scene would have been lost on me too. Also, it was blood-curdlingly cold.

"If I remember correctly, it's more or less in alphabetical order," Franck whispered to me. "Do you think they can hold out for Magny?"

Camille declared. "I cannot stand another second!"

My feet had gone numb too. I stomped them on the hard ground. I studied the next statue to pass by. "Comblanchien…Corgoloin…" We were only at the C's. There was no way we would make it to M.

"I don't remember them walking this slowly," I said to Franck.

"Let's go." He made an executive decision, and picked up a screeching Camille who accused Charlotte of tromping on her foot and took Charlotte by the hand. "Who would like a hot chocolate?"

In the end, pretty much all we saw of the festival in Beaune that day was the inside of a café and the stand selling *escargots* on the Place Carnot. The girls polished off a solid dozen each before nine o'clock in the morning and then requested multiple rides on the Merry-Go-

Round before Franck and I both decided to call it a day.

We sat in the kitchen after the girls picked at their *jambon blanc* and *puree* then left us with the dishes.

"That was a bust." I sliced away at a block of Morbier that Martial had dropped off at our house a few days before. "We didn't get any photos we can use."

"Not true," said Franck. "We have lots of photos of the merry-go-round."

I sighed.

I had gotten so used to standing at the doors of the girls' school by myself that somewhere along the way, I stopped trying to make eye contact with the other parents.

Instead I developed an aloof stance that I hoped showed I was just fine without them. It made me feel like I was back in grade four, but I had my pride.

It took me several days to notice that another woman I had never seen before was also standing at the door of Saint Coeur, not really talking to anyone. She pushed a baby stroller with what looked like a chubby cheeked specimen inside. She kept smiling at me, but I had become so unused to the experience that for many days I assumed she thought I was somebody else, someone she already knew, or that perhaps she was smiling at someone behind me.

Finally one day in mid-February it dawned on me that she was smiling at *me*.

I took a deep breath and went over to where she was standing.

"*Bonjour*," I said and then bent over the lovely olive skinned baby in the stroller. "What's her name?"

"Capucine," the woman answered with a relieved look in her warm brown eyes.

"Oh I *love* that name. We almost named our youngest Capucine but we figured that nobody would know how to pronounce it properly. I'm from Canada, the English speaking side."

"What did you name your daughter?" the woman asked.

"Camille."

"We just moved here from Paris," the woman said. *"Je m'appelle Marie."*

"I'm Laura. We moved here in the summer from Canada."

"What brought you here?"

"We're working on renovating a vacation rental in *les Hautes-Côtes*. My husband is Burgundian."

"Mine too!" Marie said. "We've come down here because he is taking over the family wine Domaine in Volnay."

Just then *La Dragonne* opened the doors and shot Marie and I dirty looks for some unfathomable reason. Like naughty schoolgirls, we caught each other's eye and laughed.

"I have to run and pick up the kids to take them to Volnay after school," Marie said. "But I'll look for you tomorrow."

"I'll look for you too," I said. Could it be that I might actually make a friend?"

When I picked up the girls Charlotte was looking rather pale, even for February. I felt her forehead and I didn't need a thermometer to know that she had a fever.

"Let's get you home," I said. "I'll give you some medicine."

"I just want to go to bed," Charlotte said.

That was never something you wanted to hear from your five year old.

"Lots of kids in my class are sick," Camille said. "Jean-Baptiste threw up on the slide during recess."

"Wonderful." I hustled them to my double-parked car. Might Jean-Baptiste's exploit usurp the notoriety of Camille's *cantine* barf, which was still referred to in reverential tones in the schoolyard?

By the time we made it back up to Villers, Charlotte had fallen asleep. She was burning up with fever by the time I got her out of the car and carried her into the house. How I would have loved to be in a house where I could give her a big warm bubble bath while I waited for her medication to kick in. Everything about our house was just so rudimentary. We were cold most of the time and had no hot water to warm us up. The kitchen was dark and impractical. Most days I had grown inured, but when I wanted to make my sick little chick comfy and cozy in a little nest, it struck me how very un-nest-like our house was.

I had to remind Luc about the bathroom, I thought, sooner rather than later.

The next week was spent in sick-child jail. Franck took Camille back and forth to school while I nursed Charlotte through sky-high fevers and a rattling cough at home.

I felt trapped. I didn't have any friends who could come and visit me and even if I did, I couldn't in all good conscience expose them to this wicked virus. My days were spent writing emails that made potential guests dream about the perfection of life in France, minutes snatched in between the hours when Charlotte needed me. In stark contrast to the utopia I conjured up with my words, I wallowed in depression. The days were foggy and dark. One seemed to blur into the next with no definition separating one hour from another. I couldn't remember feeling so depleted. I felt like I had put in so much effort before Christmas. I was ready to see some rewards, but instead I was gifted with sick children and the equivalent of house arrest.

The day before I finally got Charlotte well enough to go back to school, Camille came into my bedroom in the morning, her face pale but her cheeks bright red. "*Maman*, my head hurts," she said. I felt her head. She was burning.

Here we were, back on the *manège* of winter viruses. Another week of sleepless nights and days cooped up in the house in miserable weather with a sick child. I was becoming too disenchanted to even bother looking for my *petit bonheur du jour*. But what could I do to make things different? Nothing.

"Just wait here a second." I bent down and gave her soft forehead a kiss. "I'm going to get the thermometer."

The next morning, after finally getting Camille's fever down and having tucked her back into bed, Franck came swinging in the door. He threw me the keys.

"You have to go to the cottage now," he said.

"Why? I was just going to sit down with a magazine and…"

"You know how I was talking to you about sound proofing and how we needed it?"

"Yes."

Franck had tried to convince Luc and me that we needed to pay the extra money to have efficient soundproofing put all along the stone wall the cottage shared with the next-door neighbors. It added a significant cost to the budget that I wasn't sure we could afford, and both Luc and I felt that a stone wall that was nearly a meter thick was more than sufficient to prevent the neighbors' noises from disturbing our guests and vice versa.

"The neighbors are fighting. I want you to go over and listen for yourself."

"They've probably stopped by now."

"Given how it sounded when I left, I doubt it."

I put my boots on. At least it would get me out of the house.

The day was again encapsulated in fog, making things so dark that at times it looked like a kind of permanent dusk. The whole countryside felt like it was hibernating like the vineyards. Still, I took a deep breath of frigid, humid air. The winemakers loved the fog because it kept temperatures stable and cool which protected the precious vines

I roared past Jacky's bistro where a few ample bellied, beret topped gentleman were sauntering out the door, then past the church and down in front of the *boulangerie*. I parked there, as I couldn't get near the cottage with all of the tradesmen's white *camionettes*. I walked in and took a moment to look around. I hadn't visited for ten days due to my stint as Florence Nightingale and things had progressed nicely, thanks in large part to Franck charming the tradesmen and pouring copious quantities of wine down their throats.

We actually had a floor. I stamped my boots in satisfaction. For the moment it was merely poured concrete, but it was level and no longer dirt.

Luc appeared in the main room. He jerked his head towards the bedroom. "The show's in here." I followed him.

"I don't hear any..."

Luc held up his hand. "Wait."

"I don't care what you think of him!" The voice was strident and sounded as though it was in the bedroom with us.

"You can just leave then!" A male voice - deep and furious - answered. "Bonne chance finding the money to pay rent and gas for your car, not to mention your cigarettes!"

He too sounded as though he was here beside us, yelling. I didn't like the feeling of eavesdropping, although was it technically eavesdropping when you couldn't *not* hear an argument, short of inserting a pair of earplugs?

Auguste sidled in the room and raised his bushy eyebrows in question.

"But I love him!" The girl's voice was desperate now.

Auguste pursed his lips and shook his head. "Ah, *l'amour*," he murmured. "So cruel."

"Your little asshole on his *mobilette*?" A woman's voice now. "I don't see what there is to fall in love with there."

"She should know better," Auguste continued his running commentary. "When it comes to love, logic is a foreign country."

"Maybe we should stop listening," I said. Luc and Auguste looked equally askance at my suggestion.

"Are you joking?" Auguste said. "This is ten times better than *les Feux de l'Amour*."

"I think it's almost over," Luc said. "I remember identical fights between my parents and my sister."

"You'll never understand!" came through the wall, accompanied by a gusty sob and then some thundering footsteps, followed by a slammed door. We ran into the main room and peered out the dusty window. The neighbor's daughter leapt into her rusty Renault and sped off towards the church.

I turned to Luc. "I hereby officially change my vote on the soundproofing."

He winked at me. "I'm on it."

Camille was sick for anotherweek and the day I could finally drive both of them to school in the morning I felt like I had been released from prison. It was a welcome sight to see Marie in the courtyard of the preschool after I had dropped off the girls, smiling as though she was happy to see me.

"I haven't seen you in ages," she called over to me.

It was so nice to think that there was actually someone besides the girls' teachers who noticed that Franck had been doing all the pick ups and drop offs for the past two weeks.

She leaned in to give me *les bises*, which made me feel like I actually had a friend.

"Charlotte was sick with the flu and then the day she got better Camille caught it."

"Ah!" she said, and her rueful nod let me know that she was well acquainted with the marathon of sick children. "Mine had colds and ear infections, but no flu, thank God."

"How many children do you have?" I asked.

"Three," she said. "Eloi is in *moyenne section*, Alix is in *petit section*, and Capucine will be one in March."

"Charlotte is in *moyenne section* too!" We chatted on. Unfortunately we discovered that Charlotte and Eloi were in different classes even though they were in the same grade, and Camille because she was born after December 31st was a grade below Alix who was born only two months earlier in November.

We walked slowly up towards the wooden door, chatting all the way. When we got there we realized that *La Dragonne* had shut and locked the doors, locking us inside the school.

"*Zut!*" Marie said. "What do we do now?"

"The woman who guards the door? She's awful," I said. "I went here to school for one year when I was eighteen and she hated me then and she still hates me now. We'll have to be buzzed out the front way."

We walked through the courtyard of the elementary and high

school, which looked just the same as when I had gone to Saint Coeur.

"I have to take Capucine to the doctor now to get her ear checked," Marie said. "But would you like to drop by for coffee after drop-off at lunch?"

After my two weeks of enforced seclusion I really needed to be at the cottage and answer a bunch of questions. Still, this was the type of invitation I had been waiting months for.

"I'd love to," I said.

Franck was waiting for me when I got home from dropping the girls off. "Did you come to take me to the cottage?" I asked.

"Eventually," he said, and came over and grabbed me. "We've had a sick child in our bed for the past two weeks."

"We have," I agreed.

"I thought maybe we could enjoy a little time just the two of us before we go over to the cottage."

"A lot of time?" I asked, hopeful.

"Five minutes?"

"Fifteen?"

"Deal."

The rest of my morning was spent exploring the new "bathroom" area made out of the chicken coop. Hugo was still inordinately proud of the steel beam he placed above the hole in the wall and I spent a good five minutes exclaiming over his masonry prowess. For the moment, the floor was still dirt but I could see the beginnings of a functional little space.

"I don't know…" Franck said, standing in the middle of the room where the roof sloped steeply down towards the back wall. "Do you think we have enough ceiling height?"

While I was home with sick children, the plumbers arrived to lay their pipes. One of them was about 6'6" I guessed, unusually tall for any man, let alone a Frenchman.

"Do you mind coming here and helping us for a moment?" I beckoned him from the bedroom.

He was bright red by the time he joined us in the bathroom. I hadn't realized he was so shy.

"Would you mind standing in the corner there?" I asked. "We're trying to figure out if the ceiling height is high enough to install a shower."

He shuffled over to the spot.

"Do you have enough room to have a shower in there?" I asked.

"I take baths," he said. How could he possibly fit in a French bath? I wondered.

"Well, if you were taking a shower there would you have enough room?"

"*Oui.*" He nodded.

"Could you pretend to wash your hair?" I asked.

The plumber shot a questioning look at Franck

"It's to see if you have enough room to lift your arms over your head...you know..." Franck mimicked the action. "I would do it but I'm only five foot ten and those North Americans can come big."

"*D'accord,*" he said, and self-consciously raised his arms and made a scrubbing motion on his head.

"You see?" I said to Franck and Luc. "It's fine. *Merci,*" I said to the plumber. "That was a huge help." He grinned shyly and mumbled something about having to hurry back and attend to the radiator.

After that I ran down to pick up the girls for lunch, and fed them and Franck. Just when I was about to take them back down to Beaune and head for my café with Marie, the next-door neighbor to the cottage arrived on our doorstep. I almost couldn't look her in the eye after overhearing their family spat the other day.

"*Bonjour,*" she gave both of us a preemptory kiss and then put her hands on her hips. "You'll have to get rid of it."

"What?" Franck asked.

"The snake," she said. "I've been seeing a nasty big *colouvre* slithering around your roof but I came out this morning and he was in my courtyard. I screamed and ran back inside the house and by the time my husband got outside it had already climbed the wall and was going back into your eaves. We figure that is where it must live. It's *your* snake."

I had never seen a snake at the cottage. "It's not like it's a pet or anything..."

"You'll just have to get rid of it," she asserted.

"I've never seen it," Franck said, mystified.

"Trust me, it's there," she said. "Haven't the roofers mentioned anything?"

Franck shook his head. "*Non.*"

"It's massive." She held out her hands to illustrate a snake that was about three feet in length. "Fat too. I don't know what it eats but it's well fed, that's for sure."

I couldn't believe this was happening again. At *La Maison des Deux Clochers* we'd had a nest of baby *coulouvres* – a lazy but rather large species of snake common in Burgundian villages - in the cellar. Before they disappeared, there had been talk of me putting my hand in the pipe to see if I could get rid of them.

"I'll talk to the roofers as soon as I go back to the house and make sure we look for it."

"And you'll get rid of it if you find it?" she demanded.

"Of course," I said.

On that promise, she took her departure and I realized I was already woefully late for getting the girls back to school. Also, for my coffee with Marie.

"I've got to run," I said to Franck, and he grabbed me and planted a firm kiss on my mouth that I returned.

"Maybe it's a ghost snake?" I said, hopefully.

"Dare to dream," he said. "I love you."

CHAPTER 23

I was late getting to school to drop off the girls, so Marie must have already dropped off her crew and headed back to her house where I was to meet her.

She wasn't lying when she said she lived close to the school, I discovered. I turned left from the parking lot and her home was only three houses up from that.

I suddenly felt nervous. Would we have anything in common to talk about? Would she find my sheer Canadian-ness off-putting like so many other people who were more than happy to just keep me as a slight acquaintance?

My car tires crunched on the pea gravel that was strewn all around the front of her house. I was happy to see several weeds sprouting up from between the pebbles. I distrusted anyone with children who lived in an impeccable home.

Everything was quiet. Capucine was perhaps down for a nap, but where was Marie?

One of those moments of uncertainty washed over me that I experienced often since moving to France. Had I misunderstood her invitation? Had I gotten the time or date wrong?

I crept up the stairs to the door. If she wasn't here or busy doing something else I would sneak away and we could go on just being slight acquaintances who chatted by the school door. I swallowed back disappointment. I wanted a friend so badly and Marie seemed so nice.

There was a large set of French doors to the right of the door and I peeked inside.

Marie was sitting on the couch, an espresso cup balanced in one hand, a piece of chocolate in the other and a book balanced on her lap. She was smiling to herself.

In that instant I knew we were going to get along like a house on fire.

I knocked on the window and waved. She jumped up a little bit, laughed at herself, and motioned that she was going to come and open the door.

"*Te voilà!*" she gave me another warm bises. "I'm so glad you're here. Coffee?"

"Yes please."

"Chocolate?"

"Of course."

I followed her into her messy, cramped kitchen. The remains of lunch dishes were still sitting in the sink. Oh yes, we were going to be great friends.

She laughed – she had a lovely, warm laugh. "You caught me in the middle of my daily indulgence. Coffee and chocolate and a book! It's so lovely just to actually be able to *sit down*."

I accepted a cup of coffee and followed her back to the living room, which, although not exactly tidy, was warm and welcoming and decorated in cheery shades of yellow and red.

"Now we can finally talk!" she cut to the chase. "Don't you find *les beaunoises* unfriendly?"

And we were off, talking as though we had our whole lives to catch up on. We talked after Capucine woke up and the rest of the afternoon until it was time to walk back over to the school to pick up the children. I made a wonderful friend. That counted for something bigger than *un petit bonheur du jour*. It was amazing how things could turn on their axis in such a short space of time.

When I drove the girls home, I noticed with surprise that the spring warmth and sun of the past three days coaxed out the bright green leaves in the vineyards. Was the winter truly behind us? I changed gears up and down the hills past Pernand-Vergelesses and up into Magny-les-Villers, feeling like a racecar driver. It was difficult to believe that only a few months ago, I struggled with learning to drive standard. Maybe you could teach an old dog new tricks after all. I'd have to remember to take a detour by the lingerie stores next time I was in Beaune and show off to Cyril.

Luc had a couple of weeks downtime while the electricians and plumbers did their jobs at the cottage before he could start installing the beautiful new drywall.

He arrived at our house one morning before Franck or I had left.

"So, have you picked those tiles for your bathroom here yet?" He accepted his espresso with a nod of thanks. "I can start tomorrow if you want."

"Tomorrow? My youngest sister is arriving from California tomorrow to stay for two weeks."

"I wish I could have given you more warning. It's just that things at the cottage have been hard to predict..."

I snorted. That was the understatement of the year.

"It was just yesterday that I realized that I'm going to have a short window of time."

I thought about our aubergine bathtub with hardly any hot water and the aubergine and avocado toilet, and made up my mind. "Tomorrow's fine. I'll go and pick up the tiles this afternoon if you tell me how much I need."

"So I can start demolition today?" Luc said, eager.

"Sure. Knock yourself out."

He sucked back the rest of his espresso. "I'll just go and get some tools out of my *camionette* and then I'll be right back."

I wanted that bathroom done, of course, but the timing could have been a lot better. There was an extra toilet downstairs, but it was in a little room that had an accordion door that had never shut properly. Spiders appeared to like the dankness of the spot. I had never been bothered by spiders, but I knew Jayne had a fear of them verging on the pathological. It was not ideal, but Luc had, in his own understated way, made it clear. If I wanted a new, improved bathroom it was now or never. Well, maybe not never, but not until the cottage was finished, in any case. Besides, when was the timing for renovations ever perfect?

I left for Beaune to pick up my tiles – plain matte white - and by the time I came back home with the girls from school I was greeted by the sight of our aubergine and avocado bathtub, sink, and toilet on our front lawn.

"*Chouette!*" Charlotte and Camille dropped their school bags and ran over to begin to play on them. Competition involving who got to sit on the toilet was fierce.

Luc came outside, covered in dust although it was red this time instead of his usual white.

"*Dis-donc,*" I observed. "That was fast."

"Hugo had two guys at the house he didn't need today so I brought them over here. One of them just had a fight with his girlfriend and was very upset. All I needed to do was put a sledgehammer in his hand and stand back."

"Where are they now?" I asked.

"At Jacky's. Hugo's guy was crying by the end when Auguste came to check up on him. It was cathartic, but I think Auguste wanted to calm him down and talk things over a bit more before he tried to drive home."

"Come." He crooked his finger at me to follow him. We went to where the doors to the bathroom and the WC used to be. Both had been removed and the brick wall dividing the room into that awkward "L" shape was no longer there. Sun poured in the open window, fighting to penetrate the thick red dust in the air. I coughed.

"It's a huge improvement," I said, patting Luc's shoulder in thanks and then, gasping for breath, headed straight outside again so that I could breathe.

"I'll tarp it up now," Luc said. "I didn't have time to do that before Hugo's guy started ripping stuff out. He was on such a roll I didn't have the heart to stop him. You may have to vacuum the house a bit before your sister comes tomorrow. *Mes excuses.*"

"Right," I said, peering back inside the doorway where the late afternoon sun lit up the air inside to an ochre colour. I would be vacuuming more than a bit. "Maybe I'll wait for the dust to settle a bit first."

"Wise idea," Luc bestowed one of his warm smiles and ground out his cigarette with his heel. "Back to work for me."

I didn't want to go back inside right away so I sat on the veranda and watched as Charlotte and Camille pretended that the toilet on the lawn was the throne of a fairy universe. They played completely in French now. I wasn't certain exactly when it had happened, but now they almost never switched back to English because they couldn't find the right word in French.

A few months ago, Camille was barely speaking at all and now French was, I realized, going to be more or less her mother tongue. My earliest memories came from around her age, between three and four. If it were the same for her, her earliest memories would be of here, of Burgundy. I wondered where their lives would take them. On lots of adventures, I hoped, big and small. I hoped that thanks to this time spent here, even though reality was a far cry from the daydreams I had conjured up before moving, France would become a touchstone for them, a place where their souls felt at home, as mine did.

The sun was still warm even though it was past six o'clock. Everything felt like it was bursting into blossom at once. Compared to the past months of work at the cottage redoing masonry and plumbing when no headway was visible to my uneducated eye, things were now visibly progressing by leaps and bounds. The vineyards I could see from our front porch were doing the same. After the quiet winter weeks of seeking nourishment from the soil deep below, they had burst into a riot of the brightest imaginable green.

The walls would soon be dry walled by Luc, and after that came the part I truly loved. The paint, the fixtures, the furniture, the final decorative touches...

The tradesmen still told us every day that it was impossible to have the place ready for our first guests to arrive July 12th, and we told them every day that it had to be. Still, this was now said without much ire on either side. It was simply an acknowledgement of polarized opinions. Of course it was impossible. Franck's and my projects always were...until they weren't.

There was no time to contact Jayne and warn her of our strange bathroom situation. She was already *en route*. I did vacuum the house even though fifteen minutes after the task was accomplished, yet another fine coat of red dust had settled on everything once again. Franck and I set up an inflatable mattress in the living room and adorned it with the best set of cast-off sheets we had from Michèle and André. I even tidied up a bit, although our house was such a work-in-progress that it was difficult to really tell the difference.

I was trying to jam the girls' clothes into their four tiny dresser drawers when Luc came in the room. "You don't have any closets in this house," he observed. "That's what it's like in all the old houses here. People used to only have two sets of clothes, one for the week and one for Sundays".

I tried to push the drawer shut, but the clothes refused to be contained and kept popping out. "Maybe I should try that with Charlotte and Camille," I said. "It has to be better than this."

"I've been thinking," Luc said.

I stopped my futile attempts at making everything fit and paid attention.

"Thinking about closets?" I asked, hopeful.

"Yes." He beckoned me outside the girls' bedroom door. "You see how this hallway is much longer than it needs to be?" He waved at the four feet of wasted space at the end of it that just finished with a wall.

"I always found that strange."

"I think I could build a new wall here." Luc drew an imaginary line in the air with his hand. "And then split the empty hall space in two giving a closet to both your bedroom and the girls' bedroom."

I stared at the space, enthralled with Luc's vision. A closet in each of our bedrooms? What had once seemed impossible now appeared to be the ultimate luxury.

"What a fantastic idea," I began. "When can you…"

"Luc!" Franck rushed into the house. "I need your help. Can you come to the cottage with me?"

"What's wrong?" Luc and I both asked at the same time.

"Momo didn't send Tin-Tin for the electrical like he had promised. He sent some other guy and while I don't know much about electrical work, I do know enough to suspect this guy has no idea what he's doing."

"Let me just put the last strip of tape on to seal up the bathroom and I'll come." Luc said. "Laura just vacuumed."

Franck turned to me. "The girls are fighting over the toilet outside…" he didn't finish the question.

I shrugged. How could I explain the allure of the lawn toilet game? Besides, my mind was on closets.

"Luc thinks he can make some closets for the bedrooms by cutting the hallway here." I began to show Franck but he appeared singularly disinterested. "Am I boring you?" I asked finally.

"I'm sorry." He reached out and grabbed my hand. "I'm just really worried about this electrician Momo has sent. He not only appears drunk, but incompetent."

"We can talk about the closets later." I squeezed back. "*Vas-y.*"

Franck and Luc didn't come back. I went down to Beaune to pick up Charlotte and Camille from school and then to the train station to pick up Jayne from the TGV coming from Paris.

Jayne was eight years younger than me. But around the time she had moved in with her boyfriend and had been accepted at Berkeley for a Masters in Epidemiology, I realized that she was no longer a kid. Jayne had been to Burgundy a few times before, but this was her first visit when we were actually *living* here. I wanted to wow her, of course, but looking around at the disaster of our house, I just didn't see how that was possible. I definitely would not be able to pull off the role of the big sister who had her life together.

Jayne was waiting for us on the train platform and after we hugged tears pricked my eyes at seeing her familiar face.

"I just have to warn you," I said as soon as I loaded her suitcases in the trunk. "Our bathroom on the main floor has been ripped out. It happened suddenly."

"Your bathroom got ripped out suddenly?" Jayne asked, still groggy from her flight, or maybe just confused.

"Yes…you see…" I finally waved my hand. "Long story. Anyway, there's a toilet downstairs and a kind of makeshift shower but it's pretty rough."

"I'm sure it will be fine," said Jayne, in a tone that didn't reflect the certainty of her words.

I hadn't wanted a little sister one bit when my parents had summoned my older sister Suzanne and me to the living room to announce my mother was pregnant. I had fervently hoped that my parents' news involved a new dog or, if not that, a piano. I had long accepted that I was the youngest of our family and did not take kindly to having my position usurped. Add to this the fact that as soon as Jayne was born Suzanne became more or less her second mother and I lost my playmate, and I was seriously disgruntled with my position as the middle child – and I hadn't even been consulted! I was so indignant that when she was about three years old I brandished a couple of old report cards of Suzanne's and convinced Jayne that she had been adopted and they were her adoption papers. I was not proud, but there it is.

Jayne wasn't quick enough to hide the horrified expression on her face when I pulled up in the driveway of our house on *la route des chaumes*. The girls leapt out of the car.

"Do you see Auntie Jayne?" Charlotte asked in what I was startled to discover was rather French-accented English. "We have a toilet to play with on our front lawn. Aren't we lucky?"

Jayne's eyes were round. "Wow!" she said to the girls, then slid me a look. "Just…wow."

"It's a work in progress." I nodded towards the house. It was true that it didn't exactly look welcoming. At this point I was certain that Jayne was regretting her decision to leave San Francisco to spend her two weeks of vacation with us.

"Glamorous, isn't it?" I beckoned her inside to give her the grand tour. This didn't take long and was notable mainly for the taped off bathroom and the new layer of red dust everywhere.

I could tell from the stricken look on her face that emergency measures were required. The girls were still busy playing with the bathroom fixtures on the front lawn again. Honestly why bother with stuffies and baby dolls when kids could be happy with an old toilet?

"Do you want some wine?" I asked.

"Yes," Jayne answered immediately, looking pale.

I fetched my secret weapon, a bottle of Côte de Nuits white from the Domaine Glantenet in Magny-les-Villers which I'd popped in the fridge after lunch. Things always looked better through the glow of one of our delicious local chardonnays.

"Go sit outside on the deck," I waved her outside where luckily it was sunny and warm. "I've already taken the chairs out there. I'll bring this out. Relax."

As I cut up the saucisson and comté and baguette I wondered at the fact that Franck and Luc hadn't come back yet.

I took the bottle and glasses outside to the green plastic table we bought for the veranda and poured a glass for Jayne. Once I had fetched everything from the kitchen, I poured myself a glass and sat down beside her.

I took a sip. "Ah," I said and sat back in my chair.

Jayne took a sip. And then another. And then another. "This is amazing wine."

It was. Crisp and mineral, as well as being perfectly balanced on my tongue. Domaine Glantenet, one of our many winemaking neighbors in Magny-les-Villers, made sublime whites.

Jayne picked up a *rondelle* of dried sausage and a piece of baguette and chewed them thoughtfully. All of a sudden she looked more reconciled with her vacation plans.

The sun beat down on us, warming our skin and making the chilled wine even more extraordinary. The church bells chimed six o'clock and the bells in Magny answered shortly after. A vineyard tractor rumbled up to the vineyards on *Les Chaumes*.

"I guess it will be interesting to see a work-in-progress." Jayne kicked off her shoes and lifted her feet up on the nearest chair. I refilled her glass.

Franck and Luc didn't come back for another hour. When they did, they sported matching expressions that made me wonder if they hadn't been over at the cottage sucking lemons for the past few hours.

Jayne and I were still out on the veranda, in an attempt to habituate Jayne to the pace of life in Burgundy and to try and distract her from the disaster zone we currently lived in.

The girls came and shared in some of the cheese and *charcuterie*, then took their dolls to play in the outside bathroom so I hadn't seen any reason to hurry things along.

"What happened?" I asked, peering up at Luc through squinted eyes. The sun was still warm and bright.

"He did it all wrong," Luc told me as Franck went inside to get more glasses and a fresh bottle. I quickly introduced Luc and Jayne. One could never forget basic manners here and get away with it.

"He wired everything all wrong," Luc shook his head in disbelief. "I've never seen such a mess. It took me until now to undo it and then rewire everything properly again."

"What did he say when he saw you working on it?" Tradesmen tended to be proprietary about that sort of thing.

"He never came back to the cottage today. God knows where he is – probably in a ditch somewhere. Better off there though than wiring a house. I cannot begin to explain the dangerous mess he made in that fuse box."

"He's a drunk," Franck came back and didn't mince words. "Not the good kind."

"There's a good kind?" I asked.

"You know, like the guys who hang out at Jacky's all day long. They're happy and harmless," Franck said.

"This guy though…." Luc shook his head again. "Not only is he a mean drunk, but he's the kind that could be responsible for a house burning down."

I shifted my chair slightly to capture the last few rays of sun. "That bad?"

"That bad," Luc confirmed. He fidgeted much more than usual, incensed at such professional incompetence.

"I'm going to call Momo right now," Franck said, his brow tense. "I'll demand that he send someone else to us tomorrow. This is *ridicule*."

Jayne watched us, smiling beatifically through what I imagined was a glow of fine white wine. "Sounds complicated," she observed.

I had a strong urge to shelter her from the reality of the difficulties of our renovation project and indeed our move to France. It would be so much simpler if everything had spun out effortlessly like it had in my daydreams.

Instead, I sighed and picked up another round of *saucisson*. "You have no idea," I said and popped it in my mouth.

The next morning Jayne woke up with a green tinge to her complexion.

"Maybe too much wine," she said as she waved away my offer of a *café au lait*. "Or too much rich food. Something's just not sitting right in my stomach."

"I've got to run to the cottage," I said. "Do you want to come with me now or later?"

"Later." She put a hand over her stomach and grimaced. "It'll pass. I'm sure I'll feel better later."

I walked over to the cottage, past the *tilleul* trees on the *Place* that were bursting into leaf and past the few tradesmen and villagers trickling out of Jacky's bistro after their morning coffee or white wine.

I felt terrible I wasn't hosting Jayne in better conditions. Sleeping on a blow up air mattresss in a house filled with brick dust was really not a vacation.

When I got to the cottage, Franck and Luc stood outside, and stared up at the roof with identical tight mouths.

"What's going on?" Something was clearly going on, and not something good.

"You'll see," Franck said.

I watched for a while but didn't see anything out of order on the roof. Then over the crest of the line of tile came a lurching man wearing a tool belt and with a cigarette dangling between his lips. "*That* is the electrician Momo sent to us?"

"He's going to burn down the bloody place," Franck hissed like an angry animal. "Hey. Get that cigarette out of your mouth!" Franck yelled up at him. "And get down from there!"

"*Non!*" The man came close to the edge, clearly not steady on his feet.

"Move back!" I waved at him furiously to retreat. "Don't come near the edge!"

He stared down at me and narrowed his eyes. "*Non*," he slurred again. "I'm never listening to a woman again."

"Should you tell him Momo is on his way?" Luc hissed at Franck.

"I don't want to do anything to cause any sudden movements," Franck said. "I can't believe he hasn't fallen already."

"It's only nine thirty in the morning," I said. "How can he possibly be that drunk?"

Franck shrugged. "He was banned from Jacky's last year, so I have no idea."

Momo sped around the corner in his white *camionette*, almost flattening Franck, Luc, and me. He squealed to a stop in front of us just at the last minute.

"What are you doing in the lane?" Momo demanded after jumping out of the car. He was small but pure sinew and gristle. He had sent us Tin-Tin the intimidating electrician at *La Maison des Deux Clochers* but thanks to a few extra wine bottles and a shared recipe for boar's blood omelette that had all worked out fine in the end. I didn't feel so optimistic about his employee who was currently swaying on our roof.

"What are you all doing standing in the middle of the road?" Momo repeated. He acted affronted, as though we were standing in the autoroute instead of in front of our cottage in a tranquil country lane that was barely ever used.

"Looking up at your *protégé*," growled Franck. "Who at the moment is up on our roof with a *cigarette in his mouth*." The roof was tiles, but a cigarette could easily slip under a tile and set the entire wooden frame aflame.

Momo looked up. "What the hell is he doing up there?"

"Why don't you ask him?" Franck asked. "My guess is he's trying to burn our cottage down."

"Louis!" Momo yelled up at him. "What the hell are you doing up there?"

"Jusssssssh checking wires," Louis slurred. His cigarette dropped out of his mouth, but he somehow managed to catch it before it fell on the roof tiles.

"There are no wires up on the roof...unless...you didn't put any wires on the roof, did you?" Momo demanded.

"Not yet," Louis answered finally.

"Do I have to take you back to *La Chartreuse*?" Momo asked. Everyone in Burgundy knew of *La Chartreuse*. It was in Dijon, where alcoholics were sent for rehab. Ironically, *La Chartreuse* was also a kind of liquor made by the monks near Grenoble. Only in France would a rehab be named after a type of alcohol.

"*Non!*" Louis began to run up the roof, sending the off tile askew.

Momo looked at us and sighed. "I'm going to have to take him to Dijon. He has been sober for a long time so I thought it would be fine."

"How long?" Franck asked.

"Two weeks. He's my best electrician when he's not drinking."

Franck just arched a brow at Momo.

"I may need one of you to help me hold him in the car on the way there. He jumps out sometimes. It's not safe."

"I feel sorry for Louis, I truly do," Franck said. "But it just so happens that we have other things we need to do, such as find another electrician."

"I've taken care of that," Momo said.

Franck looked disdainfully at Momo. I knew he wanted to reject Momo's offer outright to find us another one of his employees, but we needed an eletrician right away. If only Luc's electrical ticket had come through in time…

"How exactly have you…"

Just then another *camionette* covered in mud pulled up.

A monolithic and extremely hairy man unfolded himself from the front seat.

"Tin Tin!" I gasped. I would recognize the intrepid and moody boar-hunting electrician anywhere. He was as massive and *poilu* as ever.

Ah!" he caught sight of us and came over immediately to give me *les bises* and Franck a firm handshake. "I was angry when Momo called me all the way over here for a job, but I didn't know it was you!"

"I thought you had moved away to the Saone-et-Loire," I said.

"I did. Momo called me this morning in a complete panic…"

"Now Tin-Tin…" Momo began.

"In a complete panic," Tin-Tin repeated, uncowed. "I drove all the way here. I was furious but if I'd known…Momo, why didn't you just say it was for Franck and Laura?"

Those three bottles of wine we had bought to tame Tin-Tin five years ago had certainly been money well spent.

"You are needed here," Momo said, trying to assert his authority on his employee who was almost twice his size.

"Yes," Franck said. "Please."

"But first things first," Momo said. "I need you to get Louis off the roof and help me pack him off to *La Chartreuse*.

I could see Luc examining Tin Tin's massive bulk and then looking up at our new roof, skeptical. The last thing we needed was a Tin Tin sized hole in our new tiles.

"I'd prefer *you* go up there," Franck said to Momo. "Tin Tin is too big from eating all those boars."

Tin Tin made a strange sound that, if I didn't know him better, I would almost call a laugh, and Momo sighed. He liked being a boss but had never been overly enthused about doing much actual work himself. "Fine," he grumbled.

As soon as he left Tin Tin rolled his saucer-like eyes. "I forgot how much I like working for Momo," he quipped.

A few minutes later Momo came out pulling a griping Louis behind him with a firm hand.

"I don't want to go back there," Louis mumbled, but didn't sound very convincing.

"I can't exactly let you burn down Laura and Franck's cottage, *n'est-ce pas?*" Momo pushed Louis in the *camionette*.

He jerked his head at Tin-Tin. "Hop in. I'll deliver you back here afterwards."

Tin Tin just grunted to Momo, but gave me a complicitous grin as they sped off.

Luc and Franck sped up to the roof to check for smoldering cigarette butts.

"I'll go back and check on Jayne," I called up to Franck. "Will you be coming by later Luc?" I asked. "The toilet…"

"I'll need Luc here until Tin Tin gets going," Franck said. "Even then, I think it would be better off if Luc just lingered over here. Remember the radiators at *La Maison des Deux Clochers?*"

I did. Tin-Tin was a competent electrician but esthetics was not his strong suit. It had taken three tries and three bottles of wine to get him to finally center the darn things properly under the windows. Still…how long were we supposed to live with our bathroom ripped out of the main floor?

"I'll be back to your place as soon as I can," Luc promised and disappeared again over the roofline.

I wandered back home past the mayor's office and the house of one of the village winemakers who was loading up bottles into boxes in her courtyard. She waved, as I mulled over how little time we had left to finish the cottage

"How are the renovations going?" she asked.

"Complicated!"

"You'll get there." She smiled, cheerily going about her work.

I wasn't so sure.

"Jayne?" I called when I got back home. There was no sound of anyone upstairs and our house was not that big. I went out to the front deck. She wasn't there.

The door down to the basement was slightly ajar and I stuck my head in the dank staircase.

"Jayne?" I called out even though I was highly doubtful she would be hanging out down there amongst the spiders.

There was silence and then the sound of retching.

I flicked on the light and ran down the stairs. The half broken accordion door on the WC was wide open and Jayne was crumpled over the toilet.

"Flu," she groaned. "Stomach."

"Oh no," I said. My eyes travelled up and I saw two large arachnids tranquilly making webs in the corner of the ceiling, unperturbed by the interloper. "And this is the only toilet." Shame filled me at being such a lamentable hostess. "Can I at least bring you a towel to sit on? "

Jayne's head nodded weakly. "At least I didn't see any spiders yet. You know how I hate spiders."

I eyed the two specimens above and tried to tell them via telepathy to stay up high where they belonged.

"Is there anything I can do?" I asked. Of all the bad luck, coming here for a week and then getting stomach flu at the very time that we had ripped out our bathroom. The only thing I could think to offer her was delicious food and drink but of course with the stomach flu that

277

was now off the table. Poor Jayne.

"Do you have a bowl if I go back upstairs?" she asked, turning a green face to me.

"I do," I said, but even wracking my brain I couldn't think of much else I could provide in the way of comforts. To think that we had at least twelve groups of paying guests booked in the cottage – which was in an even worse state than our house at the moment – beginning in four months' time. If Jayne's trip was indicative of my success in welcoming people to Burgundy we were in serious trouble.

Jayne began to feel marginally better on the third day, by which time Tin Tin had swung into action at the cottage. After Luc had deemed him competent, he returned to our house.

It was the weekend and our bathroom fixtures had been sitting out on the lawn for several days. The neighbors were probably beginning to wonder if this wasn't some strange Canadian thing.

"I'm back at it!" Luc said. "But you wanted to do redo the flooring in your bedrooms, right?"

Indeed I did have plans to have Luc to remove the grotty old carpet and replace it with hardwood.

I nodded. "That's the plan, but I think the bathroom is still…"

"I actually realized I need to re-run some pipes in your bedroom floor to run into the bathroom," he said. "I'll need to take up your floor anyway, so…" He let his shrug finish the sentence for him.

"OK," I said. "Let's rip up the floors too. Might as well."

I went into the living room where Jayne was lying, pale and sprawled on her inflatable air mattress.

"No bathroom for the foreseeable future," I said. Having the stomach flu when you were far from home was bad enough, but having it while you had to trek up and down to a disgusting basement toilet with very little privacy and spiders. "I'm so sorry. I feel terrible."

"Not as terrible as you will feel if you catch this bug from me," said Jayne, motioning at me to put a few feet of distance between us.

"Can you eat anything yet?" I asked. "A piece of baguette? A *patisserie*?"

Jayne held up her hand. "I think I just need to have a little nap," she said. "Please. Don't talk to me about food."

"OK." I winced, looking down at her. "Sorry again."

When I went to check on Luc a while later he had already begun ripping up the carpet in our bedroom and was starting to chisel open a hole in the floor.

"I have to be careful doing this," he said. "I don't want to hit one of the existing pipes."

"Yes," I said. "Please don't. If we have a flood I think the logical next step according to the Bible would be locusts."

Two days later no progress had been made on the bathroom front, but Luc was putting the finishing touches on our brand new hardwood floor in our bedroom. Even Jayne, who had experienced a miraculous recovery just in time to fly home, admired how much it changed the room for the better.

"Wow. Looks amazing," she said when Franck brought her home from a whistle-stop tour of the shops in Beaune.

"I know, right?" I said, admiring Luc's handiwork. "I just have one more email to answer and then we'll have the *apéritif*, OK?"

"Sounds great."

I went into our office and clicked open my inbox.

Laura, you are living our dream life… the first email began. It went on to rhapsodize about Franck's and my "glamorous" life in France in a way that bore absolutely no resemblance to our reality. I always wondered what to do with emails like this. Should I burst their bubble and explain that the fantasy of life in France is in fact just that, a fantasy or should I allow them, like the French people who dreamed of a Canada filled with dogsleds and igloos, to hold tight to their daydreams?

I pondered this question as I glanced outside in the front yard.

Charlotte was trying to dislodge her sister from the toilet and the two were yelling and scratching at each other as they fought for supremacy over the outdoor throne.

We had recently hauled an alcoholic electrician who almost burned down the cottage to rehab in Dijon. My sister had to endure one of the worst cases of stomach flu she had ever experienced in a spider-infested, *déguelasse* basement WC with a door that didn't close. We had an ex-soap opera addict who might keel over from a heart attack working with us…if there was one thing noticeably absent from our lives, it was glamour. Reality was so much more complex than the pipeline. However, I also believed that it was quite a bit more interesting.

Just then the sound of gushing water overtook my thoughts. Luc swore explosively.

"What the-?" I screeched across the hall to our bedroom where a geyser of water sprayed up from the floor with such continuous force that it hit the ceiling.

"Pipe!" Luc gasped as he scrambled to find something in his tool belt. "Must have hit it with the electric screwdriver."

Within seconds our brand new hardwood floor was under several centimeters of water.

"*Maman!*" I heard Camille call for me in a tone of voice that I knew, instantly, was demanding that I referee a dispute.

"Not now Camille!" I yelled back.

Jayne appeared in the doorway.

"Go get Franck," I screamed at her. "Run!"

Jayne took off. "Towels!" I looked beyond our bed at the suitcase that held every towel we owned. The suitcase was floating.

"Where's the water main?" Luc demanded.

"I have no idea!" I knelt down amongst the sodden floorboards and tried to help Luc stifle the exploding water with my hands. I was soaked in an instant. How could I not know where the water main was located? "Downstairs maybe?" I took a wild guess.

"Do what you can!" Luc left me with that parting advice.

After what seemed like a very long time of unsuccessfully trying to slow the water gushing into the bedroom, the geyser fell as quickly as it had begun.

Luc appeared a minute later, dripping wet and paler than usual.

"The floor is ruined." Luc pressed his thumbs against his closed eyelids. "I'm going to have to start again from scratch."

I stared out the window, catatonic with something akin to shock.

"What are you looking at?" Luc asked.

"Just watching for the locusts," I murmured, then knelt back down and got back to work.

Franck found Luc and me there, wading around in the water, trying to absorb it with the few towels that I had managed to extract from the floating suitcase.

Franck groaned when he saw it. "I'll go borrow some towels from my parents."

"When you get back I have to finish answering an email from a client," I said. "About how glamorous our life is here in Burgundy."

CHAPTER 24

Ironically, after Jayne left, the bathroom at home progressed quickly. Luc was even able, much to Charlotte and Camille's distress, to take our old bathroom fixtures off to the dump

Franck and I chose simple white fixtures to go with our white tile and I decided on a bright tropical green-blue for the walls. It wasn't a very French colour but, then again, Tahiti was part of France, right?

By the end of May even though the rest of our house was a disaster, the bathroom was bright and fresh and our bedrooms all had new wood floors. That lifted my spirits considerably.

Luc was able to begin his drywalling of the cottage shortly after and worked like a demon. The cottage of our dreams was beginning to take shape. The three skylights made the main room light and cheerful and once Luc was done in the main room, the tiler began to lay down the huge terra cotta tiles, hand fired in the south of France.

Even the bathroom began to look like more like a bathroom and less like a chicken coop. It still needed the fixtures but it was at least plumbed for a corner shower and a new toilet and sink. The room was plenty big enough – spacious even. Luc and I both agreed that Franck's idea had in fact been a stroke of genius.

Franck and I were in the bathroom one day in early June as Luc was sanding.

"The washer and dryer will fit nicely in there," said Franck waving to the space underneath the newly installed skylight in the bathroom ceiling. "Do you know what would be perfect though?"

"*Quoi?*" Luc broke off singing. He always listened to a top 40 French radio station as he drywalled and sang completely out of tune but also unselfconsciously and loudly, which was endlessly amusing.

"A wooden built-in with a little cupboard to hold detergent and stuff with a shelf above the washer and dryer to fold and sort the laundry. Could you do that?" Franck asked Luc. We'd gotten to the point where we pretty much thought Luc could do anything.

"Carpentry and plumbing are the two things I can't do," Luc said. "Trust me."

Auguste wandered in then, sweaty from helping Hugo and his boys lay down huge stone flagstones in the courtyard, and building a wall to make the space charming and private. He surveyed the bathroom.

"Coming along," he nodded. I loved how he and the other tradesmen who worked with us took real interest and pride in every aspect of the renovation as if the house was their own.

"Luc was just telling us that he can't do carpentry," Franck said. "But we don't quite believe him."

"Believe me," Luc said, then began singing offkey at the top of his lungs again.

"Is your carpentry like your singing?" Auguste asked.

"What do you mean?" Luc asked. "My singing is fantastic. I could have had a career like Johnny Halliday."

Auguste laughed so hard he had to stop and clutch his chest. "Stop!" he held up a hand to Luc. "You're going to give me a heart attack."

I studied Auguste, concerned. "Don't do that."

"I know someone who can do carpentry," Auguste said, finally.

"Who?" Franck and I both asked at the same time.

"*Moi!*" Auguste pointed at himself. "I've never done it for money but it's one of my hobbies."

"*Vraiment?*" I asked.

"Oh yes. I've built tons of things. Birdhouses. Furniture. Wine cases. What do you need?"

Franck began showing him his idea for the laundry built in.

"We also need to frame the door jambs," I reminded Franck.

"And cupboard doors for the bedroom," Luc reminded us.

"Then there's the kitchen we have to install," Franck said, as if to himself. "And those two extra shutters that are strange sizes that need making."

"And you need all that done in just over a month?" Auguste demanded.

"Yes," Franck said.

"You are going to send me into cardiac arrest."

Hugo came wandering in. "There you are!" he said to Auguste. "I was worried you'd staggered somewhere and keeled over. You looked pretty hot out there."

The thermometer had skyrocketed over the past few days and was now in the mid-thirties instead of the mid-twenties. July 12th didn't feel far away at all.

"Would you mind if I did some carpentry for Laura and Franck instead of helping you in the courtyard? Auguste said. "You know as well as I do that I'm not helping much out there. No shade, and I need shade. This way I can still be busy and do something I love."

Franck and I exchanged a glance. Neither of us had any way of knowing whether Auguste's "hobby" meant that he was any good as a carpenter or whether he was just going to cobble together something as half-hazardly as he "assisted" Hugo. However, we also had no way of getting out of this now without hurting Auguste's feelings. We both liked him far too much to do that. We would just have to take a leap of faith. It wouldn't be the first time.

Hugo's flushed face didn't hide his relief at getting rid of Auguste for a bit. "What a fantastic idea!" You better get started right away."

Auguste pulled out his measuring tape and asked Luc to borrow a piece of paper and the stub of a pencil.

"*Alors*," he said to Franck, all business. "Explain to me exactly what you had in mind."

The next day Marie invited me over for coffee again after lunch drop-off. It was an excellent distraction from obsessing whether Auguste's carpentry "hobby" would be miraculous or disastrous for us. Marie's husband Marc-Olivier, who she always referred to as Marco, was still there finishing up his cheese course. Marie introduced us and we greeted each other with *les bises*. He wore a T-shirt with the Superman insignia emblazed on the front and a pair of ratty shorts with a huge hole in the cuff.

"I was late coming in from the vineyards," he said. "The tractor broke down and the vines are running wild right now."

He also, I noticed as he sat down again across from me at the plastic table Marie had set up in the garden, had a large hole in the crotch of his shorts. Luckily he was the type of Frenchman who favored underwear.

With the warm weather and a few afternoons of rain, the vineyards were growing at an unbelievable speed, curling and sprouting so fast that I sometimes had the impression I could see it happening with my naked eye. All the winemakers we knew were happy about the good weather but exhausted by keeping up with the demands of pruning the vines.

Marie had already told me that Marc-Olivier's career change had been a dramatic one. He'd gone from being a financier in Paris to taking over his family's wine domaine in Volnay that dated back to the mid 1600's, about the same age as *La Maison de la Vieille Vigne*, I realized.

"So how do you like winemaking?" I asked him.

Marc-Olivier shrugged. "Some days I love it, some days I hate it. I know we made the right decision to move back here from Paris though."

"Paris is complicated with three children," Marie added, stretching back in her chair to better soak up the sun.

"Soon four," Marc-Olivier added.

"You're pregnant?" I gasped. Even though Franck and I had entered in the manic-busy part of the cottage renovations Marie and I had coffee together at least once a week and chatted every day at the school doors. I couldn't believe she hadn't told me...

Marie laughed. "Not yet! Although we are definitely planning on having at least one more."

She talked about it casually, as though families of four children were par for the course. On second thought, maybe they were in Burgundy.

"Do you and Franck want a third?" she leaned forward in her chair, then waved away her own question with her expressive hands. "What am I saying? Of course you must. I know! We can get pregnant around the same time! Wouldn't that be fun?"

"I'm not sure we could handle a third right now," I said, shell-shocked at the thought of caring for a newborn as well as our renovations.

"Pooh," she dismissed that argument. "Three is nothing. So is four. It's the first and second that are work. It's just a downhill coast after that."

Here in the warmth of Marie's garden and away from the tradesmen and dust and stress of the worksites, the idea had definite appeal. Franck and I were both from families of three and even though I hadn't been thrilled with Jayne's birth at the time there was a certain lack of symmetry about three children that appealed to me. Two was manageable; three teetered on the brink of chaos. I seemed to constantly make choices in life that placed me on the brink of chaos anyway, so maybe the symetrical and well-ordered life that I found so seductive on paper wasn't my destiny.

Also, family was everything in France. Children were a source of joy and pride and the French seemed to hold with the belief that the more the merrier. The French weren't as seduced by the mirage of an orderly life as North Americans. A joyful life was supposed to be complicated and messy and emotional. Also, the French system of free public school from age two, subsidized daycare, and generous family allowances didn't hurt.

As I was daydreaming under Marie's hazelnut tree, Marie and Marc-Olivier's conversation had veered off into a planned dinner with three other winemaking couples.

"I guess most of the friends you grew up with are involved in winemaking now, like Franck's are," I said. "Are they welcoming you?"

Marie and Marc-Olivier snorted in harmony.

"It's not easy to integrate with the winemakers of his generation who never left though," Marie explained. "We had a couple over for dinner last night. He's a winemaker Marco grew up with but he has a real chip on his shoulder about the fact that Marco didn't go to the wine school in Beaune but to University in Paris instead."

"You also blew the dinner," Marc-Olivier said, pouring himself another coffee after pouring one for me and Marie.

I thought she would be offended. I would if Franck said something like that, but instead she laughed.

"Oh I did," she agreed. "It was revolting. I tried to cook a bunch of new stuff but I was cursed. My little *salade en gelatine* didn't take, the chicken was undercooked…"

"And the potatoes were overcooked and the sauce separated and the *crème brulée* was far too sweet and fell apart," Marc-Olivier supplied. They both chuckled but I sat there stunned. When Franck criticized my cooking, which he did often, I always took umbrage. Here was Marie cheerfully accepting Marc-Olivier's scathing critique of a meal that she had most likely slaved over. What kind of guy was this Marc-Olivier? In Canada his criticisms would be tantamount to verbal abuse. Marc-Olivier gulped back the rest of his espresso and gave Marie a kiss and me a wave good-bye.

"Doesn't that bother you?" I asked Marie when I heard him peel out of the driveway.

"What?" she asked, mystified.

"What Marc-Olivier said about your dinner. He said it was awful."

"It *was* awful."

"He didn't need to rub it in. That wasn't very kind."

"It was honest," Marie said. "I don't need him to tell me something's good when I know it's not. I wouldn't like that at all."

"You wouldn't?"

"Of course not. You don't lie to people you love. That's just about the worst thing you can do."

"It's not exactly lying…" I tried to explain. "It's just not telling the whole truth…not being quite as harsh, do you see what I mean?"

"I do," said Marie. "But pandering to me would just be disrespectful."

I thought back to the miniature food critics at Camille's birthday party. Maybe they weren't being cruel; maybe they were just being honest because they had been brought up that way. Canadians were diplomats born and raised. We were taught to say anything, even something frankly dishonest, to prevent hurt feelings. Maybe that wasn't the only way to go. Maybe there was another way.

Then I thought back to Auguste and the built-in he was crafting for us. If it turned out hideous would I tell him that? I doubted it. I wasn't that French yet and didn't believe I would ever be.

"Do you want to go for a quick walk to La Bouzaise and into the vineyards?" Marie asked. "It's such a beautiful afternoon."

"All right," I said and we set off into the busy vineyards as I thought about honesty and kindness and how they were more complicated than I had ever realized before.

Two frantic weeks later, and the day arrived for Auguste to install the laundry cabinet. Franck and I wanted to be there to see if our gamble on Auguste's carpentry skills had failed miserably (and if it had, how were we possibly going to tell him and fix the problem in the little amount of time that remained before our first guests arrived?) or whether our altruism had paid off.

Auguste was sweating profusely when he arrived. Franck and I exchanged worried glances. Luc also stuck around to see the show.

Hugo and his guys paraded in with pieces of wood wrapped in thick blankets. "We have to protect it, you see," August said. "I chose oak and while it is very hard I don't want any scratches on the varnish."

"Good idea," I ventured.

Once the guys had deposited all the pieces against the wall in the bathroom Franck and I drew close to see what lay underneath the blankets.

"*Non!*" Auguste waved us out of our own bathroom with an imperious hand. "I need to work alone and not under everyone's gaze. You can see it when it is all installed. It should only take about three hours."

What if it was terrible? Once it was installed it would be hard to uninstall and could ruin Luc's beautiful drywall job.

Franck bit his lip and I knew similar thoughts were racing through his mind.

"*Allez!*" Auguste waved us out.

Franck, Luc, and I had no choice to but to decamp to the main room.

"I'm nervous for you," Luc confessed when we got there.

"I guess I'm going to go back home and take care of some emails before I pick up the girls," I said.

"Grab a baguette for dinner at Jacky's on your way," Franck said. Franck and Luc waved good-bye as I strode off towards the church. Waiting was never my strongpoint.

Three hours later I left Camille and Charlotte with Franck's parents and returned to the cottage. Franck and Luc were nowhere to be found so I went around the side of the house where Hugo and his guys perched on the half built wall of the courtyard, enjoying nice crisp white wine instead of coffee for their break.

"Are they inside?" I asked.

"You don't want to go in there," Hugo warned, a tragic look on his face. "Disaster."

"What do you mean?"

"What gave you the idea *notre* Auguste could do carpentry?" Hugo demanded.

"What! You brought him here!" I said. "Is it bad?" Even if it was, I knew I couldn't bring myself to say so to him. I thought back to my first meeting with Marc-Olivier and how Marie preferred the cruelest honesty to the best intentioned lie. I didn't think I could do that. Not with the endearing Auguste. I just wasn't French enough yet.

"Go and see for yourself," Hugo sighed. "Come back and see me after."

I left Hugo with a dirty look and rushed into the bathroom. Auguste, Luc and Franck were all standing around Auguste's built-ins, blocking them from my view.

"Let me see," I said, my voice choked.

Auguste turned around first and stepped aside so that I could see his work. I found myself looking at an absolutely stunning wooden unit. It looked so perfect and silky smooth that I had to run my hand over the wood which to convince myself that it was, actually, made of wood. The gorgeous honey tone of the oak Auguste had chosen was carved, sanded, and varnished to perfection. Each piece fit together like a hand crafted puzzle and it looked like the work of a master carpenter.

"*Mon Dieu*," I whispered, reverent. "You're an *artiste*. Where did you learn to do this?" I turned to Auguste who had an expression of barely contained joy and pride that warmed me down to the bottom of my toes.

"I have a workshop at home. I've always loved working with wood. I taught myself. So far I've only made furniture and things for me and some friends."

"This is stunning," I murmured, not able to tear my hand away from the luxurious feel of the built-ins curves. "You are so talented."

"I wouldn't go that far," Auguste said.

"I would," Franck disagreed.

"I will install the cupboard doors for the bedroom and start on the doors and frames tomorrow."

"That's *fantastique*."

"How do you even do this?" I asked Auguste, truly fascinated by his process.

He began to explain, joy lighting up his eyes.

A good hour later I stepped back outside again, where Hugo was fitting in a flagstone like a piece of a huge puzzle, sweat purling off his brow.

"What did you think?" He winked at me.

"I think you're a troublemaking *petit merde*," I whacked him on the shoulder. He laughed.

"Did you know he was an amazing carpenter?" I demanded.

"Yes."

"Why didn't you tell us?"

Hugo winked at me again. "This way was far more fun."

CHAPTER 25

They began building the bonfire on a Thursday. I noticed the quickly growing pile of wood in one of the fields between Magny and Villers as I drove the girls home from school. We all stopped at the cottage on the way home to admire the gorgeous handcrafted cupboard doors Auguste installed in the bedroom. Franck walked in with Charlotte and Camille as I gave Auguste a hug of delight. His woodwork truly made the cottage a work of art.

"Laura, stop molesting our carpenter," Franck said, heading outside after handing me our daughters. "Look away girls."

Auguste blushed but looked pleased all the same. He greeted Charlotte and Camille and asked them what they thought of his doors.

"*Magnifique*," Charlotte declared.

"*Chouette*," Camille chimed in.

Auguste patted their heads and said they were clearly very intelligent little girls.

"Do you know they are building a huge bonfire?" Camille asked Auguste.

Auguste nodded. "I saw it on my way here. That will be for the fire of Saint Jean. You will have a great time. Make sure you're not inside the bonfire when they light it on fire though," he recommended to the girls who stared up at him, riveted at this idea. "Gets rather warm."

I laughed. A bonfire? I wasn't sure if Auguste had his facts straight, but surely they wouldn't let the children anywhere near a fire.

I found Franck in the back courtyard with Hugo where they were admiring the first coat of stucco Hugo had laid down on the new wall. The flagstones looked like they had already been there for hundreds of years. This would be a perfect sunny place for our guests to relax outside and enjoy their meals or glasses of wine *al fresco*.

"What exactly are they building between Magny and Villers?" I asked. "In that field?

"Oh," Franck said. "That's for *Les Feux de Saint Jean* tomorrow night."

"What's that?"

Hugo looked at me, askance. "You don't have the Saint Jean in Canada? I can't believe that."

"They do in Québec," Franck explained. "But where Laura's from in Canada they're mostly pagans." He sighed. "It was my duty to marry her and save her soul."

"And how is that going?" I asked.

Franck adopted a tragic moue. "Not so well these days."

"You mean you're not Catholic?" Hugo widened his eyes, looking at me as though I had just been parachuted down to earth from Jupiter.

"Nope."

"What are you then?" he demanded.

"I don't know. Nothing, I guess."

"Nothing?" He unconsciously reached up and caressed the heavy gold cross that he always wore on a thick gold chain around his hairy neck. "You can't be nothing. Nobody is *nothing*."

I shrugged. "I like being in the forest and by the ocean, so maybe I am a pagan."

Hugo's blue eyes went round. I wondered if he wasn't going to run up the hill to the church immediately and indulge in a bit of restorative prayer with Le Père Bard.

"Anyway," I turned to Franck. "What exactly is the *Feux de Saint Jean?*"

"It's a big bonfire," Franck explained. "Honoring Saint Jean de Baptiste."

"I got that part, but why is Saint Jean honoured by a huge fire? Isn't he the saint that attracted the animals or something? "

Hugo and Franck both looked at the other to answer.

I shook my finger. "Ah hah! Both of you such good Catholics but neither of you know the answer, do you?"

"I do," Franck said. "I just forgot."

"Forgot what?" Auguste asked, coming out to sand a piece of beautiful oak that he was using to make the doorframes.

"Why we make fires for the Saint Jean," Franck said.

Auguste shook his head, looking disgusted with Franck and Hugo. "The bonfires have nothing to do with Saint Jean the Baptist, *bien sûr*," Auguste answered. "The bonfires were a pagan ritual for the summer solstice. The Catholic church just decided Saint Jean's birthday was the same day so they co-opted the tradition."

"Let me get this straight," I said. "You mean the *Feux de Saint Jean* isn't a Catholic thing at all, but a *pagan* celebration."

"*Oui*," Auguste said and turned to his sanding.

"Hah!" I said to Hugo and crossed my arms, triumphant. "So you're all a bit pagan too!"

Hugo rolled his eyes, not readily accepting defeat. "A huge bonfire is always a good idea," he said and Franck nodded in agreement. "It's not religion-specific. Besides, a fire is a very Catholic thing to do. You know, the burning bush and all that. What's not to like?"

The next night answered that question.

We walked through the vineyards over to the field at the foot of the Mont Saint Victor at seven o'clock. The light was golden but still far from fading, and massive tables were set up on the upslope of the hill. Above them festival lights were strung on what looked like the hastily constructed arches borrowed from the church in Villers-la-Faye. There was already accordion music playing on the loudspeakers and the bar set up behind the tables was doing a brisk business in local wine and kir. Huge makeshift barbeques had been lit to cook *merguez* and *chipolatas* for dinner. From what I could see, it looked like a good chunk of the villagers from both Magny-les-Villers and Villers-la-Faye were already there.

Charlotte and Camille ran immediately to the huge pile of wood which had grown exponentially since the day before. "Bonfire" seemed a paltry name for this epic construction. It towered over forty feet high and was made of random pieces of wood, entire trees, as well as broken chairs and table legs and other pieces of wooden furniture. I saw a few dented *armoires* in there as well.

It was cordoned off with a few thin pieces of twine that were blissfully ignored by all the village children. They tunneled through the bottom of the wood pile, through to the other side.

"That's dangerous," I said to Franck. "That mountain of wood doesn't look stable."

"I doubt it is," Franck said, nodding hello to several people who shouted out to him on his arrival.

"What if it collapses on top of them?"

Franck shrugged. "Kids move fast. Good reflexes."

"Can we go? Can we go?" Camille and Charlotte were tugging at our hands

Before I could open my mouth to explain to them it was just too dangerous, Franck said, "Go ahead. *Allez!* Have fun."

They quickly disappeared within the Saint Jean effigy.

"Franck!" I spluttered.

He slung his arm around my shoulder and drew me in for a kiss. "They'll be fine. Generations of village children, including me, managed to survive the *Feux de Saint Jean*. Can I buy you a glass of wine *ma belle?*"

I cast one doubtful glance at Charlotte, who had popped out of the bottom of the pile from between a desiccated pine tree and a huge oak beam. She was laughing and yelling in French with the other kids. Why was danger always so much fun? I suspected that had something to do with many of my choices in life. Maybe the tendency to seek it out was hereditary. God forbid.

A few hours, several glasses of wine, and three *merguez* later Franck and I were having a merry old time catching up with Le Zech who lived across the street from the church in Villers-la-Faye and one of Franck's many distant cousins who had just inheirited his mother's old village house down the road from us. The piping hot barbequed *merguez* were spicy and we loaded up the fresh chunks of baguette with extra spicy Dijon mustard and then poked the *merguez* inside. Food in France didn't need to be complex to be good. Often the simple things, like this French version of a hot dog, enjoyed with chilled local rosé and a chocolate Cornetto on a hot summer evening, rivaled the many gourmet meals I had enjoyed in Burgundy.

Charlotte and Camille came up to eat with the horde of other kids but returned to play in the pile as soon as they demolished a baguette *merguez* and a cornetto each. There were about fifty children now swarming in and under and around the base of the wood pile. I reasoned that French children had been doing this for centuries. Besides, there had to be safety in numbers, *n'est-ce pas?* I was sure they had a time-tested technique for ensuring all the children were out before setting it on fire.

"*Regardez!*" Le Zech pointed after we had enjoyed another glass of wine to the bonfire. "They're going to light it now!"

Indeed, dusk had begun to fall. The mayors of Magny and Villers were striding forward with huge wooden torches towards the bonfire. The torches were lit and were already blazing away.

I squinted. Where were Charlotte and Camille? I could see a lot of movement still in the dusk, what looked like little bodies leaping around in excitement.

"They'll check that there are no children underneath before they light it, right?" I said to Franck.

Franck and Le Zeck both looked at me in surprise.

"The children will see the torches coming," Le Zech surmised. "They always do."

"How will they see them coming if they happen to be underneath the pile of wood?"

"How exactly did we know when to get out when we were kids?" Franck asked Le Zech.

I wanted to kill Franck at that moment, but more pressing was saving our daughters. I ran in a blind panic towards the bonfire as flames began to lick up the pyre.

"Charlotte!" I hollered. "Camille!"

I looked wildly around, squinting to make out anything in the dark and the glare of the flames.

"Franck!" I yelled and turned my head only long enough to see him casually sauntering down the hill, now in a deep conversation with Olivier, unconcerned. Could my plan to improve our family life by moving us to France actually get one or both of my girls *killed?*

Just then I felt a tug on my hand. "Salut Maman," said Camille. In the now flickering light I could see Charlotte was standing right beside her. "Isn't it beautiful?"

"Thank God!" I leaned down and hugged them. "I couldn't believe they lit the bonfire without making sure all the children were out."

"They yelled at us a few times that they were setting it on fire," Charlotte corrected me. "We just followed the other kids."

I clutched my chest for a few seconds in a futile effort to calm my pounding heart. In Canada children would never be allowed to play under the wood pile in the first place, but even if they were, there would be fire marshalls and several checks to make sure everyone was safe before torching it.

Camille and Charlotte both turned towards the bonfire that was now raging. It generated so much heat that we all took several instinctive steps back.

Who was I kidding? This kind of event would never be allowed in Canada – there were just not enough safety precautions in the world.

"Did you two have fun?" Franck asked the girls. They smiled and nodded, the orange light making their faces glow.

"I can't believe-," I began. "I mean, did you see that?" They didn't even-. They just lit it on fire without even checking." An enormous spark burst towards us and we had to turn and run back a few more steps so as not to catch on fire ourselves.

"Laura," Franck pulled me close to him. "The girls are just fine. All the children are fine. French kids are used to looking after themselves. The kids know to get out when the fire is lit."

"Do they? How can they be sure?"

"They can't I guess, but they also don't treat the kids like they are idiots either."

"I don't know if my nerves can stand being a parent in France."

If part of me was so attracted to chaos and upheaval for me and my family, why wasn't I the type of mother who was equipped with a better set of nerves to deal with the inevitable moments of sheer terror?

My mother had always been a very calm parent, especially in emergencies. Her imagination never seemed to race straight to the worst possible scenario, unlike mine. Even though she was a homebody she was actually far better suited than me from an emotional perspective to parent in a foreign country. I knew that I was completely useless in moments of crisis. I still hadn't figured out what kind of mother I was, or wanted to be. I was a bundle of contradictions – both terror-riddled and brave, rejecting and craving comfort, energetic about some things and utterly lazy about others, pessimistic and wildly optimistic…I made no sense to myelf, how could I possibly make sense to my children?

CHAPTER 26

The next day after breakfast I washed all of our clothes from the night before because they reeked of smoke and soot The celebration of Saint Jean or, as I also thought of it, summer solstice had gone on until the wee hours of the morning. Franck had plied me with several more glasses of wine and continuous rubbing of my shoulders and – something I could never resist – the nape of my neck until I had calmed down and started to enjoy myself again.

Charlotte and Camille played with the other village children, dancing and chasing each other in the firelight.

It certainly didn't feel like a very Catholic celebration, but besides those few moments of terror when I thought Charlotte and Camille were going to meet the same end as Joan of Arc I enjoyed the pagan-like feel of the evening.

A bizarre grinding sound snapped me out of my search for a missing sock of Camille's. *Must replace that doorbell one of these days.* I went to open it up, thinking it was probably one of the tradesmen or maybe my mother-in-law.

Instead, there was a sweaty man on our doorstep holding a clipboard and overshadowed by the massive truck that blocked the street in front of our house.

"Are you Laura Bradbury?" he asked.

"Yes," I said, mystified. "But I can't remember ordering something-…"

"These are your boxes."

"What boxes?" chimed in Camille, who had appeared and attached herself to my leg. "Do they have toys in them?"

"They're your moving boxes from Canada," the man said, looking at me strangely. "You did move from Canada, didn't you?"

Our boxes. In the past few months I had completely forgotten about all the items that we had felt were so essential that we needed to have them shipped over here to France."I guess I just assumed they were at the bottom of the Atlantic by now.

The burly man shook his head as he scribbled something on his sheet. "No, they're here. All ten of them. Where should I put them?"

I opened the garage door in the basement for the mover.

A half an hour later Franck and the girls and I were cutting open the impressive taping job on the boxes with scissors.

"Were we this overzealous in sealing these?" Franck asked as sweat began to bead on his forehead.

I had a vague recollection of packing these boxes with a considerable amount of anxiety. It had felt like, under the strain of making such a large move, that what I decided to put or not put inside defined us as a family and would shape our new life over here in France. I had felt like these boxes contained not only the essence of our family so far but also my aspirations for what I wished it to become.

Franck managed to get the first box open. We all huddled around and peered inside.

I reached in and lifted out several sets of dumbbells and a set of exercise videos.

Franck laughed. "Bet you're glad you packed those!"

It did seem ridiculous now. There had hardly been any time for exercise besides my Thursday ritual of *gymnastique* and drinking *crémant* with the village ladies. I was pretty much fully occupied with the cottage and the girls and when I did get a moment to myself I struck out for a walk in the vineyards or around the Mont Saint Victor.

"Optimism is one of my best qualities." I picked up a huge camera lens of Franck's as well as a wide angle and several other photographic accoutrements "And I guess you will be taking up photography in your spare time?"

We both chuckled at this because from the moment our airplane wheels touched the runway at Charles de Gaulle airport last summer,

Franck had no spare time.

The majority of the box was filled with clothes for ourselves and the girls. Clothes that, in the case of the girls, no longer fit more often than not. Maybe it was all those *escargot* but they had both grown like weeds in the past several months. Except for a bunch of framed photos in the third box, most of the other boxes contained what seemed now to be ancient remnants of a former life, or stuff that no longer matched the direction we were headed in.

I rifled through knick knacks that no longer belonged in my streamlined new home, North American cookbooks with recipes ill suited to French grocery stores, and toys for Charlotte and Camille they had outgrown.

How had I thought we needed any of this stuff enough to warrant the cost and trouble of shipping it from the west coast of Canada to France by boat? How had I believed that leaving it behind would somehow take away from who we were as people or who we were going to become?

"I can't remember most of these stuffies," Charlotte said, going through one of the smaller, lighter boxes. "I don't really know where we're going to put them in our bedroom."

Camille squeezed her lamb stuffie that she had begun calling "mouton-y" or the Frenchified version of "lamb-y". She had brought it with her on our trip over here and it was really the only stuffy she ever seemed to care about or need. Charlotte had a plastic baby doll she called "Princess Baby" that smelled vaguely like vanilla which served the same purpose. One stuffy each was really enough.

Things came and went and sometimes they were fun to acquire and other times they were fun to purge but they could never come close to defining who we really were. Holding on to life, or a certain static vision of our lives, by holding on to things was as futile as trying to keep a handful of water from running out of our cupped hand.

I was overwhelmed by a sudden wave of fatigue at dealing with all of these *things*. I closed the lid on the box I was sorting through. "Who wants to go for a walk around the Mont Saint Victor?" I asked the girls.

"*Moi! Moi!*" They shouted and ran upstairs to put on their shoes.

Franck came home at lunch whistling and in a fine mood despite the glaring reality that our guests were arriving in two weeks and we were running out of time. We still needed to paint the entire cottage, inside and out, and we didn't have enough time to do it ourselves as we'd planned.

We also had the minor problem of furniture. We purchased a lovely new bed at the sales after Christmas and our couch was arriving from IKEA, along with our kitchen cabinets, in two days' time, but we needed a table and chairs, a coffee table, side tables for the living room and the bedroom, and a desk as well as some decorative items.

"Can your parents look after the girls so we can go look for furniture today?" I asked.

"No," Franck said. "Actually, I forgot to ask."

"You what? Don't forget that next weekend is the *kermesse* of the school so-"

"Because I found a painter and he is arriving at the cottage after lunch to start."

"Really?" I squealed with delight. That was a huge answer to our problems. We had contacted many painters who had told us they just couldn't do it in time. "How did you find him?"

"I was driving through Beaune this morning on an errand for Luc and saw his workshop. I went in and chatted and then asked. It just so happens he had a short window that fit us in perfectly." Franck handed me over a thick palette of paint colors. "You've picked your colours, right?"

Actually, I hadn't. I had a basic idea of what I wanted but it was so hard to choose from a tiny little colored square.

"Um. Yes," I said, not wanting to dampen Franck's joy. Besides, I had to bite the bullet and make my choices at some point anyway. Why not today?

"Good, because he's going to leave one of his guys at the cottage to start priming and he wants to go to Beaune this afternoon and get the colors mixed."

"Right," I said.

Franck handed me a piece of paper and a pencil stub. "Just write the colors and reference numbers on here and I'll pass them on to the painter."

"What's his name anyway?" I asked.

"Monsieur Vennard. He's kind of an odd fellow – I couldn't put my finger on it exactly - but very friendly," Franck added, as if to himself.

"Right, I said, sitting down at the kitchen table and beginning to flip through the heady number of possibilities on the palette. "How long do I have?"

Franck came over and lifted my wrist to check my watch. "About ten minutes." He planted a kiss on the inside of my wrist before lowering my arm back down on the table.

I flipped through to the blues and purples for the shutters. I had picked lavender for La Maison des Deux Clochers, maybe more towards the blue tones with the cottage?

"What do you think the Architect of French Monuments will think about turquoise shutters?" I asked.

Franck finished off a glass of water before answering. "He'll hate them of course."

"Do we care?"

"No," Franck said. "Not really. I mean, could you live with gray shutters for the cottage?"

I shook my head. "No way."

Better to ask for forgiveness than permission then."

Ten minutes later Franck came back in the kitchen and I gave him the reference numbers for a buttery yellow for the walls, a creamy white for the trim, and a bright turquoise for the shutters. Even Franck did a double take at the shutter colour.

"Wow," he said, his eyes widening as he stared at the colour. "That's...that's very colorful. Are you sure about this?"

I thanked my lucky stars that, unless I was beyond exhausted, I had never had much problem with being decisive. I always figured that I would far rather make a mistake than endure the endless limbo of indecision, or, worse yet, defer a decision to someone else and have that person make a mistake for me.

"If we're going to piss off the Architect of French Monuments, let's really piss him off," I said.

"All right," Franck said. "I can pretty much guarantee that."

"Good."

The next day I went over to the cottage in the late afternoon after arranging with Marie to pick up the girls from school for a playdate at her house. I had been busy at home lining up the renters who would be arriving at the cottage in very short order and writing all the information for the binders to leave at the cottage.

I parked behind an unfamiliar camionette that had to belong to the painters. It was painted in vibrant shades of blue, white, and red – the colors of the French flag. That was very patriotic of him, I thought to myself.

Auguste was there outside in the courtyard planing a beautiful finished door and Hugo, the Beret Rouge. and his other guys were adding another layer of stucco to the newly built wall of the courtyard. Luc seemed to be lingering beside them and they all seemed significantly more subdued than usual.

"Bonjour," I said, giving them all the ritual kisses. "What's going on with you guys?" I asked when that was accomplished.

"Nothing," Luc answered quickly.

"Something's up," I answered.

"No," he said. "We're just all tired today." He waved toward the admittedly scorching sun. "*Il fait chaud* you know."

I squinted at the lot of them, and it had nothing to do with the bright sunlight bouncing off the beautiful sandy cream shade of Hugo's freshly stucco'd walls.

"The painter's in the living room with Franck," Hugo said, jerking his head in that direction.

"All right," I said. Were the guys mad at me? Or at Franck? What was going on? I didn't like this one bit. The idea that we could have affronted them or upset them after all their hard work and friendship distressed me to the bottom of my toes.

Franck was in the living room, facing the painter, nodding as the painter kept up a constant stream of talk.

"Laura!" he looked over to me, relief palpable on his features.

"Bonjour," I said, going over to give him a kiss and then shake the hand of Monsieur Vennard.

"Ah!" Madame Germain!" he greeted me in a cheerful but obsequious way and, ignoring Franck, complimented me on my colour choices. I wasn't sure why, but his approval made me squirm. Also, I could tell that he was a talker and wasn't going to stop until he found himself alone in the room.

"Franck," I said, taking his arm and squeezing it. "Hugo needs to talk with us out in the courtyard. He has some questions."

Franck smiled a true smile. We both bid *au-revoir* and a happy continuation to Monsieur Vennard and remained otherwise silent until we were out of earshot.

"He never shuts up long enough to actually paint," Franck said.

"I know it's hard for you," I whispered, but you're just going to have to be rude and leave the room." It was one of the most ill-mannered things possible for a Burgundian to cut short a chat. "What is going on with the other guys?"

"What do you mean?" Franck said.

"Well, when I got here they were all huddled up and acting strange."

Franck didn't answer but walked out to the courtyard where Hugo and Luc and The Beret Rouge were smoking cigarettes, and Auguste was chastising them for doing so. They were laughing and seemed slightly less nefarious than when I had arrived.

"How's Vennard?" Hugo asked, sneering a bit.

"Do you know something I should know?" Franck asked Hugo, then shifted his eyes to Luc and the rest of the men who all looked down at their shoes.

Luc shrugged. "It's probably nothing. Anyway, you need a painter."

Franck studied them some more. "QUOI?" he demanded.

Just then Monsieur Vennard poked his head out the newly installed French doors. "I'm going to start in on the yellow now. Come and see it Monsieur and Madame Germain!"

Annoyance crossed Franck's features but he turned and smiled at the painter. "We'll be right there."

"I'll see you all tonight at our place for the *apéro*?" Franck confirmed with the guys.

Shockingly, the tradesmen all busied themselves with tasks while mumbling that they couldn't make it that night.

"I'll get to the bottom of this, even if you don't tell me," Franck said. "Come on." He steered me back into the house to admire the fresh shade of yellow on the living room walls.

It didn't take very long for us to figure out there was something very strange indeed with Monsieur Vennard. He came to our house and not one of the other tradesmen appeared. That in itself was unheard of. *What had he said? What had he done?*

I put in a DVD for the girls because somehow I didn't want them lurking around the kitchen table as they usually did.

Things began normally enough. Monsieur Vennard accepted a kir with alacrity and peppered Franck and me with questions about Canada.

Once we'd covered snowshoes and igloos and maple syrup he added another odd question that nobody in France had ever asked me before.

"How about social problems in Canada. Do you have those too?"

I shrugged. "Of course. Doesn't every country?"

He stroked his moustache in consternation at my answer. "But I'm sure you don't have social problems in Canada like we have here in France."

"I think we do," I said.

"But you don't have the same problem with immigrants in Canada."

"Immigrants?" I demanded, surprised. Where was he going with this?

"Yes. You know, immigrants that suck all the money out of the country and contribute nothing to society. You don't have as many immigrants in Canada as you do here in France, do you?"

I laughed loudly. "Besides the First Nations, *everyone* in Canada is an immigrant. I am. Franck is. My parents are. My grandparents were the ones who came over from Scotland and England. We are a country of immigrants."

He pressed his lips together, clearly fighting annoyance. "But you don't have *Arabs*," he said finally.

"There are many Arabs in Canada," I said. "Along with European immigrants like Franck and me and Asians and East Indians and Africans and well...probably pretty much any nationality you could think of. Like I said, we're all immigrants."

Before he could voice his discontent, Franck chimed in. "Anyway, I have always been a big believer that all the countries of the world should simply do away with their borders and allow the free flow of people. Immigration is a wonderful thing and immigrants are what make countries dynamic."

"Besides, without people from Morocco and Tunisia we wouldn't have *tagine* and *couscous* and *merguez* to eat... that would be very sad."

"It would," Franck agreed.

Maybe I wasn't one hundred per cent sure what our family believed in or what beliefs to pass on to our daughters. Franck was a Catholic who didn't believe in going to church, I was, according to Franck and Hugo, sort of a pagan ...one thing I did know for sure though - our family believed in humanity.

We believed in Auguste gaining back his dignity and purpose through his love for woodworking, in Hugo railing against the tyranny of the Architect of French Monuments, in me finding kindred spirits in Isabelle who helped me clean up Camille's vomit and Marie who also enjoyed chocolate and espresso as much as I did, in Charlotte and Camille adapting to life in France despite a rough start, even in Luc singing out of key at the top of his lungs and not caring who heard him. We believed that humans of all races and genders and beliefs had the potential to be quirky and amazing and transcendent. We didn't believe in hate. We believed in possibility, especially when a bunch of slightly crazy people came together not only to conjure up the *petits bonheurs du jour* like our shared jokes and affection, but to create things that weren't there before – like our newly renovated cottage. As far as our family beliefs went, I felt that this was a fine start.

"Would you like another drink, Monsieur Vennard?" Franck asked although I could see in his eyes that for once he wanted nothing more than for our guest to vacate our house as soon as possible.

"No. I'll be off," Monsieur Vennard said, leaving me with the distinct impression that he was angry at having his pet topic thwarted by a couple of liberals.

After shutting the door behind him, Franck turned to me. "I do believe our painter is racist," he said.

"I think you're right," I said.

"What should we do?" I asked.

"Teach him a lesson," Franck said, his eyes bright with mischief.

CHAPTER 27

The next few days Franck remained mum on exactly how he was going to teach Monsieur Vennard a lesson, but we did have a chance to discuss the matter with Hugo and Luc.

"I do believe our painter doesn't like Arabs overmuch," Franck said.

Luc snorted. "You think?"

Hugo pointed to Monsieur Vennard's truck. "Didn't you notice his truck? Le *blue, blanc, rouge*? That guy is *Front Nationale* down to his core."

Franck slapped his forehead and I felt like doing the same. *Bien sûr.* The blue, white, and red were not only the colors of the French flag but also the colors of the despicable and ultra-right wing National Front party, led by the atrocious Jean-Marie Le Pen who blamed everything on the new immigrants to France, particularly Arabs.

"I saw him once at a *Front Nationale* political rally in Nuits-Saint-Georges," Hugo said. "And to think, he doesn't even seemed ashamed of himself.

Franck recounted our conversation of the other night. "He didn't seem ashamed exactly, but we did thwart him."

"How?" Luc asked.

"Laura told him that everyone in Canada, us included, were immigrants and I waxed poetic about how open international borders would make a better world."

Luc snorted with pleasure. "Maybe I should have come after all. His reaction would have been worth seeing."

Franck furrowed his brow. "Still, I wonder if we shouldn't look for another painter."

Luc stared at Franck, aghast. "Franck, there is simply no time. You can't."

Franck chewed his lip at this. "He needs to be taught a lesson then."

"What did you have in mind?" Luc asked.

"Something," Franck said, mysterious.

By the next weekend we still didn't have any furniture for the cottage besides a wonderful bed. There were last minute details that needed attending to at the site and I was using every spare minute at home to write all the household instructions and information for our soon-to-be-arriving guests. I was very stressed at this point but Franck didn't seem to share my sense of urgency. He kept a close eye on the painters at the cottage – funnily enough Monsieur Vennard himself didn't feel the need to be present very often since his visit to our house. Instead, he sent his employees who were deemed acceptable by Luc, Hugo and the rest of our guys.

To further complicate matters, Saturday was the much anticipated *kermesse* of Saint-Coeur. This was the end of the year event where each class did a dance routine in full elaborate costumes to celebrate the end of the school year.

My girls chattered about it constantly. Camille would be ladybug and Charlotte a "rock 'n' roll girl" – whatever that meant to the French. Thankfully, someone at the school sewed all the costumes and parent volunteers applied all the make-up, so all I needed to do was show up. Of course I wouldn't miss seeing my girls on stage. Still, the stress over furniture (or lack thereof) continued to lurk in the back of my mind.

I planned to drive to Marie's house at the appointed time of ten o'clock Saturday morning so we could all go over together with the kids.

When we spun into the pea gravel courtyard still studded with weeds, Marie was frantically loading the basket underneath Capucine's stroller with wine bottles.

After I gave her a *bises* and the children ran into the backyard to play, Marie turned back to her task. "*Aie*," she said. "They're not all going to fit."

"Why do you need to take wine?" I kneeled down and turned around one of the bottles. It was a Volnay *Premier Cru Clos des Chenes* from Marco's family Domaine. I wouldn't mind a stroller full of that.

"For the wine stand," she said.

"Wine stand?"

"Yes, it's a tradition. Every parent that is involved in winemaking – which is pretty much every parent - brings twelve bottles to donate to the wine stand. The bottles are sold at about half price to raise money for the school auxiliary."

A wine sale at an event celebrating the end of preschool…only in Burgundy.

"Here," I said, looking down at my bag which was always huge and filled with random odds and ends such as a teeny pair of Petit Bateau underwear for Camille and a cork from a particularly good bottle of wine Franck and I had drunk with Martial and Isabelle a few weeks before. "I can fit at least two bottles in here, maybe three."

Marco came out of the house just then, dressed in ratty shorts and a faded red T-shirt with the communist sickle and hammer emblazoned across the front in yellow.

"I'll be off," he said, giving Marie a kiss on her lips and me *les bises* on my cheeks.

"You going to the vineyards?" I asked.

"Yes," he said. "They are *insane*. We can't keep up with the pruning and the weeds."

"You'll be there in time to see the children?" Marie asked.

Indeed, we had a good two hours of make-up and preparation before the first group of children made its way on stage.

Marco just nodded. "It's like this every year. Absolutely blazing hot."

For the first time I considered the logistics of this fact. The day had dawned baking hot already and the temperature promised to rise to at least the mid to high thirties Celius by midday. I saw them begin to construct the metal stage in the main courtyard of the school yesterday at pick-up."

"There's not going to be any shade, is there?" I asked.

"Nope," said Marco. "And combine a day like this with a shadeless courtyard and a metal stage and you get…"

"People keeling over from heat exhaustion," I said.

Marco nodded. "It's part of the *kermesse* tradition at Saint-Coeur. It was like that every year when I went to primary school there."

"Why don't they at least put up a tent or something for shade?" I asked.

Marco shrugged. "Maybe to toughen us up so when we're older we can go and prune rows upon rows of vines in the heat without passing out?" He smirked at me. "Maybe there is a method to their madness." He leapt in his camionette. "I'm off!" he said and peeled out of the gate.

Marie handed me two bottles of wine. "Here, can you take these?"

In the end we managed to fit a total of four bottles in my capacious bag. Franck was forever laughing at my need to go through life with a heavy bag of stuff on my shoulder but I could tell him this time that it had come in handy. The bottles clinked together and against my hip as Marie and I herded the children down the street and through the mayhem of the parking lot at school.

I thought briefly to the steady deterioration of my parking habits over this past year. Sometime in the past two months I began to double and even triple park, and I sometimes blocked off emergency lanes and drive-ways like the most blasé French person. People back in Canada would be horrified, but I suspected Cyril my driving instructor would be inordinately proud that the daily practice of driving in France had beaten much of the polite and law-abiding Canadian out of me, at least behind the wheel of my car.

Marie and I dropped off our superstars in their respective classrooms to be costumed and readied for the stage. I followed Marie to a series of massive tables set up in the hallway. They were already towering with wine bottles…and not just any wine bottles. Here was an astounding collection of some of the world's most expensive vintages –

Clos de Tart, Richebourg, Savigny-les-Beaune's les Serpentières, Pommard Les Charmots…I boggled at the sheer value and deliciousness of the wines set out before me. Already several fathers were buzzing around the table, making notes on sheets of paper as Marie and I added her bottles to the mix.

"When does the sale happen?" I asked. I could barely stand the anticipation.

"After the last act of the show," Marie said. "How else do you think they get the parents to stay?"

Franck arrived just in time to see Camille take the stage as a diminutive ladybug. Her costume and make-up, both bright red and black, was indeed adorable and in the typical French way executed perfectly and identically on each child. I was already sweating profusely by the time she began dancing around the hot metal stage and guzzling back my bottle of Evian. Camille seemed oblivious to the heat though, maybe because it was obvious that she loved being up above everyone, momentarily the center of attention.

Franck and I escaped into one of the classrooms to cool down while waiting for Charlotte's dance.

I was shocked that nobody else had the same idea but was instead just suffering in the courtyard. Franck and I perched on a desk in the back of the classroom. It was debatable whether it was much cooler in here although we were at least no longer under the blazing sun.

Franck loosened my grip on the Evian and took a few swigs. He leaned back against the wall and sighed.

"So this is where you were going to school when we met," he mused, examining the beaten up wooden desks and a map of France during World War II pinned up against the chalkboard.

"I had History in here," I said, thinking back on that time when I was eighteen years old and still wondering if there existed a boy out there in the big wide world who could love me for who I truly was. "I spent more of my time daydreaming about finding true love than memorizing the demarcation zones of occupied France. It is amazing to think you were so close by then - that we had already crossed paths a few times without actually meeting." I took back the bottle and swigged more water, feeling suddenly parched. "It's scary to think that we might not have met."

"But we did," Franck said, leaning over and kissing the soft spot under my earlobe. We were also a family, I realized, who believed not only in humanity but in the existence and power of true love. "Thanks to that you are now boiling at a *kermesse* at your old school with me, watching our daughters perform as a ladybug and rock 'n roll girl."

I shivered. Kissing that spot never failed and Franck knew it well. "That was all part of my life plan before I met you."

"Even the metal stage that must be about one thousand degrees and is probably melting the soles off our daughters' shoes?"

I chuckled. "Of course."

"And the racist painter? And the fact that we still don't have a table and chairs for our guests next week?"

"All part of my master plan." I tapped my temple. "*Fou comme un renard.*"

Franck grabbed me and pulled me closer. My breathing became shallow and my head spun slightly. I knew it wasn't just the heat. Thirteen years and two children since our first glance in the center of Nuits-Saint-Georges and the electricity still arced between us.

"Hey," I murmured. "Does that expression 'crazy like a fox' actually translate into French at all or does it make no sense…"

Franck shut me up with a kiss.

"It's hot," I protested feebly.

"It is." Franck continued to deepen his kisses and explore with his callused hands. We both lost track of time until we heard the announcer outside the window introduce Charlotte's class.

"*Merde!*" We both leapt up, sharing guilty smirks. I wondered if Franck's aunt Renée would deem a sweaty, slightly illicit make-out session in our old high school *un petit bonheur du jour.*

What was I thinking? Franck led me out of the school building with his fingers still possessively intertwined in mine. Of course she would.

CHAPTER 28

On Sunday, even though nobody was supposed to work on a Sunday, all of our workers were at the cottage racing to finish. As I thanked them profusely and told them about the epic wine table at the *kermesse*, decimated in minutes by the parents after the show–Monsieur Vennard drove up with his employee in his overly patriotic *camionette*.

He said a curt bonjour and began to unload our now brightly painted shutters from the back his truck.

Auguste whistled when he got a full view of the bright turquoise colour. "You *are* a brave girl!" He patted me on the back.

Monsieur Vennard's minion began to haul them out, and Hugo stepped up to help when Monsieur Vennard chose to stand back and watch him struggle.

Hugo laughed as he lined up the shutters to hang on the centuries old hinges.

"What's so funny?" I asked.

"This colour!" he said. "The Architect of the French Monuments is going to hate it so much."

"So?" I crossed my arms in front of me, defiant.

Hugo came over and gave me a kiss on the cheek. "That makes me beyond happy. Your shutters are *fantastique*. Well done Laura."

I smiled.

After several pairs were hung, Tin-Tin's truck rolled into the lane with a swirl of dust.

I went over and gave him *les bises*. "I didn't know you were coming today," I said.

"*Me voilà!*" He spread out his huge and hairy arms to emphasize this point. "There are few electrical things I need to finish up."

Just then Franck and Luc came out of the cottage.

"Bloody Arabs!" Luc shouted and Monsieur Vennard's head snapped around.

"What did they do this time?" Monsieur Vennard could hardly contain his excitement in having someone to rant to about Arabs.

"Don't you believe so many of France's problems can be blamed on them?" Luc asked Monsieur Vennard.

"All of France's problems," Monsieur Vennard said. "They are a lazy and immoral people. They come over here and sponge off our system and all of us hardworking French people have to pay for their good-for-nothing carcasses. Send them all back to where they came! France for the French, I say."

Hugo and I stood wide eyed at this toxic tirade. "Wait a sec..." I began, but Franck ushered me back and nodded slightly at Tin Tin, as if giving him a cue.

"What did the Arabs do to you?" Tin Tin asked Luc pointedly.

"I went and had a couscous last night," Luc said. "It was delicious so I ate too much and ended up having a bad case of diarrhea this morning."

"That's all?" Tin Tin asked Luc, acting scary but from where I was standing I could see they shared a complicitous smirk.

"Well yes...when I said "bloody Arabs" I was just joking. I mean, I guess I am a little angry at eating too much of their delicious couscous but I suppose I only really have myself to blame."

"Good," Tin Tin said, and slammed his cabbage sized fist into his palm.

Monsieur Vennard looked on, confused now.

"Why good?" Luc asked.

Because I'm half Arab," Tin Tin said, turning to Monsieur Vennard. "And I don't like the opinons I just heard expressed about my mother's people...*my* people."

I didn't actually think Tin Tin was Arab at all, but he was so swarthy and massive and hairy he could in fact have passed for any number of indeterminate nationalities.

Monsieur Vennard began to tremble and looked down at his shoes.

"Well, half Arab...that's different," he said. "It means you're half French."

"Actually, my father was Portuguese," Tin Tin said, taking a threatening step towards Monsieur Vennard. "So, I suppose you're going to tell me know that I sponge off the system and need to go back from where I came from?"

Monsieur Vennard began shaking and sweating for real. He fumbled to get his cell phone out of his back pocket. "Um. There's a call I've been waiting for. I need to get back down to Beaune." He leapt in his car without making any further eye contact with the hulking Tin Tin and sped off.

The rest of us collapsed in laughter, including Monsieur Vennard's employee whom he had abandoned with us. "Serves that *connard* right," the employee said. "I have had to put up with his stupid tirades long enough. My name is Jean," he said, sticking out his hand.

"So, you're an Arab now," Hugo said, slapping Tin Tin on the back.

Tin Tin was still wiping tears of laughter from his eyes. "When it serves a purpose," he said. "That went even better than I expected Franck," he said. "The most fun I've had in a long time..."

For the first time Tin Tin seemed to notice the newly hung shutters. "Great color," he said to me. "That is going to piss off the Architect of French Monuments, *sans question*."

"This day just keeps getting better and better, right?" Luc offered Tin Tin a cigarette which he accepted with a nod.

"That it does," Franck said, smiling at the guys and me. "That it does."

I really thought the day could not get any better, but after spending the morning at the cottage ticking off the endless list of things to finish, we had a delicious lunch with Mémé at Franck's parents' house. First they served a chilled terrine of zucchini freshly picked from their garden covered with a tomato coulis that they made from the first of this year's tomatoes. It was spicy and creamy and refreshing and Franck and I each ended up having seconds, groaning with how good it tasted. We mopped up the tomato coulis with slices of fresh baguette that Mémé made in the early hours of the morning. She had certainly not lost her tendency to keep bakers' hours or to make absolutely mouth-watering bread.

Next came one of my mother-in-law Michèle's specialties, a tabouleh salad with tiny shaved shallots and firm green olives from Provence as well as more tomatoes and bountiful parsley and mint and freshly squeezed lemon juice. She had also assembled a platter of charcuterie – ribbons of cured jambon de bayonne, rolls of jambon blanc, thinly sliced saucisson of all different shapes and sizes...as well as my favorite addition to any charcuterie, a cold jar of Maille *cornichons* from Dijon. Franck had brought over three bottles of rosé from our cellar that went perfectly with the heat of midday, the shade of the wisteria we sat under in the courtyard, and the chirp of crickets in the distance.

After came the cheese course of a perfectly ripe and creamy Soumatrin and a "Délice de Pommard" - a round of fresh cheese studded with macerated raisins, and several plugs of goat cheese of varying ages from a neighbouring farm in Échevronne.

I sighed in satisfaction after finishing off the last bit of Soumatrin on a slice of Mémé's baguette. "I don't care if our guests have furniture or not," I said. "I don't feel like going back to work, ever."

Next came the ice cream. How was it that they even make ice cream better in France? It was less sweet and the flavors were far more concentrated and grown up tasting. I chose a bowl of coffee ice cream that was studded with coffee beans and chocolate which was so dark as to be almost black.

Of course, last came the tiny espresso cups that had been passed down from Franck's great-grandmother to Michèle, filled with strong coffee.

"I need a nap," Franck declared and moved over to a lawn chair that Franck's parents placed behind the outdoor table. "Wake me up in twenty minutes," he said, his eyes fluttering

"He's exhausted," I observed, then stood up reluctantly and began clearing off the table.

"Non, non, non," André took the plates I was holding out of my hands. "I'll take care of the dishes.

"Can you take me over and show me your shutters? Mémé asked. "Franck told me they've just been hung."

So Michèle and Mémé and I wandered over to the cottage while the girls ran upstairs to play with Lego in the cool of the stone house.

When Mémé first caught sight of the shutters she gasped. "How did you know?" Her grip, already strong from years of kneading dough, now dug so deep in my forearm that I almost yelped.

"Know what?"

"That color. It's the bleu de Villers! It's the color of our shutters when Pépé Georges was still alive. All of our friends called it the "Blue of Villers". How did you know?"

"I didn't...I just felt drawn to that color. I can't really explain why."

Mémé drew Michèle and me closer and touched the glossy bright surface of the shutter that covered the front door. "It makes me so happy to see this color again," Mémé said. "So many wonderful memories." She laughed, lost in her own thoughts.

"*Bleu de Villers*," I said to myself. "I had no idea."

When we got back to chez Germain I gently shook Franck out of what looked like an extremely deep sleep. He blinked at me, disoriented at first and then stretched and smiled at me.

"How long have I been sleeping? he asked.

"About an hour," I said. "I think it would have been a lot longer than that if I hadn't woken you. You were like Sleeping Beauty."

Franck snorted and then sat up. "We should get going."

"Nobody's at the cottage," I said.

"No, I meant finding furniture," he said. "There's a *vide-grenier* today in Fussey. Maybe we can find some things there." Franck checked his watch. "But it's going to be over soon, so we should hurry over."

"You could have told me," I said. "I would have woken you up sooner."

Franck waved that objection away.

"Our timing is perfect," he said. "I can feel it."

"Oh, *vraiment?*" I said, rolling my eyes.

"Don't you believe in me?"

"Yes, but…"

Franck cupped a hand over my mouth. "No buts. Belief doesn't have room for any buts, remember?"

The drive over was short but lovely and took us past the property that we had been swindled out of by the dishonest notary in the village of Marey-les-Fussey.

"I'm glad we didn't get that place," I said. "If we did we wouldn't have done the cottage and we may not have moved back here with the girls."

"One thing is for sure," Franck said. "We would have been bankrupt. Now that I have a better idea of the cost of renovations I can pretty much guarantee that that property would have been our financial ruin."

I waved my hand out the car window, surfing it up and down on the air pushing against my palm. "Funny how things work out," I said.

"Yes," Franck waved at a man driving in the other direction, perched on a huge vineyard tractor. "Just like the furniture we're going to find at the *vide-grenier.*"

I was both delighted and annoyed that Franck was right. Just as we arrived a young brocanteur was packing up several lovely pine pieces of furniture that were exactly what I had in mind for the cottage.

Franck engaged him in a chat and we ended up heading home with the car full of half priced chairs and tables and a desk and even an old cutting board that had caught my fancy.

"Was I right?" Franck didn't even bother to hide the fact that he was gloating.

I punched him lightly on the shoulder. "*Oui.*"

CHAPTER 29

It was minutes before the first guests arrived, but we did it. Now it was time to celebrate.

Franck and I were out all morning with the girls buying copious amounts of wine and fresh baguettes and *merguez* sausages and cheese and, and…

We moved all of the tables we had plus a few of Steph's out on our deck. Thank God the day looked sunny and the evening promised to be a hot one.

We worked all day setting the tables, preparing salads, the cheese platter, and washing glasses, then before we knew it, Hugo arrived in our front yard with his gang.

He grabbed me for a meaty kiss on both cheeks. "Can you believe it, Laura?" he asked. "Can you believe I didn't knock your cottage down?"

"That is indeed hard to believe."

"I know!" he said. "Here, this is for you." He whipped out a stunning bouquet of pink peonies from behind his back.

"You didn't need to bring me a present!" I said. "This evening is our present to you guys for all your hard work."

"You don't want them then?" He made a mock pout.

"I do!" I took a deep sniff. "I love peonies."

I saw Auguste was lingering momentously behind Hugo, waiting for his turn. Hugo went arm and arm in the house with Franck and his other guys, leaving the two of us alone on our "lawn" that was actually more weeds than grass.

"I brought you something too," Auguste said, still red after I had given him a *bises*. "But I'm a little embarrassed. It's not as flashy as Hugo's flowers."

I wondered what on earth it could be.

"I'm not really the flashy type," I said, although given the number of times Auguste saw me arrive at the cottage in old, stained, clothing, he should know this by now. "I just want to thank you for all your beautiful woodwork. The cottage would look nothing like it does now without you."

"You know things were rough for me before Hugo dragged me to the cottage, but I'm better now - up here I mean." He tapped his head with his index finger. "I have a few paying clients lined up for carpentry projects."

I smiled. "Congratulations. They are the lucky ones."

"Here you go." He picked up my hand and placed a long metal object in it. "It's the key we found," he said. "I polished it up for you."

I examined it, amazed. He had removed the rust and the worn metal now gleamed with a deep shine. "I thought you wanted to keep it."

"I had always planned on giving this to you, ever since the day we found it and I saw your eyes light up like mine."

"Merci Auguste." I surprised him with a good old Canadian hug.

He cleared his throat and blinked when I finally pulled away.

Luc came up the path behind Auguste, his face lit up with the same giddy relief that Franck and I felt. His arms were full of bottles and his beautiful wife Céline carried a huge bowl of shiny red cherry tomatoes.

He waved a huge bottle he had in his hand. "Cognac," he said. "Magnum. Such a feat deserves nothing less."

"Definitely!" I agreed. Auguste just shook his head.

Linking my arm with Auguste's we made our way up into the house.

Half an hour later our little French house was rocking with conversation, popping corks, and the sizzle of the barbeque Franck was tending outside.

The tradesmen, many of whom brought their wives or significant others, were ensconced around the table and enjoying glass after glass of wine and Franck's gorgeous homemade *gougères*, made with Mémé's recipe of course.

Most of the conversation revolved around the extraordinary feat that we managed to pull off.

"I never thought it was possible," the plumber unfolded his long legs under the table. "Things in France – especially building projects, just don't move that fast. I really did think it was impossible. The first time you mentioned the timeline to me, actually, I thought you and Franck were perhaps a little bit insane."

"Oh, we are," I assured him.

"I think Franck needs to make a speech," Alain clanged his fork against his glass.

"Oui! That's what we need!" Luc shouted, already tipsy. "Speech!"

The demand was so loud that Franck could not possibly refuse.

He turned from the barbeque and picked up his glass of wine, still holding the long barbeque fork.

"*Mes amis*," he began. "We brought you here to thank you all. Laura and I initially bit off a bit more than we could chew with the cottage." This provoked a lot of laughs. "You have become our family over the past few months and thanks to you, our first guests are comfortably settled there now. In Burgundy, family is everything and for the past several months you have been our family. Every time we go into the cottage, we will remember the family – you – who helped us create it. Now, let's drink!"

This was met with a chorus of cheers and several rounds of the *Ban Bourgignon*. Many of the tradesmen had an admirable knowledge of the more salacious versions of the choruses that involved bare breasted women and wine vats, amongst other things.

We served the food and everyone ate heartily. There was a wedding or baptism or some kind of party going on at *La Salle des Fêtes* down the street and they had a great DJ who provided us with music for the evening.

Dancing in the living room began at some point and not long after Franck and Luc cracked open the magnum of Cognac, we were dancing on chairs while the huge bottle made the rounds.

Hugo came and clasped me from behind as I tried to take a pile of dirty bowls into the kitchen and swung me into a sweaty jig of indeterminate origins.

It was like a champagne cork popping out of a bottle, all the combined stress and work of the past several months exploding into a much-deserved and heartfelt enjoyment of a task completed, and well-completed to boot.

The wives had to drive their husbands home after asking for help to get them into the cars. Auguste, who couldn't drink too much because of all his medications, had luckily had the forethought to bring his *camionette* to haul home the almost inert carcasses of Hugo and his guys.

I gave him another warm hug as he left. "Thank you for the key," I whispered in his ear.

"Hey! Why don't I get one of those!" Hugo demanded. "I only get *les bises.*"

"Don't listen to him," Auguste pulled away and patted my shoulder. "And thank you again, you and Franck. All I have to say is the past few months have been better than any soap opera."

Momo decided he would leave his car and walk home, although I estimated a fifty per cent chance that he wouldn't make it and would likely curl up at the foot of a vine between Magny and Villers, and wake up there in the morning.

Luc was the last to leave, still clutching the now empty Magnum that, as far as I could tell, Franck and he had drained by themselves. Céline and I managed to fold him into her car but I didn't envy her the job that she would have when she arrived home.

The night was still warm, or morning, I should say. I wondered what time it was, just as I heard the village church bell chime three times.

So much had happened this year, most of it things that I never could have imagined when Franck and I made the decision to move back to France. The year had been filled with difficult times, then moments of sublime joy. One thing was certain, diving into new experiences made me feel acutely alive.

I looked around for Franck, who had been standing beside me a few minutes ago. Where could he have lurched off to?

I checked the living room and the patio but they were both empty apart from the epic detritus of the party. No husband.

I checked the bathroom where there was a high probability of finding him, but it was empty as well. I cracked open the door to the girls bedroom, not really expecting to find him there but wanting to check that they were still sleeping soundly, and miraculously, they were.

Finally I opened our bedroom door to the sounds of stertorous snoring. Franck was still fully clothed except for a few buttons on his shirt that he had attempted to undo before passing out. The problem was that he hadn't quite made it fully on to the bed either.

His torso rested on the end of the mattress, but his legs dangled over and his feet lay flat on the bedroom floor. I was overcome with a wave of tenderness for my husband, the father of my girls, my partner in crime and the only person I knew who would embark without question on one of our crazy plans.

I hooked his legs over my arms and tried to push him up the bed. I gained a few inches, perhaps, but he was an absolute dead weight.

"Franck," I tapped his cheek, then more persistent. "Franck. *Cheri*. Wake up. We have to get you into bed." I tried to give him another push, angling my shoulders into it this time. My feet slipped on the wooden floor. It did not look as though my *cheri* was going to be moved.

I stared down at him. It was a completely unnatural position but he seemed to be sleeping soundly enough. I shrugged off my clothes, and dragged the corner of the duvet Franck hadn't pinned down with his body weight over my body. I rolled over and gave him a kiss then tucked my head halfway down the bed in the curve of his neck.

CHAPTER 30

We were heading back to Canada the next day for a three week visit after our year in France. I had already phoned ahead and told my parents to bring a large spatula to the airport, as we were so exhausted we would probably need to be scraped off the tarmac.

Sleeping the day away was out of the question, however. It was the fourteenth of July – Bastille Day – and the entire village would share a meal under tents at the *Salle des Fêtes*.

It dawned hot and heavy. As the girls shook us awake and I cracked open an eye, I saw Franck still sleeping in exactly the same position where I had left him.

"We need to decorate our bikes!" Camille and Charlotte began to shake me more vigorously.

"*Quoi?*" I croaked.

"Our bikes. Lola told us that there is a bike decorating contest at the party so we need to decorate our bikes."

"I don't think we'll be doing that this year," I buried my face in the pillow.

Franck gave an almighty roar and stood up, clutching his head.

"What's wrong with Daddy?" Charlotte asked. "Why is he wearing his clothes?"

Franck collapsed beside me. I poked Franck between the ribs. "Yes. What's wrong with you, Franck? Is it anything to do with the magnum of wine and the magnum of cognac last night?"

Franck massaged his temples. "Did I do anything embarrassing?"

"You mean, besides kiss all the tradesmen?"

"I didn't!"

"You did."

"Even Hugo?" he asked.

"Even Hugo. That was maybe the best one."

"How did I get to bed?"

"I'm not sure," I said. "I tried to move you up further but you were like a sack of lead. I gave up after a while."

Franck glanced down at his jeans. "It was a great party though, *n'est-ce pas?*"

I patted him on his stomach. "Everyone said they'd never been to one like it."

"The guys deserved it. They all worked so hard…am I dreaming or have we really finished the cottage?"

"We're done," I said. "The first renters are in there now. We did it."

Charlotte and Camille had been frowning at each other, trying to follow our conversation.

"There's a bike decorating contest!" Camille said again. They each grabbed on to one of Franck's arms and began to yank.

"I don't think we're getting out of this," I said. "How about you go and figure out something for the bikes and I'll start cleaning up?"

The kitchen and living room, as I remembered it, were bombsites. The party last night was epic but unfortunately our house now reflected that.

"You mean I have to get up?" Franck asked.

"Trust me, I have no desire to either."

The church rang nine times then. The girls had actually let us sleep in. How they slept through the ruckus last night I had no idea.

"What time do we have to be down at the *Salle des Fêtes?*" I asked.

"We should head down around 11:30 for *l'apéritif.*"

"You're not actually going to drink more wine today, are you?"

"Laura! It's the 14th of July, the *fête* of the *revolution.* I must honor my country."

"I think you took care of that last night."

328

I hauled yet another garbage bag outside after turning on the dishwasher. I had already been cleaning for well over an hour and I was just starting to make a dent in the mess.

I did, however, enjoy reminiscing about last night's party as I worked. The high points in life, I reflected, were often bookended by something entirely messier and more mundane, like this morning, or something difficult or frustrating, like learning to drive standard or those bleak months of winter cooped up in the house with sick children. One could not seem to exist without the other.

At almost eleven thirty I got out of our new shower to the excited voices of Charlotte and Camille. "Mommy! Mommy! Come and look at our bikes!" they screamed.

I was still drying my hair with the towel as I stepped outside on the scorching veranda. Franck had managed to dress both girls in adorable little summer dresses and white sandals. They were each standing proudly beside their bikes, which were now arrayed with artfully constructed flourishes of branches from our bay leaf tree.

I couldn't believe what he had made from nothing.

"I'm impressed," I said, and meant it.

Franck shrugged. "The bay tree needed pruning."

"Do you think we'll win the contest, *Maman*?" Camille asked. "Do you? Do you?"

"I don't know," I said. "But I think you girls need to thank your *papa*."

Half an hour later, we made our way down *la route des chaumes* to the *salle des fêtes*.

Franck carried a cooler full of chilled rosé and wine glasses and I carried my woven market basket with plates and cutlery. The girls proudly rode their bikes down beside us.

Large white tents were set up in the square beside the *salle des fêtes* which was a blessing as the day promised to be a scorcher. My nostrils stung from the sulfur of the firecrackers that village children were lighting all around the square. Underneath the tents were long wooden tables and chairs. Franck's parents were already there and we set our plates and cutlery down beside theirs. The girls went to go park their bikes against one of the *tilleul* trees that line the square.

"Can we go and watch the firecrackers?" Charlotte asked and I had barely nodded when she grabbed Camille's hand and ran off behind the tents.

Other villagers kept arriving and every time I tried to sit down, a new person arrived who needed to be kissed and greeted. The ladies from my gymnastics group introduced me to their husbands and of course everybody knew Franck so came over to shake our hands and talk about the progress of the cottage, which seemed to have captured everybody's attention. We got many compliments on the color of the shutters, which made me particularly happy. The Architect of French Monuments could go shove his dreary gray shutters where the sun didn't shine.

Finally we sat down to a multi-course buffet meal that started with huge pitchers of chilled *rosé* and baskets of *gougères*. My friend Sandrine, who along with Stéphanie had set me up on that blind date with Franck many years ago, was there with her family. They sat beside us so we enjoyed a raucous conversation about the grape harvests when Franck's parents were in their late teens and early twenties.

As was always the case in Burgundy, the delicious food just kept coming. A variety of cold salads and charcuterie for the entrée, then a choice between poached salmon, coq au vin, or beouf bourgingon in a rich sauce redolent of wine and garlic. This was followed, of course, by a humongous cheese course and then desserts, which was our own choice of exquisite individual *patisseries*, each a work of art.

Throughout the meal the air seemed to get heavier, despite the vast quantities of varied local wines we drank to wash down the food and refresh ourselves. Sandrine's family had been winemakers in Villers-la-Faye for generations, and her father seemed to have brought a bottomless bag of bottles. He insisted I taste all of them, and wanted a detailed opinion on each one.

The girls ran back and forth between the table and behind the tents where the older village children were setting off the seemingly endless supply of firecrackers, or *pétards*.

"Do you think they could have their fingers blown off? I asked Franck at one point.

Franck shrugged. "It's been known to happen."

I meditated on this for a moment, then shrugged. Village children had been doing this for generations and clearly nobody seemed overly concerned by the danger component. The preschool schoolyard had certainly toughened me up as a parent, and taught the girls to defend themselves.

I was laughing with Sandrine over memories of Franck's and my blind date when Michèle shook my shoulder gently.

"Laura, it's time for the books now."

"Books?" I wondered.

Sandrine peered over to the other side of the tent where the mayor, the one who had approved our skylights, was tapping a microphone. "All the village children who are school age get a book at the Bastille Day celebration every year," Sandrine explained. "It's a Villers-la-Faye tradition."

Michèle nodded. "I got a book every year when I was a growing up here. Everyone does."

Charlotte and Camille must have sensed something that concerned them was going on as they rounded the corner of the tent with a horde of other village children just then. They found their way back between the chairs to us.

The mayor began his speech, outlining the tradition that reached back for as long as anyone could remember.

"This is so exciting!" Sandrine whispered to me. "Your girls will be true *Villeroises* when they get their book."

"Charlotte and Camille go to school in Beaune. I wonder if they qualify?"

Sandrine harrumphed. "They're from Villers now, *n'est-ce pas?* Of course they should get one!"

"Are we going to get books Daddy?" Charlotte asked.

"I'm not sure," Franck said, catching my eye. "I'm not certain if you have to go to the village school or not in order to qualify."

The mayor began to call out names of the village children in alphabetical order by their last names. We watched as little urchins and lanky teenagers received books. Even the daughter of the family next door, with the controversial boyfriend who did nothing but ride his *mobilette* and smoke cigarettes, received a nice looking dystopian novel.

"Every child receives a different book that is hand-picked for them," Sandrine whispered to me. "There are not two that are the same. I still have all of mine at home. I think every person from Villers-la-Faye does."

I turned back, realizing that the mayor was now calling up the Fribourg offspring one by one, all boys in that family for the past three generations, to receive their books. Unless I was missing a family, Germain would be next.

"Germain, Camille," The mayor read, and Camille went up to collect her book about *Trois Petits Canards*.

Germain, Charlotte," The mayor read again. Charlotte came proudly back with a book about a gypsy named Violette.

"Your girls are villagers now," Sandrine said as Charlotte and Camille showed their books to Franck and Michèle. "*Félicitations*

It was well after four o'clock when the final espresso had been downed, but I realized that the celebrations were far from over The square was set up with games, a fishing pond for the children, a shooting contest, a *chamboule-tout*, and a strange game made of three large wooden pins lined up in a vertical line, one behind the other, which villagers tried to knock over with a set of wooden balls.

Franck's attention was caught. "It's *les quills*," he said. "My Dad used to be village champion. I wonder if I still remember how to throw the ball."

I got up and followed him, passing Charlotte and Camille who were each hooking a plastic fish out of the garden pool that had been filled with water for the occasion.

"Franck!" Olivier spied him and handed him the three balls. "Your turn."

Franck assumed the throwing position behind a line drawn in the dust, knees together and bent, shoulders rounded and the ball held underhand. It was like a strange version of bowling.

Charlotte and Camille claimed their prizes from their successful duck captures – a pink plastic water gun for Camille and a spyglass for Charlotte - and came beside me to watch their father.

"He's going to win," Camille said.

"For sure," Charlotte agreed.

I didn't answer, but just watched as the pockmarked wooden ball flew out of Franck's hand and connected with the first pin in the line. It toppled backwards, strong enough to knock down the two pins behind it.

"*Chouette!*" Charlotte and Camille jumped around.

"There are still two more balls to throw," warned Olivier but he stood smoking his cigarette, looking pleased all the same.

We all held our breath as Franck threw the second ball and cheered when it connected with the pins exactly like the first one.

"*Six!*" Olivier made a triumphant gesture with his hand.

"Did he win? Did he win?" Camille began to jump up and down.

"Not yet," said Olivier. "He needs to throw one more."

Sweat beaded on Franck's forehead. I loved seeing him like this, in his village, in his element. Even more I loved the fact that our girls were part of it all.

"Shhhhhhhh," I squeezed Charlotte and Camille's shoulders.

A coo-coo bird sang and then the ball went flying from Franck's hand with a flick of his wrist.

It connected with the first pin with a glorious clack. The second pin fell over as well, but the third…it teetered, it teetered…

Charlotte and Camille both began to blow as hard as they could. The pin kept teetering. The pin was far too heavy to be blown over by the girls, but I crossed my fingers all the same.

"Blow harder!" Olivier commanded.

The girls' faces turned red with effort as the pin continued to teeter. And then, just when I thought it was going to steady itself, it fell over on its side. The crowd erupted in cheers. Charlotte and Camille ran forward to hug Franck. Olivier followed suit.

I gave him a kiss when he last came over to me. "Am I married to the village champion now?"

"We'll have to wait until everyone throws to see for sure," Olivier said. "But a perfect score is hard to beat."

Charlotte and Camille ran back to the ducky pond to fish some more and get some more trinkets to take home. I eyed the shooting contest.

Before I could make up my mind the mayor tapped the microphone again.

"It's time to announce the winners of the decorated bike contest!"

he said. "Could all the participants come and stand by me with their bikes?"

Charlotte and Camille hopped to it but my heart sank when I saw that a fellow villager had decorated his bike with a plethora of artfully arranged blooms from his flower garden. Franck had acquitted himself well with the bay leaf branches but they couldn't really compete with such a work of art.

On the other hand, my girls did look incredibly winsome and adorable in their summer dresses and simple white sandals. Maybe that counted? How Franck got his act together enough to have them and their bikes turned out so nicely, I would never understand.

The mayor cleared his throat and it hurt my heart a little to see my girls strain forward.

"It seems as though there is a tie this year," The mayor announced. "And not just a two-way tie, but a three way tie. Monsieur Chenu and the two Germain girls, Charlotte and Camille."

All three bike decorators were called up to receive their prize of a special set of wine glasses. Wine glasses here were considered a gift that would please any generation. More surprising still was the fact that Camille and Charlotte seemed thrilled with their gift of wine glasses emblazoned with "Villers-la-Faye" and the village crest.

"We're getting enough toys from the duck pond," Charlotte explained. "But these are *special*."

"I'll put those boxes on the table near our things," I said and then came out to watch the action at the shooting stand again, wondering...

"Do you want to try Laura?" Franck asked. "You know how to shoot, right?"

I did, thanks to the occasional trip to the rifle range with my father when I was growing and the spares I spent in high school with the gun club in the basement of the gymnasium.

"It's been a long time," I said, but Olivier and Franck hustled me over to the stand in no time.

One of the older men who spent his days walking around the village with his hands clasped behind his back looking for building infractions to report to the authorities manned the stand. He eyed me warily.

"What do we have here?" he asked. "A Canadian?"

"She grew up shooting bears," joked Franck, but I could tell that the crowd believed him.

"Let her to the front of the line then!" the older man exclaimed.

The rifles were a bit rusty and hard to cock and load. I acquitted myself well though. I loaded up the lead shot and aimed the rifle at the target. "How many shots do we get?"

"Three," the man in charge said.

"She won't need any more, right Laura?" Franck squeezed my shoulder.

I just chuckled and sited the target again. I pulled the trigger. My shot had gone a bit to the left of the bull's-eye, but not bad.

"It pulls to the left," I said.

"It does," the man said, eyeing me with respect. "You'll have to compensate."

I lined up my second shot and then my third. I didn't hit the bulls-eye but I hit the target every time, and my last one was close.

"Very nice," the man took the rifle out of my hands.

I left my spot to the next person in the long line of people behind me, and saw it was Solange from my gymnastics class.

"You're going to be a hard one to beat," she said. "But I've won the last three years in a row, you know."

Olivier and Franck and I joined Sandrine under the tent, where she uncorked a bottle of ratafia, the strong, sweet wine her family made to perfection.

The heat seemed to be pressing in on us from all sides but the children running around playing all the free games seemed oblivious.

"Look at your girls." Sandrine poked me in the ribs as I sipped a glass of ratafia. "You would never know they weren't born here." Indeed, they were chatting and playing and arguing with the other children just like any French child. Amazing to think that a mere eleven months ago they hardly spoke French. "You can tell they have Burgundian blood."

They did have Burgundian blood, but still, if we hadn't come here would they have ever known that side of themselves? Would they have appropriated Burgundy not just as something that was their father's, but their birthright as well? I doubted it.

"I think it's going to crack," Olivier mused, glancing up at the sky, which on one side had turned a menacing shade of black. "It needs to." A low rumble came from the sky in confirmation.

"I'm going to tell the girls to start gathering their things now," I said and got up. Before I got outside the tent, however, I was stopped by the hand of Madame Fribourg, a spry octogenarian who lived down a lane across from our house.

"I wanted to come over and say *bonjour*," she said, her hand still on mine. It felt like wrinkly silk. "I haven't been a very good neighbor! My boys keep having more boys and they keep having more boys so they've needed a lot of my help this past year, you see?"

"I completely understand," I assured her. "This year has been chaotic for us too."

"Was it very difficult to you adjusting to life here in the village?"

I was going to voice the same old platitudes but something about her sharp eyes changed my mind. "There were some very difficult times," I admitted. "Times when I felt as though I was just barely hanging on. I hadn't been expecting that."

"Ah, but those times do come in life, just as inevitably as they go."

I nodded.

"Do you know what a vine needs to produce truly good wine?" she tapped the back of my hand with her fingers to make sure I was paying attention.

"Sun? Rain? Warmth?"

"Of course, but the truth is that only the vines which suffer produce truly sublime grapes. They have to be thirsty and cold and stressed and challenged to survive. This makes their roots grow deep and explore places where the coddled vines never reach."

I hadn't known that.

"I always believed it was the same with people," Madame Fribourg said. "People who just glide through life…" She shrugged dismissively. "*Pas très intéressants.*"

"I'm looking forward to seeing you more next year," I said and she nodded and moved on with a wink.

So…deep roots. That's what I would tell myself next time the hard times came back, and they would. Challenge made fine wines and, it would appear, fine people.

Seconds later the rain began, a deluge worthy of the Bible and a well-constructed ark. Charlotte and Camille and everybody else who had been outside the tents now huddled inside. The lighting flashed over Magny-les-Villers.

"That was close," Franck said. "It looked like it hit the church tower."

Franck was interrupted by another massive lightning strike that looked suspiciously like it may have hit the transformer just outside of *La Maison des Deux Clochers*.

"*Merde alors!*" Olivier jumped up. "I need to go home and unplug my TV so it doesn't get fried."

"So do we." Franck and I began to collect our plates and glasses and stuff them into our bag. "Run up with the girls," Franck said. "I'll take care of this stuff."

We peered outside of the tent, waiting for a break in the lightning that was now rolling through the valley between Magny and Villers. It occurred to me that staying under the tents that were held up with metal poles wouldn't be a much safer option than trying to run home.

"We're going to get wet Maman," Charlotte said.

"Yes, we are," I admitted. "Are you ready? Let's go!"

We dashed up the street. The smell of sulfur permeated the air far more pungently than from the firecrackers that morning. Explosives manufacturers had nothing on Mother Nature. A loud crack hit behind us but I couldn't pause to look back. I ran as fast as I could, using every ounce of strength to pull the girls up the street behind me.

I instructed the girls to crouch down by the front door as I fumbled with the key. I pushed the girls inside, and slammed it behind us just as lighting struck the antenna on Victor's house beside us.

"Oh my God," I said. I ran around and unplugged everything that I could get my hands on and made sure that all of our windows were firmly closed and locked.

The girls were plastered against the French door that looked out towards Magny.

"It's beautiful *Maman*, come look." Charlotte took my hand.

Lightning forks flashed against a sky that varied from black to an unearthly color of fiery orange. I hoped that Franck had taken refuge inside the *salle des fetes* or would soon be on his way up here. It also occurred to me that I really hoped the first renters at *La Maison de la Vieille Vigne* hadn't left our three hard-won skylights open.

Just then the door swung open and Franck fell through it, his hands full of our things plus a trophy plus two bottles of wine.

"Are you OK?" I ran towards him and relieved him of some of his burden.

Charlotte and Camille spied the flashing, showy trophy immediately. "Is that yours Papa?" they demanded.

"It is!" Franck held it up in the air, triumphant. "Champion of the village for *les quills*. It appears I have fulfilled my destiny."

"Petit…non! GRAND Bonheur du jour!" I cheered. "What about the wine?" I took the boxes and opened them up to see nice local bottles inside.

"One is for me as the champion, and one is for you for coming third in the shooting competition. Solange came first."

"She told me she would," I chuckled. "I'm not going to hear the end of it come fall."

A lightning strike boomed above and rattled the windows. I jumped. "That was close. I think that may have even hit our house."

I peered out the window just in time to see another brilliant flash strike the girls rusty swing set in the front yard.

Our street beyond that was churning with muddy water like a river. The storm was washing away the dirt from the vineyards up on *les chaumes*. "Look at that!" I said. "It's washing away all the dirt."

The experiences of this year had the same rushing momentum as the storm outside, one that carried us to our future. Franck came up from behind me wrapped his arms around me, and pulled close. He nudged my ponytail away with his nose and planted a few delicious kisses up the nape of my neck.

The trick, I realized, was in letting go enough to simply accept the challenging times and experience life in all its messy glory instead of trying to predict or control our reality.

That's what I learned here The French were instinctively good at living in the moment. At the same time, I knew that the lesson was far from over for me. In fact, it had barely begun. But what path could I follow next?

"You know what I think would rent really well?" I turned my face so that I caught Franck's eye.

"What?" His lips curled into a smile.

"An apartment within the medieval walls of Beaune."

FIN

MERCI

First of all a big *merci* to Franck who continues to tolerate me writing about him and our life together. I promise my next book will be a fiction...or maybe the book after...*tu vois*, the thing is I have a few more of these memoir things to write first. This time, I also ask for the indulgence of my oldest *saucisses* Charlotte and Camille who figure prominently in this story. I know it's not easy when you are a teenager to have your mother write about all the hilarious and embarrassing things you said and did when you were little. My excuse is that a) there is no story without you two, and b) it will prove character building.

Thank you to my brilliant beta-readers, Pam Patchet and Lisa Kozleski for their eagle eyes and their never-ending support of my writing. *Santé* to Eileen Cook for doing such a spot-on edit and wisely advising me to dial up the food and wine porn. Lynne Damant is a superlative copy editor and I thank her for the generous time she spends improving my manuscripts. Also, cheers to Rebecca Sky for her amazing graphic design talents and Daisy for her invaluable feedback. Hopefully I did you all proud.

Merci to Kathy Chung, Karen Dyer, and the SIWC board for creating the best writers' conference in the universe and for including me in the fun. Same goes for all the marvelous book clubs I have been privileged to speak at – you ladies are an inspiration.

Thank you to my girlfriends – you know who you are – for being an unwavering network of awesomeness, support, and comic relief. Also thanks to the inspiring Laura Harris for introducing me to wild, messy painting and giving me another outlet for creativity. Also, thank you to my family for always rallying around during times of difficulty and uncertainty.

Thanks to all the fantastic nurses at the Royal Jubilee Hospital in Victoria, BC, particularly all the gorgeous male nurses who never failed to brighten my days at "Club Med".

As always I owe so much to all my friends on the PSC Partners Facebook Forum and in the PSC community, especially to the much missed Sandi Pearlman and Philip Burke. We will find a cure, and 10% of the royalties from the sales of all of my books (including this one) are donated to PSC Partners Seeking a Cure and earmarked for research. If you know of anyone who has PSC please encourage them to sign up for the PSC registry at:

https://pscpartners.patientcrossroads.org/

It is our best tool for finding treatments and a cure.

I never realized how dire the shortage of organ donors was until I had a doctor tell me that I would most likely die of liver failure due to my rare autoimmune bile duct and liver disease before ever receiving a transplant. Please sign up to be an organ donor and support opt-out organ donation where you live.

Last but certainly not least, thank you to all my readers who send me lovely emails, photos, mugs and other treats and who write kind reviews on Amazon and Goodreads. To the wonderful guests we have had through the years at **La Maison de la Vieille Vigne** and our other properties (which you can see on our website www.graperentals.com), it is a privilege to share our special corner of the world with you.